PRACTICE
MAKES
PERFECT™

French Conversation

Eliane Kurbegov

Mc
Graw
Hill

New York   Chicago   San Francisco   Lisbon   London   Madrid   Mexico City
Milan   New Delhi   San Juan   Seoul   Singapore   Sydney   Toronto

Contents

Preface

Have you already spent considerable time learning French vocabulary and grammar? Are you ready to learn the language that real Francophones speak in a spontaneous and authentic manner? In that case, this is the right book for you. You have some knowledge of French, and you probably want to embark on activities that will allow you to engage in conversations with native speakers of French. That is precisely the aim of this book!

My personal experience as a student of languages as well as a teacher of French is that the most appealing aspect of language study lies in your ability to interact with other people in the target language, gaining ever greater insights into new cultures.

Although learning vocabulary and grammatical concepts is important, it is but one avenue toward real communication. Therein lies the fun! Once you have established the fundamentals of language, it is time to aim at practical applications, setting the stage for personal interactions, and above all, an understanding of the target culture.

Language does not merely consist of words and structures; it is a representation of the perspectives and points of view of real people. Growing up in France, I became accustomed to acting humbly, for instance questioning whether I truly deserved a compliment, instead of simply accepting it and thanking the giver for it—as Americans do. So, when I first came to the States, it took me a while to understand that an appropriate reply to a compliment such as *What a pretty dress!* is *Thank you* rather than *Really, you think so?*

Therefore, to help you gain an understanding of cultural differences between U.S. culture and French culture, I have tried to create as many culturally appropriate scenarios as possible in this conversation book, so that you can appreciate situations you might encounter in France: transportation strikes, Bastille Day celebrations, shopping at the Fnac (a chain of stores specializing in electronics, books, CDs, and videos). I also created Chris, an American student in France, so that you could meet French people and face authentic French situations through his eyes. Although the cultural focus is on France, the communicative aspects of language emphasized throughout the book are applicable to all Francophone cultures. Furthermore, because my goal is to give you the skills required for conversation, dialogues are often written in the informal register (with **tu**) except for interactions that require the formal register (with **vous**), for example, with salespeople, waitpersons, or business associates.

The book is divided into ten units. Each unit is guided by a theme, such as current events, leisure time, or asking for help. You can focus on specific units or themes of interest, or you may opt to travel through the chapters in the order they are presented. The latter approach will allow you to become familiar with the characters who reappear throughout the chapters and meet new ones as you go through the book.

The conversational style of the lessons aims at developing a confident speaking style. Beginning with an opening conversation, followed by grammatical notes, syntactical structures, and study of word usage, all elements are focused on the typical problems of native English speakers.

Each unit features several engaging dialogues that illustrate practical, interesting, and culturally relevant conversational situations. For example, in one chapter, you will learn that travel and leisure activities in France are at times impacted by labor strikes. Useful, high-frequency conversational phrases are highlighted in the dialogues, then clarified and illustrated for your use. A variety of exercises help you put new knowledge into practice. The Answer key provides quick and easy feedback. You will get practice in using new concepts and will be encouraged to construct personalized conversations.

This book will enhance your conversational skills by exposing you to high frequency phrases and sentences used in spontaneous conversations and provide opportunities to practice them in a variety of formats.

À vous de jouer!

Meeting people

Dialogue 1

Chloé meets a young American at a party. She has never met him face to face, but she seems to know him . . .

CHRIS: **Bonjour**, je m'appelle Chris. **Ça va bien?**

Hello, my name is Chris. How's it going?

CHLOÉ: Oui, très bien, merci. **Moi, je** suis Chloé. Tu es le copain américain de Didier, n'est-ce pas?

Yes, very well, thanks. I'm Chloé. You're Didier's American friend, right?

CHRIS: Oui, **c'est ça**. Comment le sais-tu?

Yes, that's it. How do you know (it)?

CHLOÉ: Parce que j'aide souvent Didier avec l'anglais.

Because I often help Didier with English.

CHRIS: **Je vois.** Alors quand il m'envoie des méls, c'est **toi** qui écris?

I see. So when he sends me e-mails, are you the one who writes?

CHLOÉ: Disons que **lui, il** écrit, et **moi, je** traduis et je corrige.

Let's say that he writes, and I translate and correct.

CHRIS: Tu es très bonne en anglais. **Je pige** toujours très bien.

You're very good in English. I always understand very well.

CHLOÉ: Et moi, je vois que tu parles bien français, **même** l'argot.

And I see that you speak French well, even slang.

CHRIS: **Merci pour** le compliment.

Thanks for the compliment.

CHLOÉ: **Pas de quoi.**

Don't mention it.

EXERCICE

1·1

Jugez de votre compréhension. *Check your comprehension. Write* T *for true or* F *for false.*

1. _____ Chris connaît déjà Chloé.

2. _____ Chris est français.

3. _____ Chloé est américaine.

4. _____ Chris est l'ami de Didier.

5. _____ Chloé traduit des méls en français.

Improving your conversation

Review the following explanations of some interesting phrases found in the previous dialogue. Make them your own.

Bonjour

To say *hello*, the words **bonjour** (literally, *good day*), **bonsoir** (literally, *good evening*), or **salut** (*hi*) may be used. **Bonjour** is usually used until around six P.M., whereas **bonsoir** is used after six P.M. On the other hand, **salut** can be used any time of day.

—**Salut,** Paul. Ça va bien?	—**Hi**, Paul. Is everything going well?
—Très bien, merci.	—Very well / Great, thanks.
—**Bonjour**, Pierre. Comment ça va?	—**Hello**, Pierre. How are you?
—Bien, merci.	—Fine, thank you.

Ça va bien?

This question has several variations. **Ça va?** may be interpreted as *How are you?*, *How's it going?*, or *Is everything OK?* Therefore, there is flexibility in the response.

—Bonsoir, Sophie. **Ça va?**	—Hello, Sophie. **Is everything OK?**
—Oui, **ça va.**	—Yes, **everything is OK.**
—Bonsoir, Sophie. **Ça va?**	—Hello, Sophie. **How are you?**
—(**Ça va**) pas mal.	—(**I'm**) not bad.

The question **Ça va bien?** is more specific and requires a *yes* or *no* answer.

—**Ça va bien**, Sophie?	—**Are you fine / Is it going well**, Sophie?
—Oui, très bien, merci.	—Yes, quite fine, thank you.
—**Ça va bien**, Sophie?	—**Are you fine / Is it going well**, Sophie?
—Non, pas trop bien.	—No, (I'm) not (doing) very well.

Moi, je/toi, tu/lui, il/elle, elle

In English, voice inflexion and tone are used to emphasize the subject; in French, emphasis is conveyed by adding a stress pronoun before the subject pronoun.

moi, je	*I*		**nous, nous**	*we*
toi, tu	*you* (familiar)		**vous, vous**	*you* (formal)
elle, elle	*she*		**elles, elles**	*they* (f.)
lui, il	*he*		**eux, ils**	*they* (m.)

Didier, **lui, il** écrit.	*Didier, **he** writes.*
Moi, je corrige ses méls.	*I correct his e-mails.*

C'est ça

Use this phrase to confirm what someone says to you.

—Il va nous rejoindre?	—*Is he going to join us?*
—**C'est ça.** À dix-sept heures.	—*Yes, **he is (that's it)**. At five P.M.*

Je vois

Use this phrase to confirm that you understood what was conveyed to you.

—Je ne peux pas sortir. Je suis malade.
—**Je vois.** Repose-toi bien!

—*I can't go out. I'm sick.*
—*I see. Rest well!*

Je pige

This phrase is slang for **Je comprends** (*I understand*).

—Il faut vouvoyer les gens qu'on ne connaît pas.
—Ah oui! **Je pige.**

—*You have to use* vous *with people you don't know.*
—*Oh yes! I understand (I get it).*

Merci pour...

Use this phrase to thank someone for something specific.

Merci pour ce beau cadeau.

Thanks for this beautiful gift.

Pas de quoi / il n'y a pas de quoi

Use either of these phrases as a reply for a *thank you*. Know that **pas de quoi** is an abbreviated version of **il n'y a pas de quoi** and is therefore more informal than the longer phrase.

—Merci pour cette carte.
—**Il n'y a pas de quoi. / Pas de quoi.**

—*Thanks for this card.*
—*Don't mention it.*

Même

Use this word to intensify and give emphasis to what you just said.

Je sais parler français, **même** l'argot.

I know how to speak French, **even** *slang.*

EXERCICE

1·2

Entre amis! *Between friends! Complete the sentence with the appropriate word or phrase from the list provided. Capitalize when necessary.*

bien	ça	je pige
même	pas	sais
salut	suis	toi

1. JOËL: _____, Karina. _____ va?

2. KARINA: _____ mal. Et _____, Joël?

3. JOËL: Très _____, merci. Tu _____, je _____ toujours content, moi.

4. KARINA: Moi aussi, je suis toujours contente, _____ aujourd'hui.

5. JOËL: _____, Karina. Tu as un examen aujourd'hui.

EXERCICE
1·3

Insistons sur la différence! *Let's emphasize the difference! Complete each sentence with a stress pronoun:* **moi, toi, elle, lui, nous, vous, elles,** *or* **eux.**

1. Vous, _____ parlez bien français.

2. Elle, _____ s'appelle aussi Karina.

3. _____, tu es François, n'est-ce pas?

4. Non, _____, je m'appelle Nicolas.

5. Ah! Alors, _____, il s'appelle François.

Dialogue 2

The following week, Chloé and Chris meet again at another party.

CHRIS: Bonsoir, Chloé.	*Hello, Chloé.*
CHLOÉ: Bonsoir, Chris. Comment ça va?	*Hello, Chris. How are you?*
CHRIS: Pas mal du tout. **Et toi?**	*Not bad at all. And you?*
CHLOÉ: Ça va. Je suis contente de te revoir.	*Fine. I'm happy to see you again.*
CHRIS: **Moi aussi.** Je suis là avec Didier.	*Me too. I'm here with Didier.*
CHLOÉ: Ah oui, **le voilà** avec Marie-Josée!	*Ah yes, there he is with Marie-Josée!*
CHLOÉ: Salut, Didier. Salut, Marie-Josée. Ça va, **vous deux?**	*Hi, Didier. Hi, Marie-Josée. Are you doing OK, you two?*
DIDIER: Salut, ma chère Chloé. Oui, **nous deux**, ça va très bien.	*Hi, dear Chloé. Yes, we're doing great, both of us.*
MARIE-JOSÉE: Parle pour toi, Didier. Moi, je suis **fatiguée à mourir.**	*Speak for yourself, Didier. I am dead tired.*
DIDIER: Marie-Josée **est en train de** travailler à sa thèse.	*Marie-Josée is working on her thesis.*
CHLOÉ: Oh là là, **ma pauvre**, je vois. **Tu n'as pas bonne mine.**	*Oh my poor friend, I see. You don't look so good.*
MARIE-JOSÉE: **Je compte** rentrer à la maison très bientôt.	*I intend to go home very soon.*

EXERCICE
1·4

Jugez de votre compréhension. *Check your comprehension. Write T for true or F for false.*

1. _____ Chris connaît déjà Chloé.

2. _____ Chris ne va pas bien aujourd'hui.

3. _____ Marie-Josée est la copine de Chris.

4. _____ Marie-Josée est une étudiante.

5. _____ Marie-Josée est extrêmement fatiguée.

Improving your conversation

Et toi?

Et followed by a stress pronoun is used to elicit reciprocal information.

<table>
<tr><td>Moi, ça va bien. Et toi?</td><td>I'm fine. How about you? (And you?)</td></tr>
<tr><td>Papa et maman vont au travail. Et nous?</td><td>Dad and Mom go to work. What about us?</td></tr>
</table>

Moi aussi

The stress pronoun **moi** followed by the adverb **aussi** expresses *me too*. All stress pronouns may be used this way.

<table>
<tr><td>Je dois étudier et toi aussi.</td><td>I have to study and you do too.</td></tr>
</table>

Le voilà / la voilà / les voilà

These phrases are used to indicate that something has been found or someone has appeared. The definite article is **le**, **la**, or **les**, depending on the gender and number of the noun it replaces.

<table>
<tr><td>Tu cherches Marie? La voilà.</td><td>Are you looking for Marie? There she is.</td></tr>
<tr><td>Où est le mobile? Ah! Le voilà.</td><td>Where's the cell phone? Oh! There it is.</td></tr>
<tr><td>Où sont tes copains? Ah! Les voilà.</td><td>Where are your friends? Oh! There they are.</td></tr>
</table>

Nous deux / vous deux / eux deux / elles deux

Use the appropriate stress pronoun followed by the word **deux** to express *both of us*, *both of you*, or *both of them*.

<table>
<tr><td>Nous parlons anglais, nous deux.</td><td>We speak English, both of us.</td></tr>
</table>

Fatigué(e) à mourir

This expression describes a state of extreme fatigue.

<table>
<tr><td>Après un voyage de vingt-quatre heures, elle est fatiguée à mourir.</td><td>After a twenty-four hour trip, she is dead tired.</td></tr>
</table>

Être en train de + *infinitif*

In French, there is no progressive present tense equivalent to the English *I am traveling, she is singing*. However, to emphasize that an action is in progress, use the phrase **être en train de (d')** followed by an infinitive.

<table>
<tr><td>Ils sont en train de manger.</td><td>They are eating (in the midst of eating / in the process of eating).</td></tr>
</table>

Mon pauvre / ma pauvre

Use these phrases to show compassion or sympathy for a friend or relative. Note that the noun described by **pauvre** is omitted and implied in French.

> Henri! Tu as perdu ton portefeuille, **mon pauvre**.

> *Henri! You lost your wallet, **my poor** (**friend/brother/husband/son . . .**).*

Avoir bonne/mauvaise mine

These idiomatic **avoir** expressions indicate that somebody looks good or bad (in the context of looking rested/tired or well/ill).

> Vous **avez bonne mine** malgré votre long voyage.

> *You **look good** in spite of your long trip.*

Je compte + *infinitif*

Compter followed by an infinitive is used to express intentions.

> **Je compte chercher** un nouveau travail.
> **Mes parents comptent faire** un voyage en décembre.

> *I'm planning to look for a new job.*
> *My parents plan to go on a trip in December.*

Grammar notes

Review the following grammatical concepts that help structure and perfect your communicative skills.

Conjugating -er verbs in the present tense

aider (*to help*)	
j'/il/elle/on aide	vous aidez
tu aides	ils/elles aident
nous aidons	

s'appeler (*to be named, called*)	
je m'appelle	nous nous appelons
tu t'appelles	vous vous appelez
il/elle/on s'appelle	ils/elles s'appellent

Conjugating irregular verbs in the present tense

avoir (*to have*)	
j'ai	nous avons
tu as	vous avez
il/elle/on a	ils/elles ont

dire (*to say / to tell*)	
je/tu dis	vous dites
il/elle/on dit	ils/elles disent
nous disons	

écrire (to write)
j'/tu écris
il/elle/on écrit
nous écrivons

vous écrivez
ils/elles écrivent

être (to be)
je suis
tu es
il/elle/on est

nous sommes
vous êtes
ils/elles sont

savoir (to know [a fact])
je sais
tu sais
il/elle/on sait

nous savons
vous savez
ils/elles savent

traduire (to translate)
je/tu traduis
il/elle/on traduit
nous traduisons

vous traduisez
ils/elles traduisent

voir (to see)
je/tu vois
il/elle/on voit
nous voyons

vous voyez
ils/elles voient

Je **suis** ici et ma copine **est** là aussi.
Elle, elle **s'appelle** Chloé.
Elle **traduit** le français en anglais.
J'**écris** et j'**envoie** beaucoup de méls.
   Et toi?
Je **vois** que mes copains **sont en train
de parler**.
On **dit** toujours bonjour.
Je **suis** content pour lui.
Elle **travaille** trop. Elle **a mauvaise
mine**.

*I **am** here and my friend **is** here also.*
*Her **name is** Chloé.*
*She **translates** French into English.*
*I **write** and **send** many e-mails.*
   How about you?
*I **see** that my friends **are talking**.*

*We/You always **say** hello.*
*I **am** happy for him.*
*She **works** too much. She **doesn't look
good**.*

EXERCICE

1·5

Que disent-ils? *What are they saying? Write the correct form of each verb in parentheses
on the line provided.*

1. DIDIER: Chloé, je _____ (être) content quand tu m'_____ (aider)
avec mon anglais.

2. CHLOÉ: Pas de problème, Didier! J'_____ (adorer) _____ (écrire)

en anglais.

3. DIDIER: Je _____ (savoir). Tu _____ (traduire) vraiment bien du
français en anglais.

4. CHLOÉ: Alors, comment _____ (s'appeler) ton correspondant? C'_____ (être) Chris?

5. DIDIER: Oui. Il _____ américain. Et lui, il _____ bien français.

6. CHLOÉ: Super! Je _____ (conditional form of **vouloir**) _____ (connaître) Chris.

7. DIDIER: Je _____ (voir). Tu _____ (compter) pratiquer l'anglais avec lui!

8. CHLOÉ: Bien sûr. Ça _____ (aider) de pratiquer avec une personne de langue maternelle anglaise.

Ne vous disputez pas! *Don't argue! Write* **moi** *or* **toi** *as appropriate in the space provided.*

1. MARIE-JOSÉE: _____, je rentre à la maison, Didier.

2. DIDIER: Ah non! Tu es toujours fatiguée, _____.

3. MARIE-JOSÉE: Et _____, tu es égoïste et tu ne penses qu'à _____!

4. DIDIER: Non! Mais quand je suis avec _____, tu es toujours fatiguée.

5. MARIE-JOSÉE: Parce que _____, je travaille toujours!

En train de faire quelque chose. *In the midst of doing something. Follow the model, writing two similar sentences expressing first that one is doing something, and second, that one is in the midst of doing something.*

EXAMPLE: J'(écrire un mél) *J'écris un mél.*

Je suis en train d'écrire un mél.

1. Tu (travailler) _____

_____

2. Nous (envoyer une lettre) _____

_____

3. Ils (traduire un article) _____

_____

4. Vous (lire un mél) _____

_____

5. On (présenter un ami) _____

_____

6. Elle (corriger une faute) _____

_____

Dialogue 3

Now Chloé walks over to greet Didier, who is talking to Marie-Josée.

DIDIER: Dis, Chloé, je voudrais te présenter **mon pote**, Chris.

Say, Chloé, I would like you to meet my pal, Chris.

CHLOÉ: Trop tard, mon cher! Je le connais déjà.

Too late, my dear! I already know him.

DIDIER: Ah bon? **Comment ça?**

Really? How is that?

CHLOÉ: On s'est rencontré tout à l'heure, et il sait maintenant que je lis ses méls et que j'écris les tiens.

We met a little while ago, and now he knows that I read his e-mails and that I write yours.

DIDIER: Quelle copine tu es! Tu ne sais jamais rien garder pour toi. **Comment se fait-il?**

What a friend you are! You never know how to keep anything to yourself. How come?

CHLOÉ: Pourquoi garder des secrets, Didier? On est tous copains. Bonsoir. **À un de ces jours!**

Why keep secrets, Didier? We're all friends. Good night. See you around!

DIDIER: **Salut**, Chloé! **À bientôt!**

Bye, Chloé! See you soon!

MARIE-JOSÉE: Au revoir, Chloé. **À un de ces jours.**

Good-bye, Chloé. See you around.

EXERCICE
1·8

Jugez de votre compréhension. *Check your comprehension. Write* T *for true or* F *for false.*

1. _____ Chris est un bon ami de Didier.

2. _____ Chloé aide Didier avec ses méls à Chris.

3. _____ Marie-Josée aime écrire les méls de Chris à Didier.

4. _____ Didier n'aime pas Chloé.

5. _____ Didier est aimable avec Chloé.

Improving your conversation

Review the following conversational concepts that help structure and perfect your communicative skills.

Mon pote

This phrase is very colloquial and is used for only a *male friend*, to replace **mon ami** or **mon copain**.

Je peux tout te dire, **mon pote**.	*I can tell you everything, **my friend**.*

Comment ça se fait-il? / comment se fait-il?

This question is used to show surprise and elicit more information.

Tu connais ce jeune homme? **Comment ça se fait-il?**	*You know this young man? **How is that?***
Elle parle parfaitement français. **Comment se fait-il?**	*She speaks French perfectly. **How can that be?***

Salut

This familiar term is used to say *Hi* but can also be used to say *Bye*.

Salut, mon pote. Ça va?	***Hi**, buddy. How are you?*
Salut, Jean-Jacques. À demain.	***Bye**, Jean-Jacques. See you tomorrow.*

À un de ces jours / à bientôt / à demain

Here, the preposition **à** helps express *see you*; **un de ces jours** literally means *one of these days*. This structure can be used with specific days of the week or moments in time.

Au revoir et **à dimanche**.	*Good-bye; **see you Sunday**.*
Au revoir et **à demain**.	*Good-bye; **see you tomorrow**.*
Salut, Dominique. **À un de ces jours!**	*Bye, Dominique. **See you later!***
Je file maintenant. **À bientôt**, tout le monde.	*I'm taking off now. **See you soon**, everybody.*

Grammar notes

Review the following grammatical concepts that help structure and perfect your communicative skills.

Mon/ma/mes

The masculine singular possessive adjective is **mon** (*my*); this form is also used in front of feminine singular nouns starting with a vowel sound. The feminine form of **mon** is **ma** (used before feminine singular nouns starting with a consonant), and the plural is **mes**.

mon ami / **mon** copain	*my friend* (male)	**mon** amie / **ma** copine	*my friend* (female)
mes amis / **mes** copains (*m. pl.*)	*my friends* (male)	**mes** amies / **mes** copines (*f. pl.*)	*my friends* (female)

Je voudrais voir **mon** amie Marie-Josée.	*I would like to see **my** friend Marie-Josée.*

Ton/ta/tes and son/sa/ses

Similarly, the possessive adjective for the familiar *your* has three forms: **ton**, **ta**, **tes**; and the possessive adjective for *his* or *her* has three forms: **son**, **sa**, **ses**. **Ton** and **son** also precede a feminine singular noun that starts with a vowel sound.

Tu as **ton** argent?	*Do you have **your** money?*
Elle a **son** ticket?	*Does she have **her** ticket?*
Sarah, c'est **ton** amie?	*Is Sarah **your** friend?*

Connaître and savoir

Connaître and **savoir** both mean *to know*. However, **connaître** is generally used to express *being familiar* with a place or person, whereas **savoir** is used to express *knowing a fact* or *knowing how to do something*.

Je **connais** ton copain. Il **sait** parler anglais.	*I **know** your friend. He **knows how** to speak English.*
—Chris **connaît** bien Paris?	*—Does Chris **know** Paris well?*
—Je ne **sais** pas.	*—I don't **know**.*

The verb **connaître** has an irregular conjugation in the present tense: **je/tu connais, il/elle/on connaît, nous connaissons, vous connaissez, ils/elles connaissent**.

Tu **connais** mon copain Bill?	*Do you **know** my friend Bill?*

The verb **savoir** has an irregular conjugation in the present tense: **je/tu sais, il/elle/on sait, nous savons, vous savez, ils/elles savent**.

Ses parents **savent** toujours où elle est.	*Her parents always **know** where she is.*

EXERCICE 1·9

Quelle est la réponse? *What is the answer? Write the letter of the appropriate response on the line provided.*

1. _____ Tu connais bien Paris?

2. _____ Tu sais bien parler anglais?

3. _____ Ça va?

4. _____ Il est là, Chris?

5. _____ Marie-Josée est avec Chris?

6. _____ Je voudrais rentrer à la maison.

7. _____ C'est vous deux, Al et Bob?

8. _____ Je voudrais te présenter Sophie.

a. Bonjour. Je m'appelle Kathy.

b. Bon, au revoir.

c. Oui, c'est nous deux.

d. Oui, c'est ma ville.

e. Oui, le voilà!

f. Oui, je suis américain.

g. Non, je suis fatigué.

h. Non, elle est avec moi.

Dialogue 4

Didier takes his friend Chris home to meet his parents. Only his father is at home.

DIDIER: Bonsoir, papa. **Je te présente** mon ami Chris.	*Hello, Dad. I'd like you to meet my friend Chris.*
CHRIS: Bonsoir, monsieur Dupoint.	*Hello, Mr. Dupoint.*
M. DUPOINT: **Enchanté de faire votre connaissance**, jeune homme!	*Delighted to make your acquaintance, young man!*
DIDIER: Tu sais, papa, c'est mon correspondant des États-Unis.	*You know, Dad, he's my pen pal from the United States.*
M. DUPOINT: Oui, oui, bien sûr! Mais vous ne restez pas **chez nous**?	*Yes, yes, of course! But aren't you staying with us?*
CHRIS: J'ai une tante et un oncle qui habitent en ville. Je reste **chez eux**.	*I have an aunt and an uncle who live in town. I'm staying with them.*
M. DUPOINT: Ah! D'accord. Je comprends.	*Ah! OK, I understand.*
CHRIS: Il est quelle heure? **Chez ma tante**, nous dînons à dix-neuf heures.	*What time is it? At my aunt's, we eat dinner at seven P.M.*
M. DUPOINT: Vous ne pouvez pas dîner avec nous?	*Can't you have dinner with us?*
CHRIS: Pas aujourd'hui. Mais **peut-être une autre fois**.	*Not today. But perhaps another time.*
M. DUPOINT: Considérez-vous invité pour samedi. D'accord?	*Consider yourself invited for Saturday. OK?*
CHRIS: Merci, monsieur. Je veux bien! Au revoir, monsieur.	*Thank you, sir. Gladly! Good-bye, sir.*
M. DUPOINT: À samedi. Au revoir.	*See you on Saturday. Good-bye.*
DIDIER: Salut, Chris. Dis, tu prends le métro ou le bus?	*Bye, Chris. Say, are you taking the subway or the bus?*
CHRIS: Le métro.	*The subway.*
DIDIER: Tu sais où est la station la plus proche?	*Do you know where the nearest station is?*
CHRIS: **Ne t'inquiète pas. Je sais me débrouiller.**	*Don't worry. I can manage.*
DIDIER: Bon, je t'appelle demain.	*Good. I'll call you tomorrow.*

EXERCICE 1·10

Jugez de votre compréhension. *Check your comprehension. Write T for true or F for false.*

1. _____ Didier présente Chris à son père.

2. _____ Le père de Didier est très aimable avec Chris.

3. _____ Chris peut dîner aujourd'hui avec la famille de Didier.

4. _____ Chris peut dîner un autre jour avec Didier.

5. _____ Chris habite chez sa tante.

Improving your conversation

Je te présente

Use this expression to introduce someone to a friend or relative. Use the same expression, substituting **vous** for **te**, to introduce someone in a formal setting.

Sonia, **je te présente** Damien.	Sonia, **I'd like you to meet** Damien.
Madame Chartier, **je vous présente** le nouvel employé.	Mrs. Chartier, **I would like you to meet** the new employee.

Enchanté(e) de faire votre connaissance

This rather formal expression is used when meeting someone. The expression is often abbreviated to **Enchanté(e)**.

—Mademoiselle, je suis **enchanté de faire votre connaissance**.	—**Delighted to make your acquaintance**, miss.
—**Enchantée**, monsieur.	—**Delighted**, sir.

Chez...

Use this preposition followed by the name or identity of a person to express *at* or *to that person's place/house/home*.

Il habite **chez sa tante**.	He lives **at his aunt's**.
Nous allons **chez Rémy**.	We are going **to Remy's house**.

The preposition **chez** is followed by a stress pronoun (**moi/toi/lui/elle/nous/vous/eux/elles**) when you want to replace the person's name.

Je suis **chez moi**.	I'm **at home (at my house)**.
Nous allons **chez eux**.	We're going **to their house**.

Peut-être une autre fois

Use this expression to tell someone that you would like to take a rain check on an offer.

Je ne peux pas rester aujourd'hui, mais **peut-être une autre fois**.	I can't stay today, but **perhaps another time**.

Ne t'inquiète pas

Use this phrase to tell a friend that there is no need for concern or worry.

Je sais comment rentrer chez moi. **Ne t'inquiète pas.**	I know how to get home. **Don't worry.**

Je sais me débrouiller

Use this phrase to say that you do not need help; you can manage.

Il y a beaucoup de lignes dans le métro, mais **je sais** déjà **me débrouiller**.	There are lots of subway lines, but **I** already **know how to manage**.
Je suis débutant en français, mais **je sais me débrouiller** au restaurant pour commander.	I'm a beginner in French, but **I can figure out** how to order at the restaurant.

Grammar notes

Review the following grammatical concepts that help structure and perfect your communicative skills.

Prendre and comprendre

The verbs **prendre** and **comprendre** follow the same irregular pattern in the present tense: **je/tu (com)prends**, **il/elle/on (com)prend**, **nous (com)prenons**, **vous (com)prenez**, **ils/elles (com)prennent**.

Moi, je **prends** le bus. Et toi?	*I **take** the bus. How about you?*
Tu le **comprends**?	*Do you **understand** him?*

Pouvoir and vouloir

Conjugations for the verbs **pouvoir** and **vouloir** follow similar irregular patterns in the present tense: **je/tu peux/veux**, **il/elle/on peut/veut**, **nous pouvons/voulons**, **vous pouvez/voulez**, **ils/elles peuvent/veulent**. They are both often followed by an infinitive.

Je **veux** absolument apprendre le français.	*I definitely **want** to learn French.*
Nous **pouvons** étudier ensemble.	*We **can** study together.*

Vouloir

When the verb **vouloir** is followed by the adverb **bien**, with or without an infinitive, it expresses willingness.

Je **veux bien**.	*I **would be happy to**. / **Gladly**.*

EXERCICE 1·11

Une invitation à dîner. *A dinner invitation. Complete the blanks in the following dialogue according to the English guidelines in parentheses.*

1. —Tu peux dîner avec nous?

   —Oui, _____. (*I can*)

2. —Tu prends le bus?

   —Non, je préfère _____ le métro. (*to take*)

3. —Tes parents peuvent venir aussi?

   —Non, pas cette fois, mais _____. (*perhaps another time*)

4. —Tu peux arriver à dix-huit heures?

   —Oui, je pense que _____ arriver vers dix-huit heures. (*I can*)

5. —Ta famille habite à Paris?

—Non, seulement ma tante _____ à Paris. (*lives*)

6. Et toi, comment _____ que tu habites à Paris? (*how is it*)

EXERCICE
1·12

Visite chez les Dupoint. *Visiting the Dupoints. Reconstitute the following dialogue by filling in the blanks with the appropriate words from the list. Capitalize when necessary.*

là	très	bonjour
pote	voilà	enchanté
l'ami	madame	monsieur
je m'appelle	va	

1. CHRIS: _____ Madame Dupoint. _____ de faire votre connaissance.

2. MME DUPOINT: Bonjour, _____. Vous êtes _____ de Didier.

3. CHRIS: Oui, _____. _____ Chris.

4. MME DUPOINT: Didier, ton ami est _____. Ah! Le _____!

5. DIDIER: Salut, mon _____. Ça _____?

6. CHRIS: _____ bien, merci.

Dialogue 5

Today is Saturday. Chris comes to Didier's house to have dinner with him and his parents. He is surprised when he walks into a room filled with people.

CHRIS: Salut, Didier. **C'est bien** samedi aujourd'hui? Ce n'est pas dimanche, **n'est-ce pas?**

Hi, Didier isn't it Saturday today? It's not Sunday, right?

DIDIER: Oui, mais **le samedi**, on dîne généralement en famille. Je vais te présenter.

Yes, but on Saturdays, we generally eat dinner with the family. I'm going to introduce you.

CHRIS: **Bonjour, monsieur** Dupoint.

Hello, Mr. Dupoint.

M. DUPOINT: Bonjour, Chris!

Hello, Chris!

DIDIER: Maman, je te présente Chris.

Mom, let me present Chris.

MME DUPOINT: Bonjour, Chris. Je vous **fais la bise**.

Hello, Chris. Here's a kiss for you.

CHRIS:	**Bonjour, madame.**	Hello, madam.
DIDIER:	Je te présente ma sœur Hélène et son mari.	This is my sister Hélène and her husband.
CHRIS:	Bonsoir, madame. Bonsoir, monsieur. **Comment allez-vous?**	Hello, madam. Hello, sir. How are you?
HÉLÈNE:	Bien, merci. Et vous?	Fine, thank you. How about you?
CHLOÈ:	Moi, je suis Chloé, la cousine de Didier.	I'm Chloé, Didier's cousin.
CHRIS:	**Ça alors!** Tu es vraiment sa cousine?	How about that! Are you really his cousin?
CHLOÈ:	Eh bien, oui! Et voilà Marie-Josée. Tu sais, c'est la copine de Didier.	Well, yes! And here's Marie-Josée. You know, she's Didier's girlfriend.

EXERCICE 1·13

Jugez de votre compréhension. *Check your comprehension. Write T for true or F for false.*

1. _____ Chris va chez Didier dimanche.

2. _____ Chris fait la connaissance de la mère de Didier.

3. _____ La maman de Didier est affectueuse avec Chris.

4. _____ Chris connaît déjà la sœur de Didier.

5. _____ Chloé est la cousine de Didier.

Improving your conversation

C'est bien...

Use this expression to confirm that you are right about an assumption you made.

| **C'est bien** l'adresse correcte? | *Isn't it (this) the correct address?* |
| **C'est bien** lundi aujourd'hui? | *Isn't it Monday today?* |

N'est-ce pas?

This is another expression to confirm that you are right about an assumption you made.

| On va au concert vendredi, **n'est-ce pas?** | *We are going to the concert on Friday, aren't we?* |
| Ta copine s'appelle Chloé, **n'est-ce pas?** | *Your girlfriend's name is Chloé, isn't it?* |

Le samedi

Use a day of the week with the definite article **le** in front of it to indicate that you mean *regularly* on that day.

Je ne vais pas au cours **le samedi**.   *I don't go to school **on Saturdays**.*
Nous sortons dîner **le dimanche**.   *We go out to dinner **on Sundays**.*

Bonjour, monsieur / bonjour, madame

Use the title **monsieur, madame**, or **mademoiselle** with or without the last name of the person whenever you address someone in a formal setting. Don't forget to use the titles in the evening, when say **bonsoir**.

—**Bonjour, monsieur** Ramu.   —*Hello, **Mr.** Ramu.*
—**Bonsoir, madame**.   —*Good evening, **madam**.*

Faire la bise

Faire la bise reflects a cultural habit. It is customary in France to give two or more kisses on the cheek when greeting friends or relatives.

Je ne te fais pas la bise parce que j'ai   *I'm not kissing you, because I have*
un rhume.   *a cold.*
Jean, **fais la bise** à ta tante!   *Jean, **kiss** your aunt!*

Ça alors!

Use this expression to express surprise.

Tu es déjà là? **Ça alors!**   *You're already there? **How about that!***

Comment allez-vous?

Use this phrase to ask a person whom you address formally (someone older, a store clerk, employee, server, etc.) how he or she is. This expression is followed by the person's title (**monsieur, madame**, or **mademoiselle**).

Comment allez-vous, monsieur?   *How are you, sir?*

Grammar notes

Days of the week

When introducing a day of the week, do not try to translate the English preposition that precedes the day (*on Mondays*). Say simply **le lundi**, or, in the case of a single event, just **lundi**.

le lundi   *on Mondays (every Monday)*
Mercredi, je vais voir Guy.   *I'm going to see Guy **(on) Wednesday**.*

Relationships and possessions

To express relationships and possession, use the appropriate structure and include the preposition **de** (*of*) as in the following examples:

la famille **de** Didier   *Didier's family*
la copine **de** Didier   *Didier's girlfriend*
la maison **de** Didier   *Didier's house*

Votre and vos

There are two words for formal *your*: **votre** (used before all singular nouns) and **vos** (used before all plural nouns).

J'admire **votre** mère.   *I admire **your** mother.*
J'admire **vos** parents.   *I admire **your** parents.*

C'est / ce sont

Use **C'est / ce sont** before noun phrases.

C'est Didier. **C'est** mon meilleur ami.   *This is Didier. He's my best friend.*

Faire

Remember that the verb **faire** (*to do/make*) is irregular in the present tense: **je/tu fais, il/elle/on fait, nous faisons, vous faites, ils/elles font. Faire** is used in numerous idiomatic expressions where the English equivalent is not always *to do* or *to make*.

Tu fais du vélo?   ***Are you riding** a bike?*
Les voisins **font** du bruit.   *The neighbors **are making** noise.*

EXERCICE 1·14

La famille de Didier. *Didier's family. Write the appropriate possessive adjective* **son, sa,** *or* **ses** *in the blank spaces.*

Dans la famille de Didier, il y a (1). _____ mère, Mme Dupoint; il y a (2). _____

père, M. Dupoint; il y a (3). _____ sœur Hélène; il y a (4). _____ beau-frère; il

y a aussi (5). _____ cousins et (6). _____ cousines.

Qui est-ce? *Who is this? Translate the sentences in parentheses into French.*

7. M. Dupoint? _____. (*He is Didier's father.*)

8. _____. (*He is delighted to make Chris's acquaintance.*)

9. Mme Dupoint? _____. (*She is his mother.*)

10. _____. (*She is affectionate.*)

11. Hélène? _____. (*She is his sister.*)

12. _____. (*She is married.*)

La rencontre d'Hélène et de Chris. *Hélène's and Chris's meeting. In this dialogue, Chris meets Didier's sister Hélène for the first time. Write the dialogue between these two people using the English guidelines provided.*

1. Hélène greets Chris in a formal manner by saying hello and asking him how he is.

   HÉLÈNE: _____

2. Chris says he is fine and then expresses how delighted he is to make her acquaintance.

   CHRIS: _____

3. Hélène asks Chris if he is indeed Didier's English friend.

   HÉLÈNE: _____

4. Chris tells her that is not exactly the case. Then he explains that he is his American friend.

   CHRIS: _____

5. Hélène apologizes. Then she adds that she does know that he is American.

   HÉLÈNE: _____

6. Chris states that today being Saturday, they both have a little free time.

   CHRIS: _____

7. Hélène says that it's nice. Then she adds that on Saturdays, the family always eats together and that everyone wanted to meet him.

   HÉLÈNE: _____

Making conversation and making plans

Dialogue 1

Chris approaches a young woman he meets at his friend's house and finds out she was interested in meeting him because he is American.

CHRIS: Bonjour, mademoiselle. Je m'appelle Chris.

Hello, miss. My name is Chris.

ANNE: Je m'appelle Anne et je suis la cousine de Didier.

My name is Anne, and I'm Didier's cousin.

CHRIS: Et moi, je suis son copain. J'habite aux États-Unis et **je suis ici en visite**.

I'm his friend. I live in the United States, and I am here visiting.

ANNE: Ah oui, **j'ai entendu parler de vous. J'avais justement envie de** vous rencontrer.

Oh yes, I've heard about you. It just so happens I wanted to meet you.

CHRIS: Ah bon. Je ne savais pas que j'étais célèbre!

Well. I didn't know I was famous!

ANNE: Célèbre? Je ne sais pas! Mais j'étais aux États-Unis il y a deux ans et j'ai des copains américains, moi aussi.

Famous? I don't know about that! But I was in the United States two years ago, and I too have American friends.

CHRIS: **Je plaisantais**, bien sûr! Où est-ce que vous étiez aux USA?

I was joking, of course! Where were you in the U.S.?

ANNE: J'étais en Californie et au Colorado.

I was in California and in Colorado.

CHRIS: Ah bon, à l'ouest! Moi, j'habite au Nevada, à Las Vegas!

Oh, in the West! I live in Nevada, in Las Vegas!

ANNE: Las Vegas, pour moi, c'est les casinos au milieu du désert.

For me, Las Vegas is casinos in the desert.

CHRIS: **Je comprends qu'on pense cela**, mais il y a aussi des gens tout à fait ordinaires là-bas.

I understand that people think that, but there are also very ordinary people there.

ANNE: **C'est vrai qu'**on peut imaginer Paris comme la ville de la Tour Eiffel, de l'Arc de Triomphe, des Champs-Élysées et du Louvre.

It's true that we could imagine Paris as the city of the Eiffel Tower, the Arch of Triumph, the Champs-Élysées, and the Louvre.

CHRIS: **Exactement. Et pourtant** c'est tellement plus que cela, n'est-ce pas?

Exactly. And yet, it's so much more than that, isn't it?

EXERCICE
2·1

Jugez de votre compréhension. *Check your comprehension. Write* T *(true) or* F *(false).*

1. _____ Didier a deux cousines, Chloé et Anne.

2. _____ Anne connaît les États-Unis.

3. _____ Chris habite en Californie.

4. _____ Anne était sur la côte ouest des États-Unis.

5. _____ Anne pense que Chris est célèbre.

Improving your conversation

En visite

This phrase helps you say you are visiting without specifying whom or what you are visiting.

> Nous sommes ici **en visite**.   *We are here **visiting**.*

J'ai entendu parler de vous

This expression can be used when you meet someone you've heard about prior to your meeting.

> Enchanté de faire votre connaissance.   *Delighted to make your acquaintance.*
> **J'ai** souvent **entendu parler de vous**.   *I've often **heard about you**.*

J'avais justement envie de (d')...

This expression can be used when you meet a person you've heard of prior to your meeting. In this case, you are saying that you expected and looked forward to your meeting.

> Ah! Voilà ta copine. **J'avais justement**   *Ah! Here's your girlfriend. **It just so***
> **envie** de la rencontrer.   ***happened I wanted** to meet her.*

Je plaisantais

This nice ice-breaker is for people who like to use humor in their conversation.

> Je parle dix langues!... Bon, pas vraiment.   *I speak ten languages! . . . Well, not really.*
> **Je plaisantais.**   *I was joking.*

Je comprends qu'on pense...

This expression can be used to confirm or deny a preconceived notion.

> J'ai un petit accent en français.   *I have a little accent in French. **I understand***
> **Je comprends qu'on pense** que je   ***(that) people think** I am a foreigner.*
> suis étranger.

C'est vrai que (qu')...

These expressions are transitions or replies that confirm a previous statement.

Je parle assez bien le français. **C'est vrai que** je passe beaucoup de temps en France.

*I speak French pretty well. **It's true that** I spend a lot of time in France.*

Exactement

This short phrase is used to confirm an interlocutor's statement.

—Vous êtes américain, monsieur?
—Oui, **exactement**.

—Are you American, sir?
*—Yes, **that's right**.*

Et pourtant...

This short phrase can be used to deny or temper a preconceived notion or statement.

Elle parle très bien l'anglais, **et pourtant** elle ne l'étudie que depuis deux ans.

*She speaks English very well, **and yet** she's studied it for only two years.*

Grammar note

En and au/aux

When mentioning where you live, use the preposition **en** followed by the name of a feminine country, state, or province, or use **au/aux** followed by the name of a masculine country, state, or province.

J'habite **en** France / **en** Normandie / **au** Colorado / **aux** États-Unis.

*I live **in** France / Normandy / Colorado / the United States.*

EXERCICE
2·2

On est intéressé! *We're interested! By completing the sentences of the following dialogue with words or expressions from the list provided, you will reconstruct a meeting between Chris and Anne.*

au Colorado	J'ai entendu parler	exactement
grandes villes	moi	vous
c'est vrai	aux États-Unis	plaît
j'avais envie	des copains	m'appelle
Qu'est-ce qui		

1. ANNE: C'est _____, Chris, le copain de Didier?

2. CHRIS: Oui, c'est bien _____. Et qui êtes-vous?

3. ANNE: Je _____ Anne et je suis la cousine de Didier.

4.–5. CHRIS: Ah oui. _____ de vous. Vous avez voyagé _____.

6. ANNE: Oui, _____ que tout le monde le sait.

7. CHRIS: Et où _____?

8.–9. ANNE: En Californie et _____. La Californie me _____ beaucoup.

10. CHRIS: Ah oui? _____ vous plaît surtout là-bas?

11. ANNE: J'adore ses _____.

12. CHRIS: Vous avez _____ américains?

13. ANNE: Mais oui! C'est pourquoi _____ de vous parler.

Dialogue 2

As Chris and Anne continue their conversation, Chris finds out about Anne's American experience.

CHRIS: Dites, Anne, **cela vous dérangerait si on se tutoyait**?

Say, Anne, would it bother you if we used the familiar?

ANNE: Mais non, pas du tout.

Of course not, not at all.

CHRIS: Alors, **dis-moi, qu'est-ce qui te plaît** aux États-Unis?

So, tell me, what do you like in the United States?

ANNE: Beaucoup de choses. Les grandes villes de Californie et la personnalité ouverte de ses habitants, par exemple.

Lots of things. The big California cities and the open personality of the people, for example.

CHRIS: J'ai de la famille à San Francisco. Je connais et **j'aime bien** la ville.

I have family in San Francisco. I know and like the city well.

ANNE: Au Colorado, j'adore les paysages et la nature.

In Colorado, I love the scenery and nature.

CHRIS: Tu as fait de l'escalade et des randonnées au Colorado, je suppose.

You went climbing and hiking in Colorado, I suppose.

ANNE: On s'est promenés en montagne, bien sûr, mais l'escalade, c'est pour les professionnels.

We went walking in the mountains, of course, but climbing is for pros.

CHRIS: Tu n'aimes pas les sports?

Don't you like sports?

ANNE: Oh! Tu sais, pour moi, la marche **me suffit** et elle **fait partie** de ma vie quotidienne.

Oh you know, for me, walking is enough and it's part of my daily life.

CHRIS: C'est vrai que je marche beaucoup depuis que je suis à Paris.

It's true that I walk a lot since I've been in Paris.

ANNE: Tu vois. Tu t'adaptes à la vie parisienne.

You see, you are adapting to Parisian life.

CHRIS: **Il le faut! Et puis je veux bien aussi.**

It's necessary! And also I don't mind.

Jugez de votre compréhension. *Check your comprehension. Write* T *(true) or* F *(false).*

1. _____ Chris peut tutoyer Anne.

2. _____ Anne n'aime pas les États-Unis.

3. _____ Anne aime faire des promenades.

4. _____ Anne est très sportive.

5. _____ Chris marche beaucoup à Paris.

Improving your conversation

Cela te/vous dérangerait?

This expression allows you to ask for a favor in a very courteous manner because you acknowledge that you might be imposing on someone.

Cela vous dérangerait, madame, si je parlais anglais?	***Would it bother you***, *madam, if I spoke English?*

Dis / dis-moi

This expression is best used in familiar settings. Note that you are using the command form of the verb **dire** as a direct approach to someone.

Dis, Joël, tu peux me chercher?	***Hey/Say***, *Joël, can you pick me up?*
Dis-moi, elle te plaît, cette voiture?	***Say***, *do you like that car?*

Qu'est-ce qui te plaît?

This familiar question is frequently used instead of **Qu'est-ce que tu aimes?** Note that the literal translation of the question is *What is pleasing to you / pleases you?*

—**Qu'est-ce qui te plaît** ici, Suzanne?	—***What do you like*** *here, Suzanne?*
—J'aime bien les montagnes.	—*I like the mountains.*

Asking this question in a formal manner requires substituting the pronoun **vous** for **te**.

Qu'est-ce qui vous plaît, mademoiselle?	***What do you like***, *miss?*

J'aime bien

Since the verb **aimer** means both *to like* and *to love*, use the adverb **bien** to specify or emphasize that you mean *to like*.

J'aime bien les comédies.	***I like*** *comedies.*
J'aime bien cette actrice.	***I like*** *this actress.*

Cela/ça me suffit

This versatile expression is used to express that you have had enough of something. The word **ça** is simply an abbreviated form of **cela**.

—Tu veux encore du café?	—*Do you want more coffee?*
—Non merci. **Ça me suffit**.	—*No, thanks. **That's enough.***
Ah non! Plus de télé ce soir. **Cela me suffit.**	*Oh, no! No more TV tonight. **I've had enough.***

Faire partie de (d')...

Use this idiomatic **faire** expression to express being a part of or belonging to something.

Ma sœur **fait partie d'**une sororité à l'université.	*My sister **belongs to** a sorority at the university.*
Cette ceinture **fait partie d'**un ensemble que j'ai depuis longtemps.	*This belt **is part of** an outfit I've had for a long time.*

Il le faut

Use this impersonal phrase to express that something is a *must*.

—Tu réponds toujours?	—*Do you always answer?*
—Bien sûr. **Il le faut**.	—*Of course, **I must / It's necessary.***
—Vous travaillez le week-end?	—*You work on weekends?*
—**Il le faut.**	—*We have to.*

Et puis...

This phrase is used to add a detail. It is used as a somewhat emphatic *and* or *in addition*.

J'ai faim, **et puis** je voudrais goûter ces hors-d'œuvre.	*I'm hungry, **and** I would like to taste these appetizers.*

Je veux bien

Use the verb **vouloir** with the adverb **bien** when you mean *I want to* as in *I don't mind* or *I'm willing*.

—Tu veux aller au restaurant?	—*Do you want to go to the restaurant?*
—Oui, **je veux bien**.	—*Yes, **I don't mind.***

EXERCICE
2·4

Quelle est la réponse appropriée dans le dialogue suivant? *What is the appropriate reply in the following dialogue? Write the letter of the response on the line provided.*

1. _____ Je connais très bien les États-Unis.

a. Oh non! La marche me suffit.

2. _____ Je connais, par exemple, la Californie.

b. Ah! Je vois! Tu as voyagé aux États-Unis.

3. _____ J'adore les grandes villes.

c. Pas du tout. Un peu d'exercice, c'est on!

4. _____ Dis, tu aimes bien Paris?		d. Oui, j'adore la ville et ses habitants.
5. _____ Tu marches beaucoup.		e. Je veux bien. Allons-y!
6. _____ Tu fais des sports?		f. Ah bon! Tu connais San Francisco?
7. _____ On va au parc?		g. Oui, comme les Parisiens. Il le faut.
8. _____ Cela te dérangerait si on marchait?		h. Moi aussi.

Dialogue 3

Now Anne is interested enough to want to know more about Chris and what he is doing this summer in Paris.

ANNE: Alors, **combien de temps** tu vas rester en France?

So, how long are you going to stay in France?

CHRIS: Je suis là pour l'été. Mais, avec ma tante qui habite à Paris, nous allons voyager.

I'm here for the summer. But, with my aunt who lives in Paris, we're going to travel.

ANNE: **Comment se fait-il que** tu aies une tante à Paris?

How is it that you have an aunt in Paris?

CHRIS: Elle est tout simplement mariée à un Français.

She is simply married to a Frenchman.

ANNE: Ah! Je vois. **Depuis quand** elle est mariée? **Et ça fait longtemps qu'**elle habite à Paris?

Oh, I see. How long has she been married? And has she lived in Paris long?

CHRIS: **Depuis** à peu près dix ans, je crois.

For about ten years, I think.

ANNE: Et où est-ce que vous comptez aller alors?

And where do you intend to go then?

CHRIS: En Normandie et en Touraine.

To Normandy and Touraine.

ANNE: Vous n'allez pas en Provence comme la moitié de la population française?

Won't you go to Provence like half the French population?

CHRIS: Eh bien non. Ma tante dit qu'il y a **trop de monde** sur la côte méditerranéenne en été.

Well no. My aunt says that there are too many people on the Mediterranean coast during the summer.

ANNE: Elle a raison! Et pourtant elle est belle, la Côte d'Azur!

She's right! However, the Riviera is beautiful!

EXERCICE
2·5

Jugez de votre compréhension. *Check your comprehension. Write* T *(true) or* F *(false).*

1. _____ Chris va passer l'été en France.

2. _____ La tante américaine de Chris est mariée à un Français.

3. _____ La tante de Chris habite en Normandie.

4. _____ Chris et sa tante vont voyager en Provence.

5. _____ Anne aime la Côte d'Azur.

Improving your conversation

Combien de temps... ?

Use this expression when you want to ask for how long an event took place, is taking place, or will take place.

Combien de temps dure le film?	*How long does the movie last?*
Combien de semaines passeras-tu là-bas?	*How many weeks will you spend over there?*

Comment se fait-il que (qu')... ?

This expression shows your puzzlement or surprise that something is true or may be happening. Note that the verb in the dependent clause is in the *subjunctive* mood.

Comment se fait-il qu'il neige en été?	*How can it snow in the summer?*
Comment se fait-il que vous étudiiez encore à cette heure?	*Why are you still studying at this hour?*

Depuis quand / ça fait combien de temps que (qu')... ?

Use one of these expressions to ask for how long something has been going on. Be sure to use the present tense to indicate that the action is still going on.

Depuis quand est-ce qu'il a cette voiture?	*How long has he had this car?*
Ça fait combien de temps qu'elle attend?	*How long has she been waiting?*

Trop de monde

Use this expression to talk about *too many people*.

Il y a **trop de monde** dans ce café. Allons ailleurs!	*There are **too many people** in this café. Let's go somewhere else!*

EXERCICE 2·6

Une rencontre. *A meeting. Reconstitute the following dialogue. The first sentence is identified as **a**. Write **b**, **c**, **d**, **e**, or **f** for each of the remaining sentences, putting them in the appropriate chronological order.*

1. _*a*_ Bonjour, je m'appelle John. Enchanté de faire votre connaissance.

2. _____ Mais oui, c'est mon copain aussi.

3. _____ Vous le connaissez depuis longtemps?

4. _____ Bonjour. Je m'appelle Hélène. Vous êtes l'étudiant américain?

5. _____ Oh oui. Depuis à peu près dix ans.

6. _____ Oui, je passe l'été chez Jean-Luc. Vous le connaissez?

Une conversation. *A conversation. Complete this exercise as you did the one above.*

7. __*a*__ J'avais justement envie de faire votre connaissance, Hélène.

8. _____ Vous savez que j'ai voyagé aux États-Unis, c'est ça?

9. _____ C'est vrai. Je connais bien la Californie.

10. _____ Ah bon. Pourquoi?

11. _____ Parfaitement.

12. _____ Parce que j'ai entendu parler de vous.

Dialogue 4

Now Chris is curious about how Anne plans to spend her summer and is surprised to find out that she loves to stay home.

CHRIS: Et toi, Anne, **qu'est-ce que tu fais**, cet été?

And you, Anne, what are you doing this summer?

ANNE: Moi, **je profite de** Paris pendant que tout le monde quitte la ville.

I enjoy Paris while everybody leaves the city.

CHRIS: Super bonne idée! Tu as la ville pour toi toute seule.

What a great idea! You have the city to yourself.

ANNE: J'ai les berges de la Seine où je peux me bronzer.

I have the banks of the Seine where I can tan.

CHRIS: Pas mal! Mais tu ne peux pas te baigner!

Not bad! But you can't swim!

ANNE: Non, mais j'adore lire, couchée dans l'herbe ou sur le sable.

No, but I love to read lying in the grass or on the sand.

CHRIS: Du sable à Paris?

Sand in Paris?

ANNE: Mais oui, le long de la Seine. **Et puis**, tu sais, **je suis des cours** aussi.

Of course, along the Seine. And, you know, I also take classes.

CHRIS: Ah oui? De quoi?

Really? In what?

ANNE: Je suis un cours de littérature anglaise en ce moment. C'est fascinant.

I'm taking an English literature class at the moment. It's fascinating.

CHRIS: **Tiens**, tu sais **donc** bien l'anglais?

What do you know, so you know English well?

ANNE: Pas trop mal, mais je sais **mieux** lire que parler.

Not too badly, but I read better than I speak.

Jugez de votre compréhension. Check your comprehension. Write T *(true)* or F *(false)*.

1. _____ Anne va voyager cet été.

2. _____ Anne aime se promener le long de la Seine.

3. _____ Anne nage dans la Seine.

4. _____ Anne va à l'université pendant l'été.

5. _____ Anne va suivre des cours de français.

Improving your conversation

Qu'est-ce que tu fais?

Use this phrase to ask what someone is doing or will do soon.

Qu'est-ce que tu fais en ce moment?	***What are you doing*** *at the moment?*
Qu'est-ce que tu fais demain?	***What will you do*** *tomorrow?*

Profiter de (d')

Use this verb and structure to express that you are enjoying and taking full advantage of an opportunity.

Je n'ai pas classe aujourd'hui. **Je profite de** ma journée de congé.	*I don't have class today.* ***I'm enjoying*** *my day off.*
Il habite près de la mer. Alors **il en profite** pour se bronzer souvent sur la plage.	*He lives near the sea. So* ***he takes advantage of it*** *by sunbathing often on the beach.*

Mais oui!

Use this emphatic phrase to express a most definite *yes* as in *of course.*

—Tu viens ce soir?	*—Are you coming tonight?*
—**Mais oui!**	*—Of course!*

Et puis...

This expression, which, in its literal sense, means *and then,* can be used to mean *on top of that.*

Je vais finir cet exercice **et puis** je vais dormir.	*I'm going to finish this exercise **and then** go to sleep.*
Je ne peux pas sortir. Je suis fatigué. **Et puis** j'ai encore du travail.	*I can't go out. I'm tired. **On top of that** I still have some work.*

Tiens!

This interjection has a variety of uses and meanings. It usually conveys surprise.

Ils vont en France? **Tiens**, je ne savais pas.	*They're going to France? **Well**, I didn't know.*
Où sont les clés? **Tiens**, les voilà!	*Where are the keys? **Look**, there they are!*

Donc...

This adverb also has a variety of uses and meanings. It often accompanies an urgent command, in which case it has no translation. It can also be used to indicate a *cause* (*so/therefore*).

Viens **donc**!	*Come on! / Let's go!*
Ils sont à la retraite. **Donc** ils voyagent beaucoup.	*They are retired. **So** they travel a lot.*
Tu es **donc** déjà professeur?	***So** you're already a teacher?*

Suivre un cours

This idiomatic phrase includes the irregular verb **suivre** (literally meaning *to follow*); it is used to indicate that you are *taking a class*.

Nous **suivons un cours d'anglais**.	*We're **taking an English class**.*

Mieux

This adverb modifies the meaning of the action verb to say it's being done *better* than before or than in other circumstances.

J'étudie **mieux** tout seul.	*I study **better** alone.*
Vous jouez **mieux** aujourd'hui.	*You're playing **better** today.*

With a verb that indicates a state (rather than an action), such as **être** (*to be*), the superlative adverb **le mieux** means *the best*.

Tout est pour **le mieux**.	*All is for **the best**.*

Grammar notes

Meilleur(e)(s) and mieux

Remember to distinguish the adjective (**le/la/les**) **meilleur(e)(s)** (*better; best*) from the adverb (**le**) **mieux** (*better; the best*). **Aimer mieux** is a synonym for **préférer**.

C'est **le meilleur** film de cette année.	*It is **the best** movie this year.*
J'**aime mieux** rester à la maison.	*I **prefer** staying home / I **like** staying home **better**.*

Reflexive verbs

Many regular -**er** verbs such as **se baigner**, **se promener**, and **se bronzer** are also reflexive. So remember to add the appropriate reflexive pronoun before the conjugated verb.

se baigner (*present tense*) (*to bathe / to swim*)	
je me baigne	nous nous baignons
tu te baignes	vous vous baignez
il/elle/on se baigne	ils/elles se baignent

se promener (*present tense*) (*to go for a walk*)	
je me promène	nous nous promenons
tu te promènes	vous vous promenez
il/elle/on se promène	ils/elles se promènent

se bronzer (*present tense*) (*to tan*)	
je me bronze	nous nous bronzons
tu te bronzes	vous vous bronzez
il/elle/on se bronze	ils/elles se bronzent

Nous **nous baignons** dans ce lac en été.	*We **swim/bathe** in this lake during the summer.*
On **se bronze** sur l'herbe.	*We **are sunbathing** on the grass.*
Tout le monde **se promène** aujourd'hui.	*Everybody **is going for a walk** today.*

Suivre

The conjugation of the irregular verb **suivre** (*to follow; to take* [*a class*]) in the present tense is as follows: **je/tu suis, il/elle/on suit, nous suivons, vous suivez, ils/elles suivent**.

Vas-y! Je te **suis** dans une minute.	*Go ahead! I'll **follow** you in a minute.*
Ma sœur **suit** un cours d'anthropologie.	*My sister **is taking** a class in anthropology.*
Ils **suivent** bien nos instructions.	*They **follow** our instructions well.*

EXERCICE

2·8

Quelle coïncidence! *What a coincidence! Write the letter of the most appropriate reply to each line of dialogue in the space provided.*

1. ___*a*___ Qu'est-ce que tu fais pendant l'été?   a. Je profite des vacances.

2. _____ Oui, mais tu voyages par exemple?   b. Tiens! Quelle coïncidence!

3. _____ Pourquoi? Tu as de la famille là-bas?   c. Ah oui, je connais très bien.

4. _____ Ah. Je comprends. Tu y vas toute seule?   d. Pas trop mal? Moi, j'adore cette petite ville.

5. _____ Tu sais, moi aussi, je vais en Normandie!   e. Bien sûr! Je vais toujours en Normandie.

6. _____ Oui, tu vois, j'ai un oncle qui habite là-bas.   f. Exactement. Mes parents ne quittent pas Paris.

7. _____ Il habite à Caen. Tu connais?   g. Justement oui: mes grands-parents.

8. _____ Ce n'est pas trop mal comme ville.   h. Où en Normandie habite-t-il?

J'aime me détendre. *I like to relax. Complete each sentence with an appropriate term or expression from the list provided.*

suis	quitter	lire
me suffit	profite	tout seul
Et puis	me baigner	me bronzer
me promener		

En été, je _____ (1) de mes vacances. Je ne _____ (2) généralement pas de

cours à l'université. J'adore _____ (3) le long des berges de la Seine. Les Parisiens

aiment _____ (4) la ville en été; moi, non. C'est vrai, je ne peux pas _____ (5),

mais je peux _____ (6) et _____ (7) un bon livre, couché dans l'herbe ou sur

le sable. Cela _____ (8). _____ (9) j'adore la tranquillité et le calme; cela ne

me dérange pas d'être _____ (10).

Dialogue 5

Since Chris is going to be in Paris for a few more weeks, he wonders if Anne could show him around town.

CHRIS: Tu sais, Anne, Didier va bientôt partir en Italie avec sa famille.

You know, Anne, Didier is soon going to leave for Italy with his family.

ANNE: C'est parce qu'ils ont une maison de campagne en Toscane où ils vont chaque été.

It's because they have a house in Tuscany where they go every summer.

CHRIS: **Dommage** pour moi! Je perds mon copain.

Too bad for me! I'm losing my friend.

ANNE: Si tu veux, je peux te montrer mes endroits favoris à Paris.

If you want, I can show you my favorite places in Paris.

CHRIS: C'est gentil, Anne! Mais tu vas être occupée avec tes études, non?

That's nice, Anne! But you're going to be busy with your studies, aren't you?

ANNE: **Mais non, pas tout le temps, voyons**!

Of course not, not all the time, come on!

CHRIS: Tu vas m'emmener promener le long de la Seine?

Are you going to take me for a walk along the Seine?

ANNE: Ah non! Ça, je le fais toute seule. Mais on peut sortir le soir.

Certainly not! That I do alone. But we can go out in the evenings.

CHRIS: Ah! **Ça m'intéresse!** Où par exemple?

Oh! I'm interested! Where for example?

ANNE: Il y a mille choses à faire. Tu aimes la musique, la danse, le théâtre, la bonne bouffe?

There are a thousand things to do. Do you like music, dance, theater, good food?

CHRIS: J'adore le théâtre.

I love the theater.

ANNE:	Eh bien, moi aussi. **Alors**, on va décider ensemble **ce qui est le plus** intéressant à voir.	*Well, me too. So we'll decide together what is the most interesting to see.*
CHRIS:	D'accord! Je suis prêt!	*OK, I'm ready!*

EXERCICE 2·10

Jugez de votre compréhension. *Check your comprehension. Write T (true) or F (false).*

1. _____ La famille de Didier a une maison en Italie.

2. _____ Didier va partir en vacances cet été.

3. _____ Anne ne veut pas sortir avec Chris.

4. _____ Chris et Anne vont faire des promenades le long de la Seine.

5. _____ Chris et Anne adorent le théâtre.

Improving your conversation

Dommage!

Use this adverb to show empathy or express disappointment.

Élaine est malade. **Dommage!**	*Élaine is sick. **Too bad!***
Il pleut. **Dommage** pour le pique-nique.	*It's raining. **Too bad** for the picnic!*

Mais non, voyons!

The expression **mais non** is an emphatic *no* or *of course not*. The verb **voyons** (literally, *let's see*), added to the phrase, makes a reply more forceful and somewhat indignant.

—Tu as encore eu un accident de voiture?	*—Have you had another car accident?*
—**Mais non, voyons!**	*—**Of course not!** (implying "How can you think that?")*

Ça m'intéresse!

Use this structure to express that you are interested in something (rather than trying to make a literal translation of *I'm interested*).

La politique? **Ça m'intéresse** beaucoup.	*Politics? **It interests me** a lot.*

(Pas) tout le temps

This is one of several expressions that include the noun **le temps** with the meaning of *time*.

J'aime lire, mais **pas tout le temps**.	*I like to read but **not all the time**.*
Lui, il regarde **tout le temps** la télé.	*He watches TV **all the time**.*

Alors...

Use this transitional adverb, at the beginning or end of a sentence, to predict an effect or draw a conclusion.

Tu aimes les films d'aventures. **Alors,** trouvons-en un!

*You like adventure movies. **So** let's find one!*

Ce qui est le plus...

Use this phrase to talk about something that's the most boring, interesting, expensive, etc., in a given circumstance.

Ce qui est le plus ennuyeux ici, c'est qu'il faut toujours attendre.

***What is most** annoying here is that you always have to wait.*

Grammar note
The near future tense

The near future tense (*to be going to*) uses a conjugated form of the verb **aller** followed by an infinitive:

Je **vais partir.**

*I'm **going to leave.***

Remember that the verb **aller** has an irregular conjugation in the present tense: **je vais**, **tu vas**, **il/elle/on va**, **nous allons**, **vous allez**, **ils/elles vont**.

Ils **vont voyager.**
Mes copains **vont organiser** une fête.
Nous **allons nous amuser.**

*They **are going to travel.***
*My friends **are going to organize** a party.*
*We're **going to have fun.***

EXERCICE
2·11

Un petit incident! *A little incident! Complete each line of dialogue with an appropriate term or expression from the list provided. Capitalize as necessary.*

c'est gentil	c'est parce que	si tu veux
alors	d'accord	mais non, voyons!
dommage	ce qui est intéressant	il y a mille choses à faire
prêt		

1. DENISE: Tu es _____, chéri? Voilà le taxi!

2. JEAN-LOUIS: Oui, oui, _____. J'arrive. Mais ce n'est pas un taxi, c'est un autobus, c'est un car de tourisme!

3. DENISE: _____! Tu exagères toujours!

4. JEAN-LOUIS: _____, c'est que tu adores quand j'exagère, n'est-ce pas?

5. DENISE: C'est vrai. _____ tu es drôle!

6. JEAN-LOUIS: Merci pour le compliment. _____.

7. Denise: _____ on y va?

8. Jean-Louis: Oui, _____, allons-y!

9. Denise: Oui, je veux. _____ ce soir. Mais... où est le taxi?

10. Jean-Louis: _____ pour nous! Le taxi est parti avec d'autres clients.

Dialogue 6

Anne and Chris are planning to see a modern play at Anne's university and then go out to a café for a bite to eat.

Anne: Allô, Chris. Ici, Anne. J'ai deux billets pour une pièce à l'université samedi soir. Ça t'intéresse?	*Hello, Chris. This is Anne. I have two tickets for a play at the university Saturday night. Are you interested?*
Chris: Bien sûr, Anne! C'est sympa de ne pas m'avoir oublié. Mais **dis-moi** un peu **de quoi il s'agit**.	*Of course, Anne! It's nice that you didn't forget me. But tell me something about it.*
Anne: Écoute, tout ce que je peux dire, c'est que mon professeur d'anglais a vu la pièce et l'a trouvée **géniale**.	*Listen, all I can say is that my English professor saw it and found it amazing.*
Chris: Tu ne sais pas **quel en est le sujet**?	*You don't know what it's about?*
Anne: C'est une adaptation de *La Tempête* de Shakespeare, mais dans un contexte moderne.	*It's an adaptation of Shakespeare's* The Tempest, *but in a modern context.*
Chris: Bon, d'accord. **On verra bien**!	*OK, good. We'll see!*
Anne: **Tu veux me chercher chez moi ou me rejoindre** au théâtre?	*Do you want to pick me up at home or meet me at the theater?*
Chris: Donne-moi ton adresse et l'heure où je dois être chez toi et **j'y serai**.	*Give me your address and the time I have to be at your house and I'll be there.*
Anne: Ça va! Tiens, je vais t'envoyer tout ça à ton adresse e-mail, d'accord?	*Fine! Hey, I'm going to send all that to your e-mail address, OK?*
Chris: Ça va. Parfait.	*Fine. (It's) perfect.*
Anne: Si tu veux, après la pièce, on peut aller dans un café avec quelques amis.	*If you like, after the play, we can go to a café with a few friends.*
Chris: **Volontiers.** Je te suis **n'importe où**, Anne!	*Gladly. I'll follow you wherever you want, Anne!*

EXERCICE 2·12

Jugez de votre compréhension. *Check your comprehension.* Write T *(true)* or F *(false)*.

1. _____ Anne invite Chris au cinéma.

2. _____ Le prof d'Anne recommande une pièce à ses étudiants.

3. _____ Chris veut chercher Anne chez elle.

4. _____ Anne va envoyer l'adresse du théâtre à Chris.

5. _____ Anne et Chris vont aller au café samedi soir.

Improving your conversation

Dis-moi / dites-moi de quoi il s'agit

This expression may be used to ask what something is about, such as a movie, a play, a book, or a lecture.

Je veux bien aller voir cette pièce, mais **dis-moi de quoi il s'agit.**	*I don't mind going to see this play, but* **tell me what it's about.**

Génial!

This adjective may be used in multiple contexts to express admiration or excitement.

Quel beau tableau! Il est **génial!**	*What a beautiful painting! It's* **brilliant!**
Tu as acheté les tickets de concert? **Génial!**	*You bought the concert tickets?* **Great!/ Fabulous!**

Quel en est le sujet?

This question asks what the subject or topic of an article or a book is. The pronoun **en** (*of it / in it*) replaces the article or book being discussed.

Tu as lu ce livre. **Quel en est le sujet?**	*You read this book.* **What is its topic?**

On verra bien

Use this expression to show skepticism or restrained optimism.

Je ne sais pas si on pourra apprécier le spectacle de si loin. **On verra bien.**	*I don't know if we'll be able to appreciate the show from so far away.* **We'll see.**

Tu veux me chercher ou me rejoindre?

Ask this question to find out if your friend will pick you up or if he or she prefers to meet you at the venue.

Je ne sais pas où c'est. **Tu veux me chercher?**	*I don't know where it is.* **Do you want to pick me up?**
Je suis devant le cinéma. **Tu veux me rejoindre?**	*I'm in front of the movie theater.* **Do you want to meet me?**

J'y serai

This phrase assures your friend you'll get to your agreed-upon rendezvous on time. Change the subject and the form of the verb to adapt the expression as necessary.

Le cinéma Rex? D'accord. **J'y serai!**	*The Rex cinema? OK,* **I'll be there!**

Rendez-vous devant le restaurant?	*Rendez-vous in front of the restaurant?*
D'accord, **nous y serons**.	*OK, **we'll be there**.*

Volontiers

Use this adverb to agree with or accede to a request.

—Tu peux me rejoindre au théâtre?	*—Can you join me at the theater?*
—**Volontiers.**	*—**Gladly.***

N'importe où

Use **n'importe** followed by an interrogative adverb (**quand/où/comment**) to indicate *any time/ any place* or *by any means.*

Tu peux téléphoner **n'importe quand**.	*You can phone **any time**.*
J'irai **n'importe où** avec toi.	*I'll go **any place**/**anywhere** with you.*

Grammar note

Commands

The command forms of verbs are the conjugated **tu/nous/vous** forms of the verb *without* the subject pronouns that normally precede them in statements.

Dis-le!	*Say it! (familiar)*
Disons-le!	*Let's say it!*
Dites-le!	*Say it! (formal or plural)*

For regular -**er** verbs and the verb **aller**, remember to drop the -**s** ending of the conjugated **tu** form of the verb (**vas**) to create the familiar command.

Écoute!	*Listen!*
Va!	*Go!*

EXERCICE
2·13

Tu vas me rejoindre? *Are you going to meet me? Write the letter of the most appropriate reply on the line provided. The first one has been done for you.*

1. __a__ J'ai des billets pour un récital de danse.

2. _____ C'est à dix-neuf heures. Tu peux y aller?

3. _____ C'est de la danse expérimentale.

4. _____ Oui, je sais. Tu veux me rejoindre au théâtre?

5. _____ D'accord. Tu arrives à quelle heure?

6. _____ L'heure où il y a le plus de circulation.

a. Génial, c'est à quelle heure?

b. Non, je vais te chercher chez toi.

c. Je sais, mais on verra bien.

d. Je serai chez toi à dix-sept heures.

e. Volontiers! Ça m'intéresse!

f. Écoute, tu sais que j'adore n'importe quelle danse.

EXERCICE 2·14

Allons au cinéma! *Let's go to the movies! In the following dialogue, write Marc's replies to his friend Juliette according to the English guidelines in parentheses.*

1. JULIETTE: Allô, Marc. Ici Juliette. J'ai les billets de cinéma. Tu veux me chercher ou me rejoindre?

   MARC: _____ (*I am going to pick you up.*)

2. JULIETTE: À quelle heure?

   MARC: _____ (*Any time.*)

3. JULIETTE: D'accord. Je serai prête. On peut prendre le taxi.

   MARC: _____ (*Gladly*)

4. JULIETTE: Ça va être génial.

   MARC: _____ (*It is about Facebook. I'm interested.*)

5. JULIETTE: Ah oui. Bien sûr! Et moi aussi!

   MARC: _____ (*The topic is good, but the movie? We'll see.*)

6. JULIETTE: Tout ce que je peux dire, c'est que c'est un film à voir.

   MARC: _____ (*Listen, I'll be at your house at six.*)

EXERCICE 2·15

Karen et François deviennent amis. *Karen and François become friends. In this dialogue, Karen tells François she is taking an art history class on Wednesdays with Professor Pouce. Write the dialogue between these two people using the English guidelines provided.*

1. Karen tells François that she's taking an art history class on Wednesdays with Professor Pouce.

   KAREN: _____

2. François is surprised because he is also taking an art history class with Professor Pouce, but on Mondays.

   FRANÇOIS: _____

3. Karen tells François that her course is only an introduction and asks about his course.

   KAREN: _____

4. François replies that his course is a second year course and that he loves it.

    FRANÇOIS: _____

5. Karen asks François if he goes regularly to museums then.

    KAREN: _____

6. François says that, of course, he spends all his free time in museums and art galleries. Then he asks if she wants to join him tomorrow for a modern art exhibit.

    FRANÇOIS: _____

7. Karen says that she would be glad to and asks at what time.

    KAREN: _____

8. François says they can go any time after seven P.M.

    FRANÇOIS: _____

Discussing leisure activities

Dialogue 1

During intermission, Chris and Anne discuss the play they are watching.

CHRIS: **Qu'est-ce que tu penses de** cette pièce, Anne?

What do you think of this play, Anne?

ANNE: Je suis fascinée. Certains des thèmes me semblent tout à fait **actuels**.

I'm fascinated. Some of the themes seem totally current.

CHRIS: **Ah oui, tu crois?** Quel thème par exemple?

Really, you think so? Which theme, for example?

ANNE: Celui de la quête de pouvoir absolu et de l'abus de pouvoir, par exemple.

The quest for absolute power and the abuse of power, for example.

CHRIS: C'est vieux comme le monde, ça! Je suis un peu **déçu**.

That's as old as the hills! I'm a little disappointed.

ANNE: **Mais justement!** On peut constater que la psychologie humaine ne change pas au cours du temps.

That's just it! We (You/One) can observe how human psychology doesn't change over time.

CHRIS: Oui, bon, je vois ça. Mais **tu ne penses pas que** le jeu des acteurs laisse un peu à désirer?

Yes, well, I do see that. But don't you think that the acting leaves a bit to be desired?

ANNE: **Tu es vraiment dur**, toi! Ce sont tous des amateurs, voyons!

You're really tough! They're all amateurs, you know!

CHRIS: **Je le sais bien**, mais **je ne les trouve pas très bons**, tu sais!

I know that, but I don't find them very good, you know!

ANNE: Eh bien. Je suis désolée. **Tu n'as pas l'air d'apprécier** la pièce ni les acteurs.

Well. I'm sorry. You don't seem to appreciate the play or the actors.

CHRIS: Mais j'apprécie beaucoup ta compagnie. Retournons à nos places!

But I do appreciate your company. Let's go back to our seats!

ANNE: Je suis **ravie**. J'espère que la seconde partie va te **plaire**.

I'm delighted. I hope (that) you'll like the second part.

Jugez de votre compréhension. *Check your comprehension. Write* T *(true) or* F *(false).*

1. _____ Chris pense que les thèmes de la pièce sont actuels.

2. _____ Chris apprécie beaucoup la pièce.

3. _____ Anne pense que Chris est dur.

4. _____ Chris aime bien Anne.

5. _____ Anne est déçue.

Improving your conversation
Qu'est-ce que tu penses de (d')... ?

Ask this question to elicit an opinion about a thing or a person.

—**Qu'est-ce que tu penses de** cet acteur?   —***What do you think of*** *this actor?*
—Je le trouve médiocre.   —*I think he's mediocre.*

Actuel(le)

Use this adjective to describe what is *current* or *present-day*. Beware that it is a false cognate and does *not* mean *actual*.

Le thème de l'environnement est **actuel**.   *The environmental theme is **current**.*

Ah oui, tu crois?

Use this expression to express a slight doubt while listening to an opinion.

—Je pense que ce couple va divorcer.   —*I think this couple is going to divorce.*
—**Ah oui, tu crois?**   —***Really?***

Mais justement!

Use this expression to play devil's advocate, that is, to pretend to support the "wrong" opinion.

—Ton argument n'est pas logique!   —*Your argument is not logical!*
—**Mais justement.** Je veux voir si tu peux me contredire.   —***That's just it.*** *I want to see if you can contradict me.*

—Tu portes ça d'une façon bizarre.   —*You wear that in a strange way.*
—**Mais justement!** Je vais lancer une mode!   —***That's just it!*** *I'm going to start a trend!*

Déçu(e)

Use this adjective to express *disappointment*, not deception. Beware that it is a false cognate and does *not* mean *deceived*.

Il est **déçu** de ne pas avoir été admis.	*He is **disappointed** he was not accepted.*

Tu ne penses pas que (qu')... ?

Use this expression to elicit someone's agreement while stating your own opinion.

Tu ne penses pas qu'ils exagèrent?	***Don't you think** (that) they're exaggerating?*

Tu es vraiment dur(e)

Use this expression to show that someone's opinion seems harsh to you.

—Cette actrice est minable.	*—This actress is pitiful.*
—**Tu es vraiment dur.**	*—**You're really harsh.***

Je (le) sais bien

Use the adverb **bien** after **je sais** or **je le sais** when you want to emphasize that you already know something, in the context of defending yourself.

—Tu devrais mieux écouter.	*—You should listen better.*
—**Je le sais bien**, mais c'est difficile.	*—**I know it** (**well**), but it's difficult.*

Je le/la/les trouve + *adjectif*

This structure is used to express an opinion using adjectives that describe things or people.

La soupe à l'oignon, **je la trouve** trop **salée**.	*The onion soup, **I think it's** too **salty**.*
Le nouveau prof, **je le trouve strict**.	*The new teacher, **I find him strict**.*

Je suis désolé(e)

Use this expression to convey *regret* or *sympathy* or to apologize.

Tu es malade? **Je suis désolé(e).**	*You're sick? **I'm sorry.***
Je suis désolé(e) d'être en retard.	***I'm sorry** to be late.*

(Ne pas) apprécier...

Use this expression to express appreciation or show displeasure.

J'apprécie beaucoup votre invitation.	***I appreciate** your invitation a lot.*
Je n'apprécie pas cette façon de parler.	***I do not appreciate** this manner of speaking.*

(Ne pas) avoir l'air

Use this idiomatic **avoir** expression to describe someone. Note that the adjective may agree with the subject of the verb *or* with the masculine noun **l'air**.

Marie **n'a pas l'air** heureux/heureuse.	*Marie **does not seem** happy.*
Paul **a l'air** furieux.	*Paul **looks** furious.*

Ravi(e)

Use this adjective to express *delight*. Beware that it is a false cognate and does *not* mean *ravished*.

Je suis **ravi** que le concert te plaise.   *I'm **delighted** that you like the concert.*

Plaire

The verb **plaire** (*to please*) is expresses *likes* and *dislikes*. Note that it requires a special construction in French. The French indirect object pronoun **me** (**m'**) is translated as the English subject pronoun *I*. In the question, the French indirect object pronoun **te** (**t'**) or **vous** will become the English subject pronoun *you*.

La pièce **me plaît**.	*I like the play. (The play **pleases me**.)*
Les thèmes ne **me plaisent** pas.	*I do not like the themes. (The themes don't **please me**.)*
Qu'est-ce qui **te plaît**?	*What do you (familiar) like? (What **pleases you**?)*
Qu'est-ce qui ne **vous plaît** pas?	*What don't you (formal, plural) like? (What doesn't **please you**?)*

Grammar notes

Croire, penser, and espérer que (qu')...

The verbs **croire** (*to believe*), **penser** (*to think*), and **espérer** (*to hope*) are followed by the conjunction **que** (**qu'**) (*that*) when a new clause is introduced, even though the English word *that* may be omitted and implied.

Je **crois/pense que** la pièce est bonne.	*I **believe/think** (**that**) the play is good.*
Nous **espérons que** la pièce va être appréciée.	*We **hope** (**that**) the play is going to be appreciated.*

Gender and number

French adjectives agree in gender (masculine or feminine) and in number (singular or plural) with the noun they describe.

Chris n'est pas **fasciné**.	*Chris is not **fascinated**.*
Anne est **fascinée**.	*Anne is **fascinated**.*
Ils sont **contents**.	*They (m.) are **happy**.*
Elles sont **contentes**.	*They (f.) are **happy**.*

EXERCICE
3·2

Thomas et Josette ne sont pas d'accord. *Thomas and Josette do not agree. Provide the replies to Thomas's comments in French as indicated in parentheses. Remember that you are Josette in this dialogue.*

1. THOMAS: Cette pièce ne me plaît pas du tout.

   JOSETTE: _____. (*I'm sorry. Why don't you like it?*)

2. THOMAS: Je ne comprends vraiment pas. Quel en est le sujet?

   JOSETTE: _____. (*It is human psychology.*)

3. THOMAS: Vraiment? Alors ça!

   JOSETTE: _____. (*Yes, I know. It's old!*)

4. THOMAS: Ça, tu peux le dire!

   JOSETTE: _____. (*I do like that play!*)

5. THOMAS: Tu adores toutes les pièces.

   JOSETTE: _____. (*I appreciate good plays.*)

6. THOMAS: Bon, d'accord. Mais pour moi, cette pièce, je la trouve ennuyeuse.

   JOSETTE: _____. (*Don't you think you are a bit tough?*)

7. THOMAS: Non, pas du tout! C'est mon opinion!

   JOSETTE: _____. (*What do you think of the actors?*)

8. THOMAS: Ils sont bien!

   JOSETTE: _____. (*You see! You appreciate something!*)

9. THOMAS: Tu es contente, Josette?

   JOSETTE: _____. (*I am delighted.*)

10. THOMAS: Eh bien, retournons à nos places. J'espère que la seconde partie va être bonne!

   JOSETTE: _____. (*I hope you are not going to be disappointed.*)

EXERCICE 3·3

Thomas et Josette discutent d'une autre pièce. *Thomas and Josette discuss another play. For each of Thomas's lines of dialogue write the letter of the most appropriate reply by Josette.*

1. _____ Cette seconde partie est bonne.

2. _____ Mais je trouve vraiment le thème pas très actuel.

3. _____ Tu trouves les acteurs bons ou mauvais?

4. _____ Tu es toujours indulgente, toi.

5. _____ Je sais, mais justement, j'aime critiquer.

6. _____ Ah oui. Tu crois?

a. Oui, je pense que tu n'apprécies pas assez les bonnes choses.

b. Je te trouve un peu trop critique!

c. Pourtant on voit ça tous les jours!

d. Ah! Je suis ravie que tu l'aimes.

e. Pas trop mauvais pour des amateurs!

f. Oui, mais tu es toujours trop dur!

Dialogue 2

Chris and Anne agree that the movie they just saw was really bad.

ANNE: **Quel navet**, ce film! Je suis furieuse. Quelle perte de temps!

What a bad movie! I am furious. What a waste of time!

CHRIS: Je suis tout à fait d'accord avec toi. Je suis même dégoûté. **Rien que** du sang et des massacres!

I totally agree with you. I am disgusted even. Nothing but blood and massacres!

ANNE: Quelle horreur! Qui t'a recommandé ce film?

How awful! Who recommended this movie?

CHRIS: C'est Didier! Tu crois que c'est **son genre de** film?

It's Didier! Do you believe that this is his type of movie?

ANNE: Ah non. Je le connais trop bien. C'est une de ses plaisanteries.

No. I know him too well. This is one of his jokes.

CHRIS: Une blague? Tu es sérieuse?

A joke? Are you serious?

ANNE: Oui, il adore **jouer des tours** à ses amis.

Yes, he loves to play jokes on his friends.

CHRIS: **On devrait** lui **faire le même coup**.

We should play the same trick on him.

ANNE: Oui, mais pas tout de suite. **Il ne faut pas qu'**il s'en doute.

Yes, but not right away. He must not suspect it.

CHRIS: En attendant, on peut **faire croire** qu'on a aimé le film, qu'on est ravis.

Meanwhile, we can pretend that we liked the movie, that we are delighted.

ANNE: Ça va être difficile, ça!

That's going to be tough!

EXERCICE 3·4

Jugez de votre compréhension. *Check your comprehension. Write* T *(true) or* F *(false).*

1. _____ Anne et Chris pensent que le film est mauvais.

2. _____ Le film est violent.

3. _____ Anne pense que Didier aime ce genre de film.

4. _____ Chris veut jouer un tour à Didier.

5. _____ Anne et Chris vont faire croire qu'ils aiment ce film.

Improving your conversation

Quel navet!

Use this expression to express a negative opinion of a show, a movie, or other performance.

Le nouveau feuilleton à la télé est horrible. **Quel navet!**

*The new TV series is horrible. **What a failure / a dud!***

Rien que...

Use this phrase to make a clear point that something is limited or restricted to the best or the worst.

Rien que des amateurs! Super!	***Nothing but** amateurs! Great!*
Rien que de la violence? Ah non!	***Nothing but** violence? Oh, no!*

Un genre de (d')...

Use this expression when discussing types of movies, books, etc.

Quels genres de film te plaisent le plus?	***What types of** movies do you like the most?*
Quel genre d'actualités te plaît?	***What type of** news do you like?*

Jouer un tour à...

This expression refers to *playing a joke on someone*. Note that it requires an *indirect object* (**à** + noun or pronoun).

Nous allons **jouer un tour à notre copain**.	*We're going **to play a joke on our friend**.*
C'est vrai? Tu **lui as joué un tour**?	*Is it true? You **played a joke on him/her**?*

Faire le même coup à...

This expression refers to *playing the same trick on someone*. Note that it requires an *indirect object* (**à** + noun or pronoun).

On va **faire le même coup à Jean et à Marc**.	*We're going **to play the same trick on Jean and Marc**.*
Tu veux vraiment **leur faire le même coup**?	*You really want **to play the same trick on them**?*

On devrait...

Use the verb **devoir** in the conditional mood to suggest a moral obligation.

On devrait travailler aujourd'hui.	***We should** work today.*
On ne devrait pas mentir.	***We should not** lie.*

Faire croire (à)

Use this phrase to express *to pretend, to make (others) believe,* or *to convince (others)*. It takes an indirect object.

Je vais **faire croire** que le film me plaît.	*I'm going **to pretend** that I like the movie.*
Il **fait croire aux gens** qu'il parle français. Quel comédien!	*He **makes people believe** that he speaks French. What a joker!*

Grammar notes

Quel/Quels/Quelle/Quelles + *nom!*

Use the appropriate form of the adjective **quel(le)(s)**, followed by a noun, to exclaim and state a positive or negative opinion. It has four forms, agreeing in gender and number with the noun it precedes.

Quel film!	*What a movie!*
Quels films!	*What movies!*
Quelle pièce!	*What a play!*
Quelles pièces!	*What plays!*
Je suis déçu(e) par ce concert. **Quel** navet!	*I am disappointed by this concert. What a bad performance!*
Le film était horrible. **Quelle** perte de temps!	*The movie was horrible. What a waste of time!*

Il faut...

Il faut (literally, *it is necessary*) is an impersonal expression often followed by an infinitive. The translation of this expression is usually *must / has / have to*. Note however that **il ne faut pas** translates only as *must not*.

Il faut apprécier ceci.	*We/You/One must appreciate this.*
Il faut apprécier ceci.	*We/You have (One has) to appreciate this.*
Il ne faut pas critiquer.	*We/You/One must not criticize.*

Il faut que (qu') is followed by a subject and a verb in the *subjunctive* mood.

Il faut qu'il s'en doute.	*He must / has to suspect it.*
Il ne faut pas qu'ils s'en doutent.	*They must not suspect it.*

EXERCICE 3·5

Qu'en penses-tu? *What do you think? Complete each sentence with an appropriate word or expression from the list provided. One of the expressions will be used twice.*

as l'air dégoûté	On devrait plaît	horreur Quelle	Il ne faut pas navet

1. JOSETTE: Il te _____, ce film?

2. THOMAS: Non, je suis _____. Quel _____!

3. JOSETTE: Tu _____ vraiment furieux.

4. THOMAS: Quelle _____! Rien que des assassinats!

5. JOSETTE: Tu es sérieux? _____ terrible perte de temps!

6. THOMAS: Tu peux le dire! _____ dire à tous nos amis de ne pas y aller.

7. JOSETTE: Bonne idée! _____ qu'ils perdent leur temps comme nous!

8. THOMAS: _____ nous rembourser le prix de nos tickets!

EXERCICE

3·6

J'ai envie de voir ce film. *I feel like seeing this movie. Write the following dialogue in French.*

1. JULIE: _____. (*We should go see this movie.*)

2. THOMAS: _____. (*OK. There's nothing but sports on TV today.*)

3. JULIE: _____. (*Nicole says that it's terrible, but I don't believe her.*)

4. THOMAS: _____? (*What kind of movie is it?*)

5. JULIE: _____. (*It's the biography of the founder of Facebook.*)

6. THOMAS: _____. (*Jean told me it's a good movie. Let's go!*)

Dialogue 3

Chris and Anne pretend to have a surprise for Didier. In fact, they are just playing a joke on him.

ANNE: **Je suis aux anges**! Ça va être **la soirée de ma vie**!

I'm on Cloud Nine! This is going to be the best evening of my life!

DIDIER: Moi, **je me laisse** emmener **je ne sais où** pour **je ne sais quoi**. Quand est-ce que vous allez me révéler votre surprise?

I am being taken who knows where for who knows what. When are you going to tell me your surprise?

CHRIS: **Pour faire son effet**, une surprise doit rester une surprise jusqu'au dernier moment!

To have an effect, a surprise must remain a surprise until the last moment!

DIDIER: Vous m'inquiétez un peu tous les deux.

You worry me a little, both of you.

ANNE: **Prépare-toi!** Tu ne vas en croire ni tes yeux ni tes oreilles!

Get ready! You're not going to believe your eyes or your ears!

DIDIER: Un spectacle! On va à un spectacle! Un concert, un cirque, un film en 3D? Qu'est-ce que ça peut être?

A show! We're going to a show! A concert, a circus, a 3D movie? What can it be?

CHRIS: Dis, dépêche-toi! Il ne faut pas qu'on soit en retard.

Hey, hurry up! We can't be late!

DIDIER: Mais calmez-vous tous les deux. Nous courons comme si nous avions **le feu aux trousses**.	*Calm down, both of you. We're running like we were escaping a fire.*
ANNE: Dis donc, Didier, **tu n'es pas en forme**. Tu es tout **essoufflé**.	*Hey, Didier, you are out of shape. You're completely out of breath.*
DIDIER: Écoute, Anne, cesse de me taquiner et dis-moi où on va.	*Listen, Anne, stop teasing me and tell me where we're going.*
CHRIS: Arrête-toi, Didier. **On y est!**	*Stop, Didier. We're there!*
ANNE: **Tiens-toi bien!** Voilà ta surprise! Regarde le panneau!	*Brace yourself! There's your surprise! Look at the sign!*
DIDIER: Les Rappeurs de Sous-Sol. Ah non! Je déteste ces chanteurs!	*The Basement Rappers. Oh no! I hate these singers!*
CHRIS: **Remets-toi**, Didier. On ne va pas te forcer à **assister à** ce spectacle.	*Don't have an attack, Didier. We're not going to force you to attend this show.*
ANNE: Oui, mais **que ça te serve de leçon**. La prochaine fois, ne nous envoie pas voir un film détestable **non plus. Compris?**	*Yes, but let it be a lesson to you. Next time, don't send us to see a horrible movie either. Understood?*
DIDIER: Dites, les gars, vous m'avez bien eu!	*Say, guys, you really got me!*
ANNE: **Pressons-nous**, Chris! Toi et moi, nous allons nous amuser ce soir avec Les Rappeurs de Sous-Sol! Au revoir, Didier.	*Let's hurry, Chris! You and I, we're going to have fun tonight with the Basement Rappers! Bye, Didier.*
CHRIS: Ne t'en fais pas, Didier. Elle continue de plaisanter, notre petite Anne. **Allons-nous-en!**	*Don't worry, Didier. She won't stop kidding around, our little Anne. Let's leave!*

EXERCICE 3·7

Jugez de votre compréhension. *Check your comprehension. Write* T *(true) or* F *(false).*

1. _____ Anne et Chris font semblant d'avoir une surprise pour Didier.

2. _____ Ils marchent tous très vite.

3. _____ Les Rappeurs de Sous-sol sont des artistes de cirque.

4. _____ Chris veut absolument que Didier assiste au spectacle.

5. _____ Anne plaisante quand elle dit qu'elle veut rester.

Improving your conversation

Je suis aux anges!

Use this expression to express how ecstatically happy you are. It literally means that you are *among the angels.*

C'est le meilleur anniversaire! **Je suis aux anges!**

This is the best birthday! ***I am so happy!***

La soirée de ma vie

Use this expression to refer to *the best evening of your life*. The word *best* (**[la] meilleure**) is omitted and implied.

Je viens de recevoir une bague de fiançailles! C'est **la soirée de ma vie!**

*I just received an engagement ring! It is **the (best) evening of my life!***

Je me laisse + *infinitif*

Use this expression plus an infinitive to convey that *you're allowing something to happen to you*.

Je me laisse guider.
Je me laisse aller.

I allow myself to be guided.
I let myself go.

Je ne sais où / je ne sais quoi

Use the first expression to express *who knows where* and the second to convey *who knows what*.

J'ai acheté ça **je ne sais où.**
Il cherche encore **je ne sais quoi.**

*I bought this **I don't know where**.*
*He's still looking for **who knows what**.*

Pour faire son effet

This idiomatic expression refers to having an effect or making an impression.

Le café doit être fort **pour faire son effet**.

*Coffee must be strong **to have an effect**.*

Prépare-toi!

Use this expression to tell a friend or relative *to get ready*.

Marc, il faudra partir bientôt à l'école. **Prépare-toi!**

*Marc, you'll have to leave soon for school. **Get ready!***

Avoir le feu aux trousses

Use this phrase, which literally means *there is a fire right behind you*, to dramatize how fast someone is running.

Jean **a toujours le feu aux trousses** le matin quand il va au travail.

*Jean **is always running like mad** in the morning when he goes to work.*

Être en forme

Use this phrase to refer to *being in shape*.

Je suis en forme grâce à tout le sport que je fais.

***I'm in shape** thanks to all the exercise I do.*

Être essoufflé(e)

Use this phrase to refer to *being out of breath*.

Il a grimpé les escaliers à toute vitesse!   *He climbed the stairs at full speed!*
Il **est essoufflé**.   *He**'s out of breath**.*

On y est

Use this phrase to convey that you have arrived at your destination.

Arrête la voiture. **On y est!**   *Stop the car. **We have arrived!** /*
*   **We are there!***

Remets-toi!

Use this phrase to encourage a friend or relative to get better or to get over his or her surprise or shock.

Tu as eu peur, mais **remets-toi**   *You got scared, but **get a hold of***
maintenant. Tu es sain et sauf.   ***yourself** now. You're safe.*

Assister à...

Use this verbal expression to refer to attending a show, a meeting, or a conference.

Nous **avons assisté à** un excellent   *We **attended** an excellent concert.*
concert.
Il doit **assister à** la réunion des   *He has **to attend** the teachers'*
professeurs.   *meeting.*

Que ça te serve de leçon!

Use this expression to admonish a friend or relative.

Tu as eu un accident. **Que ça te serve**   *You had an accident. **May that be a***
de leçon! Il faut conduire plus   ***lesson to you!** You have to drive*
doucement.   *more slowly.*

Non plus

Use this phrase to express *not either / neither*.

Je ne sors pas ce soir. Et demain **non plus**.   *I'm not going out tonight. And **not** / **nor***
*tomorrow **either**.*
Tu n'aimes pas ce groupe. **Moi non plus!**   *You don't like this band. **Me neither!***

Compris?

Use this word to ask whether something has been understood.

Tu dois respecter les règles. **Compris?**   *You have to respect the rules. **Understood?***

Pressons-nous!

Use this expression to urge everyone to *hurry up*.

Le spectacle commence dans dix   *The show starts in ten minutes.*
minutes. **Pressons-nous!**   ***Let's hurry!***

Allons-nous-en!

Use this expression to convey the urgency to leave.

Ce film est horrible. **Allons-nous-en!**   *This movie is horrible.* ***Let's leave!***

Grammar notes

Emmener and acheter

Emmener and **acheter** are stem-changing verbs. All forms of the present tense except for the **nous/vous** forms include an -è-.

emmener *(to take [somebody or something] along)*	
j'/il/elle/on emmène	vous emmenez
tu emmènes	ils/elles emmènent
nous emmenons	

acheter *(to buy)*	
j'/il/elle/on achète	vous achetez
tu achètes	ils/elles achètent
nous achetons	

J'**emmène** souvent mes amis en boîte.	*I often* ***take*** *my friends to nightclubs.*
Nous **emmenons** nos chiens au parc.	*We* ***take*** *our dogs to the park.*
Tu **achètes** tes vêtements ici?	*Do you* ***buy*** *your clothes here?*
Vous **achetez** beaucoup de choses.	*You're* ***buying*** *lots of things.*

Remember that the verb **acheter** has an **accent grave** (-è-) in the stem of the *future tense:*

j'achèterai	nous achèterons
tu achèteras	ils/elles achèteront
il/elle/on achètera	vous achèterez

Demain, mes parents **achèteront** une nouvelle télévision.	*Tomorrow my parents* ***will buy*** *a new television.*

In the conditional mood, the verb **acheter** also has an **accent grave** (-è-) in the stem.

j'achèterais	nous achèterions
tu achèterais	vous achèteriez
il/elle/on achèterait	ils/elles achèteraient

Si je n'étais pas fauché, j'**achèterais** un nouvel ordinateur.	*If I weren't broke, I* ***would buy*** *a new computer.*

Reflexive commands

Remember that in the affirmative command forms of reflexive verbs, pronouns *follow* the verb.

Dépêche-toi!	*Hurry (up)!* (familiar)
Dépêchons-nous!	*Let's hurry!*
Dépêchez-vous!	*Hurry!* (formal or plural)

The reflexive verb **s'en aller** (*to go away, to leave*) always includes the object pronoun **en**. Note its position in the affirmative commands.

Va-t'**en**!	*Go away!* (familiar)
Allons-nous-**en**!	*Let's go away!*
Allez-vous-**en**!	*Go away!* (formal or plural)

EXERCICE 3·8

Veux-tu assister à un concert? *Do you want to attend a concert? Complete each sentence with an appropriate word or expression from the list provided. Capitalize as necessary. Some expressions may be used more than once.*

dépêchons-nous	emmènerai	achètes
emmènes	génial	emmenons
pressons-nous	acheter	

1. JOSETTE: Mon groupe favori est en ville. Tu m' _____ les voir?

2. THOMAS: Si tu _____ les billets, je veux bien.

3. JOSETTE: Regardons s'il y a des billets pas trop chers qu'on peut _____ en ligne.

4. THOMAS: Bonne idée! _____!

5. JOSETTE: Je suis d'accord. Il faut faire vite. Ce groupe est _____.

6. THOMAS: Regarde, il y en a encore à un prix raisonnable. _____ d'en acheter!

7. JOSETTE: Voilà ma carte de crédit! _____ aussi ma sœur si ça ne te dérange pas!

8. THOMAS: Bien sûr. Je vous _____ toutes les deux puisque tu m'invites. Merci. C'est gentil.

EXERCICE 3·9

En retard pour le concert! *Late for the concert! Translate each person's lines into French to find out whether Josette and Karen make it to the concert.*

1. JOSETTE: Hurry, Karen. We're late.

_____

2. KAREN: I'm out of breath. Stop running like there is a fire behind us.

_____

3. JOSETTE: I can't be late for this concert. It's my favorite group. Understood?

_____

4. KAREN: I understand, but I can't go faster than this.

_____

5. JOSETTE: Well, you aren't in shape, my little one.

_____

6. KAREN: Neither are you, Josette.

_____

7. JOSETTE: Good, here we are!

_____

8. KAREN: I'm in heaven!

_____

9. JOSETTE: There's Thomas with the tickets!

_____

10. KAREN: Let that be a lesson to us that it is better to leave early.

_____

11. JOSETTE: Yes, you're right. I got scared!

_____

12. KAREN: Get a hold of yourself. Let's have fun!

_____

Dialogue 4

Anne took Chris to a little café where they are enjoying the friendly atmosphere and good food.

ANNE: Super, ce café! Je suis ravie! **La bouffe** est excellente et l'ambiance sympa **comme tout**.

This café is super! I am delighted! The food is excellent, and the atmosphere is really friendly.

CHRIS: **Tu as raison.** Mon steak-frites est **super-bon**!

You're right. My steak and fries is super-good!

ANNE: **Tant mieux!** Mais tu devrais essayer quelque chose de moins typique pour changer.

So much the better! But you should try something less ordinary for a change.

CHRIS: **Quoi par exemple?**

Like what, for example?

ANNE: Eh bien. Ce café a des spécialités alsaciennes. Leur tarte flambée est une des **meilleures**.

Well. This café has Alsatian specialties. Their tarte flambée is one of the best.

CHRIS: Une tarte flambée?	*A tarte flambée?*
ANNE: Oui, regarde la table voisine. Ils en partagent une. Elle a l'air délicieuse, non?	*Yes, look at the next table. They're sharing one. It looks delicious, don't you think?*
CHRIS: **Ça ressemble à** de la pizza.	*It looks like pizza.*
ANNE: Oui, **mais** c'est très différent **quand même**. Il y a des oignons, du lard et de la crème fraîche dessus.	*Yes, but it's quite different. There are onions, bacon, and crème fraîche on it.*
CHRIS: **Ça me fait envie.** On en commande une?	*I'm tempted. Should we order one?*
ANNE: Je voudrais bien en partager une avec toi, mais j'ai assez mangé.	*I would like to share one with you, but I ate enough.*

EXERCICE 3·10

Jugez de votre compréhension. *Check your comprehension. Write* T *(true) or* F *(false).*

1. _____ Anne et Chris adorent le café où ils sont.

2. _____ Chris mange une spécialité alsacienne.

3. _____ La tarte flambée ressemble à une pizza.

4. _____ Chris n'aime pas les oignons.

5. _____ Chris et Anne partagent leur dîner avec les voisins.

Improving your conversation

La bouffe

Use this word only in very familiar (colloquial) settings as it is a slang word for *food*.

C'est de la bonne **bouffe**, ça.   *This is good **food**.*

Adjectif + comme tout!

Use this structure to emphasize what something or someone is like (*really*).

Ils sont gentils **comme tout**.   *They are **really** nice.*
Vous êtes accueillants **comme tout**.   *You are **really** welcoming.*

Avoir raison

Use this idiomatic **avoir** expression to state that someone *is right*.

Tu as raison. Le film joue à dix-huit heures.   ***You're right.** The movie goes on at six P.M.*

Super + *adjectif*

Add the adjective **super-** before any other adjective to reinforce and emphasize its meaning. This is a colloquial construction.

Ce gâteau est **super-bon**.	*This cake is **really good**.*
Ta copine est **super-sympa**.	*Your girlfriend is **really nice**.*

Tant mieux!

Use this expression to show and share your approval and pleasure.

Tu aimes cette bouffe? **Tant mieux!**	*You like this food? **So much the better!**/ **Glad you do!***

Quoi par exemple?

Ask this question when you want an *example*.

Tu dis que Marc te joue toujours des tours. Mais **quoi par exemple**?	*You say that Marc always plays jokes on you. **Like what?***

(Le/la/les) meilleur(e)(s)

Remember to use this adjective to describe a thing or a person as *better* or *best*. Remember that it agrees in gender and number with the noun described.

Cette tarte est **meilleure** ici.	*This tart is **better** here.*
Ils ont **le meilleur** chef du monde.	*They have **the best** chef in the world.*

Ça ressemble à...

This expression may be used to make comparisons.

Intéressant, ce plat. **Ça ressemble à** une pizza.	*Interesting, this dish. **It looks like** pizza.*

Mais quand même...

Use this expression to introduce a very strong argument for or against something.

Je sais que tu aimes avoir raison, mais **quand même**!	*I know that you like to be right, **but really!***
Cet artiste est inconnu, mais **quand même** reconnaissez qu'il est génial!	*This artist is unknown, but **(you have to) admit** that he is great!*

Ça me fait envie

Use this idiomatic **faire** expression to express envy or temptation. Note that the indirect object pronouns **me (m')**, **te (t')**, **nous**, **vous**, **lui**, and **leur** are used to indicate who is tempted, and the subject of the verb **faire** is the object of his or her desire.

Elle adore nager. Alors, la mer, **ça lui fait envie**.	*She loves to swim. So the sea **tempts her**.*
Regardez ce beau plat. **Ça vous fait envie?**	*Look at this beautiful dish! **Are you tempted? / Does it tempt you?***

Grammar notes

Mieux versus meilleur(e)

Remember to use the adverb **mieux** (*better*) to modify a verb and the adjective **meilleur(e)(s)** (*better*) in the appropriate form (agreeing in gender and number) to describe a noun.

J'aime **mieux** les frites.	*I prefer fries. / I like fries **better**.*
Les frites sont **meilleures** ici.	*Fries are **better** here.*

Devoir

The verb **devoir** in the conditional mood has the special meaning of the English auxiliary verb *should*: **je/tu devrais, il/elle/on devrait, nous devrions, vous devriez, ils/elles devraient**. It is followed by an infinitive.

Je **devrais faire** plus attention à mes fautes.	*I **should pay** more attention to my mistakes.*
Nous **devrions commander**.	*We **should order**.*

Vouloir

The verb **vouloir** in the conditional mood has the special meaning of the English phrase *would like*: **je/tu voudrais, il/elle/on voudrait, nous voudrions, vous voudriez, ils/elles voudraient**. Like **devoir**, it is followed by an infinitive.

Ils **voudraient venir**?	*Would they **like to come**?*
Tu **voudrais manger**.	*You **would like to eat**.*

Partitive articles

The partitive articles **du, de la, de l'**, and **des** are used to express *some*, even though *some* may be omitted in the English sentence.

Je voudrais **du** café, **de la** crème, **de** l'eau et **des** petits gâteaux.	*I would like (**some**) coffee, (**some**) cream, (**some**) water, and (**some**) cookies.*

En

The pronoun **en** is used in a French sentence to replace an English noun phrase that includes the quantitative adverb *some*.

—Tu voudrais **de la tarte**?	*—Would you like **some tart**?*
—Oui, j'**en** voudrais.	*—Yes, I would like **some**.*

Beware that the pronoun **en** can be translated in a variety of ways and is not necessarily translated by the English adverb *some*.

—Tu veux **des chocolats**?	*—Do you want **some chocolates**?*
—Oui, j'**en** veux **un**.	*—Yes, I want **one** (**of them**).*

Pronouncing the various accented e sounds

The French sound **é** (*acute accent*) resembles the vowel sound you hear in the English word *bay* (nongliding). The French sound **è** (*grave accent*) makes the same vowel sound as in the English word *bare*. The French sound **ê** (*circumflex accent*), as in **même** (*even/same*), makes the same sound as **è**, but slightly elongated.

The infinitive **célébrer** (*to celebrate*) has an **é** in the first two syllables. Since an **-er** infinitive ending sounds just like **é**, the infinitive repeats the same sound in all three syllables. Furthermore, since the **-ez** ending of the conjugated verb is pronounced just like **é** and **-er**, three forms of this verb are pronounced alike: **célébrer** (*to celebrate*), **vous célébrez** (*you celebrate*), and the past participle **célébré** (*celebrated*).

However, when this stem-changing verb is conjugated in the present tense, the accent over the second **e** becomes *grave* (**è**), *except* in the **nous** and **vous** forms: **je/il/elle/on célèbre**, **tu célèbres**, **nous célébrons**, **vous célébrez**, **ils/elles célèbrent**.

Note that the same patterns are found in conjugations of the verbs **espérer** (*to hope*), **répéter** (*to repeat*), and **préférer** (*to prefer*). Also keep in mind that there are several other letter combinations that produce the same sound as **é**: **m<u>ai</u>son** (*house*), **<u>é</u>couter** (*to listen*), and **pren<u>ez</u>** (*take*).

EXERCICE
3·11

Qu'est-ce que tu voudrais? *What would you like? Complete each sentence in the following dialogue with an appropriate word or expression from the list provided.*

Depuis	fait envie	Tant mieux
quand même	de la tarte flambée	en
mieux	meilleures	

1. MICHEL: Qu'est-ce que tu voudrais, Monique? Du steak ou _____?

2. MONIQUE: Pas de steak pour moi. J'aime _____ la tarte flambée végétarienne.

3. MICHEL: Ah bon. _____ quand tu es végétarienne?

4. MONIQUE: Je ne suis pas strictement végétarienne. Mais _____ j'aime mieux ne pas manger trop de viande.

5. MICHEL: La tarte me _____, moi aussi.

6. MONIQUE: On _____ commande une à partager entre nous deux?

7. MICHEL: Oui, allons-y! Ils font les _____ tartes flambées ici.

8. MONIQUE: _____! On va en profiter!

Qu'en penses-tu? *What do you think? Find Monique's replies to Michel in the following dialogue by writing the letters **a** through **f** on the lines provided. The first one has been done for you.*

1. __*a*__ MICHEL: Quelle excellente tarte!

2. _____ MICHEL: Tu en voudrais encore une part?

3. _____ MICHEL: Oh! Écoute, il y en a encore beaucoup. Prends-en encore une part, s'il te plaît!

4. _____ MICHEL: Bravo! Tu voudrais encore de l'eau?

5. _____ MICHEL: On devrait célébrer avec du Champagne, tu ne penses pas?

6. _____ MICHEL: Les vacances, bien sûr!

a. Tu as raison. Elle est super-bonne!

b. Célébrer quoi?

c. Je voudrais du vin, s'il te plaît!

d. Tu as raison. Mais quand même c'est cher, le Champagne?

e. Non merci. Je ne devrais pas. Je crois que j'en ai assez mangé.

f. Ça me fait vraiment envie! Bon, encore une petite part quand même!

On n'est pas d'accord! *We do not agree. In this dialogue, Michel would really like to see a movie while Monique prefers going to the ballet. Write the dialogue using the English guidelines provided.*

1. Michel tells Monique that the comedy he has been waiting to see for weeks is finally playing in the neighborhood. He can't wait to see it.

   MICHEL: _____

2. Monique reminds Michel in a slightly condescending manner that they are going to the ballet tonight.

   MONIQUE: _____

3. Michel first says that Monique is right. But then he acts very disappointed about not being able to see his movie.

   MICHEL: _____

4. Monique says she understands, but she already has expensive tickets for the ballet tonight.

   MONIQUE: _____

5. Michel tells Monique that he really does not care for ballet and adds that he only goes to please her.

   MICHEL: _____

6. Monique reminds Michel that she goes to the movies and watches rugby on television to please him.

   MONIQUE: _____

7. Michel concedes that this is true. Then he agrees that the ballet is not so bad and that they can go to the movies next week.

   MICHEL: _____

Discussing current events

Dialogue 1

Didier and his family can't get back from Italy by train because of a railroad workers' strike.

ANNE: Allô, Chris. Ici Anne. Ça va bien?

Hello, Chris. This is Anne. Is everything OK?

CHRIS: Oui, très bien, Anne. Et toi? **Quoi de neuf?**

Yes, fine, Anne. How about you? What's new?

ANNE: Moi, **j'ai des nouvelles de** Didier. Je viens de lui parler.

I heard from Didier. I just spoke to him.

CHRIS: Il devrait **être de retour** bientôt, **non?**

He should be back soon, shouldn't he?

ANNE: **Tu n'es pas au courant?** Les employés de la SNCF **sont en grève.**

Don't you know? The workers of the French National Railroad Company (the SNCF) are on strike.

CHRIS: **Zut! Ça veut dire** pas de trains pour quelques jours!

Darn! That means no trains for a few days!

ANNE: Exact! **C'est** déjà **assez embêtant. Mais en plus**, les conducteurs d'autobus veulent se joindre à la grève.

Correct! That's already pretty annoying. But in addition, the bus drivers want to join the strike.

CHRIS: Ah oui, par solidarité, sans doute. **À mon avis**, c'est admirable.

Of course, out of solidarity, no doubt. In my opinion, it's admirable.

ANNE: **C'est toujours comme ça** en France. **Quelle poisse!**

It's always like that in France. What a pain!

CHRIS: Je sais. Ma tante m'en a souvent parlé.

I know. My aunt often talked to me about it.

ANNE: **Tu trouves ça bien que** les travailleurs emploient tant de force de persuasion contre leur employeur?

Do you think that's good that workers use so much persuasive force against their employers?

CHRIS: **Ça dépend.** C'est bien pour les travailleurs, **c'est sûr et certain**!

That depends. It's good for workers, that much is certain!

ANNE: Pas si bien pour les voyageurs et les touristes. **Ça arrive** toujours **en pleine saison**, ces grèves!

Not so good for travelers and tourists. It always happens in the high season, those strikes!

CHRIS: Alors **on dirait que** Didier et sa famille seront coincés en Italie.

So it looks like Didier and his family will be stuck in Italy.

ANNE: Pour l'instant. On verra si la SNCF et le syndicat de travailleurs pourront **se mettre d'accord** bientôt.

For the moment. We'll see if the SNCF and the workers' union can come to an agreement soon.

Jugez de votre compréhension. *Check your comprehension. Write* T *(true) or* F *(false).*

1. _____ Anne voudrait des nouvelles de Didier.

2. _____ Anne sait où est Didier.

3. _____ Anne pense que les grèves sont embêtantes.

4. _____ Chris trouve que les grèves sont bonnes pour les travailleurs.

5. _____ Chris pense que Didier est de retour à la maison.

Improving your conversation

Quoi de neuf?

Use this familiar expression with friends to start a conversation.

Salut, Marie-Josée. **Quoi de neuf?**	*Hi, Marie-Josée.* ***What's up?***

Avoir des nouvelles de (d')...

Use this expression to inquire or give updates about what is happening with friends.

Tu **as des nouvelles d'**Arnaud?	*Do you **have any news from** Arnaud?*
Aujourd'hui j'**ai eu des nouvelles de** Lucie.	*Today I **got news from** Lucie.*

Non?

Always placed at the end of a statement, this word is a synonym for the expression **n'est-ce pas?** (*isn't it so?*).

Tu comprends, **non?**	*You understand, **don't you?***
Elle est là, **non?**	*She's there, **isn't she?***

Être idioms

There are many expressions using the verb **être**; some do not translate literally from French into English.

Arnaud **est** finalement **de retour**.	*Arnaud **is** finally **back**.*
Nous **ne sommes pas au courant** de ce qui se passe.	*We **are not abreast** of what's happening. (We **are not in the loop**.)*
Les travailleurs **sont en grève**.	*The workers **are on strike**.*

Zut!

Use this short interjection to express dissatisfaction or annoyance colloquially.

Je vais arriver en retard à mon rendez-vous. **Zut!**	*I'm going to arrive late for my appointment. **Darn!***

Ça veut dire...

Use this phrase to paraphrase, clarify, or summarize statements.

Ils ne téléphonent pas. **Ça veut dire** qu'ils sont fâchés.

*They aren't calling. **That means** that they're angry.*

C'est embêtant!

This colloquial expression expresses annoyance.

Le café est fermé. **C'est embêtant!**

*The café is closed. **That's annoying!***

Assez

Use this adverb before an adjective to convey the meaning of *rather*, *pretty*, or *quite*.

Tu es **assez grand** pour ton âge.
C'est **assez gênant**.

*You're **rather tall** for your age.*
*This is **pretty embarrassing**.*

Et en plus...

Use this transitional phrase to add details to statements.

J'ai faim et soif, **et en plus** je suis fatiguée.

*I am hungry and thirsty, **and on top of that** I'm tired.*

À mon avis...

Use this phrase to indicate that you are about to express your personal opinion.

À mon avis, nous ne pourrons pas avoir de tickets.

In my opinion, we will not be able to get tickets.

C'est toujours comme ça

Use this transitional phrase to trivialize or generalize occurrences.

Il y a trois pharmacies en plein centre. **C'est toujours comme ça.**

*There are three pharmacies in the city center. **It's always like that.***

Quelle poisse!

This slang expression, which shows extreme exasperation, should only be used in very colloquial settings.

Il faut attendre trois heures pour l'arrivée du train? **Quelle poisse!**

*We have to wait three hours for the arrival of the train? **What a pain!***

Tu trouves ça bien que (qu')... ?

Start a question with this expression to ask someone's opinion about something. The verb after **que (qu')** will be in the subjunctive mood.

Tu trouves ça bien que le pourboire soit inclus?

Do you think it's right that the tip be included?

Ça dépend de (d')...

Use this transitional phrase to interject nuances, details, or examples.

Tu penses que nos amis vont arriver à l'heure? **Ça dépend de** la circulation.

*You think our friends are going to arrive on time? **It depends on** the traffic.*

C'est sûr et certain!

Use this expression to agree vehemently with a statement.

Je t'assure qu'il va neiger. **C'est sûr et certain.**

*I assure you it's going to snow. **It is absolutely certain.***

Ça arrive

Use this transitional phrase to trivialize or generalize occurrences.

Il y a des accidents de voiture sur l'autoroute? Oui, **ça arrive**.

*There are traffic accidents on the highway? Yes, **it happens**.*

En pleine saison

This expression is generally used in the context of tourism.

Les prix des chambres sont plus élevés **en pleine saison**.

*The prices of rooms are higher **in high season**.*

On dirait que (qu')...

Use this phrase to express an opinion or a point of view.

On dirait que beaucoup de célébrités ont des problèmes de drogue.

***It would seem that** many celebrities have drug problems.*

Se mettre d'accord

Use this **mettre** idiom to refer to a negotiation that leads to an agreement. Note that the verb **mettre** is an irregular verb in the present tense; it normally means *to put* or *to put on*.

Peut-on **se mettre d'accord** qu'il vaut mieux lire les journaux que de regarder le journal télévisé?

*Can we **agree** that it is better to read the newspapers than watch the televised news?*

Grammar notes

Pas de (d') + *nom*

Pas de (**d'**) + *noun* is an invariable expression used before a noun, regardless of the noun's gender or number. Note that the noun is expressed without an article.

Il n'y a **pas de trains**?
Pas de nouvelles aujourd'hui?

*There are **no trains**?*
***No news** today?*

En

The pronoun **en** replaces **de** (**d'**) + *noun* or *verb*. The translation of the pronoun **en** varies according to what it replaces and can sometimes be omitted in the English sentence.

—Tu es de retour **d'Italie?**   —*You're back **from Italy**?*
—Oui, j'**en** arrive.   —*Oui, I'm arriving (**from there**).*

—Tu as envie **de manger?**   —*You feel like **eating**?*
—Oui, j'**en** ai envie.   —*Yes, I feel like **it**.*

The **futur simple**

The **futur simple** tense consists of the infinitive (minus the **-e** ending for infinitives ending in **-e**) used as a stem and the following endings: **je (j') -ai, tu -as, il/elle/on -a, nous -ons, vous -ez, ils/elles -ont**.

J'**arriverai** bientôt.   *I **will arrive** soon.*
Nous **répondrons** demain.   *We **will answer** tomorrow.*

The **futur simple** tense of some common verbs have irregular stems. They should be memorized.

être	→	**ser-**
pouvoir	→	**pourr-**
voir	→	**verr-**
vouloir	→	**voudr-**

Ce **sera** super.   *That/It **will be** great.*
On **pourra** rentrer.   *We'**ll be able** to go back home.*
On **verra**!   *We'**ll see**.*
Tu **voudras** rester.   *You'**ll want** to stay.*

EXERCICE 4·2

Tu es au courant? *Do you know what's happening? Complete the following lines of dialogue with words or expressions from the list provided.*

poisse	Pas de	comme ça
Ici	Quoi de neuf	Ça arrive
Zut	ce sera super	non
On dirait	grève	en pleine saison

1. MARC: Allô, Sabine. _____ Marc.

2. SABINE: Bonjour, Marc. _____?

3. MARC: Les conducteurs de bus font _____.

4. SABINE: Quelle _____! Heureusement qu'il y a le métro.

5. MARC: Désolé! _____ métro non plus!

6. SABINE: _____! C'est vraiment embêtant!

7. MARC: C'est toujours _____ pendant les vacances.

8. SABINE: _____ que tu n'es pas surpris!

9. MARC: _____ assez souvent, non?

10. SABINE: Tu as raison, mais vraiment, _____, ce n'est pas bien!

11. MARC: C'est une bonne excuse pour ne pas aller au cours, _____?

12. SABINE: Pour nous, bien sûr, _____.

EXERCICE
4·3

Tu plaisantes? *Are you kidding? Write Sonia's replies to Luc's statements or questions as indicated.*

1. LUC: Tu es au courant? Tous les travailleurs des transports publics font la grève.

   SONIA: _____

   (*Darn! What a pain!*)

2. LUC: Tu as des cours aujourd'hui?

   SONIA: _____

   (*Yes, I do have some.*)

3. LUC: Mais non, Sonia! Pas de cours aujourd'hui!

   SONIA: _____

   (*Are you kidding?*)

4. LUC: Non! Crois-moi! C'est sûr et certain! Tu n'as pas de nouvelles de tes profs ou de ta faculté?

   SONIA: _____

   (*No news at all!*)

5. LUC: Regarde la télé! Tu verras!

   SONIA: _____

   (*I see. It looks like you're right!*)

6. LUC: Tu devrais être contente. Une journée de vacances!

   SONIA: _____

   (*That depends! Not so good when you like your class.*)

7. LUC: Tu es assez bonne élève. Tu pourras te débrouiller (manage).

SONIA: _____

(*We'll see.*)

8. LUC: Et en plus, il fait si beau aujourd'hui. Tu voudras sans doute te promener avec moi.

SONIA: _____

(*You think they're great, those strikes, don't you?*)

Dialogue 2

Chris and Anne talk about the weather forecast and particularly about the upcoming heat wave.

ANNE: **Dis donc**, Chris. On annonce qu'il va y avoir une vague de chaleur la semaine prochaine.

Say, Chris. They announce that there's going to be a heat wave next week.

CHRIS: Zut! Il fait déjà assez chaud.

Darn! It is pretty hot already.

ANNE: Tu sais, ici **c'est grave**. Les maisons et les bureaux n'ont généralement pas l'air conditionné.

You know, here it is serious. Houses and offices generally don't have air conditioning.

CHRIS: **Pas drôle, ça!**

That's no fun!

ANNE: Tout le monde transpire dans les bus et dans le métro. **Tu verras.**

Everybody sweats in the buses and in the subway. You'll see.

CHRIS: **Plus personne** aux terrasses des cafés! Ce sera parfait pour toi qui aimes être seule.

Nobody left on the terraces of the cafés! That will be perfect for you who likes to be alone.

ANNE: **Tu m'énerves**, tu sais. J'espère que tu souffriras bien.

You are getting on my nerves, you know. I hope you'll suffer.

CHRIS: Désolée, Anne. Je serai en Normandie où je profiterai de la brise atlantique.

Sorry, Anne. I'll be in Normandy where I'll enjoy the Atlantic breeze.

ANNE: **Veinard!** Moi, il faudra que je supporte la canicule avec ses températures extrêmes. On prédit quarante-deux degrés Celsius.

Lucky you! I will have to bear the heat wave with its extreme temperatures. They predict forty-two degrees Celsius.

CHRIS: Quelle horreur! **Franchement** j'espère que les météorologues se trompent. Ça arrive!

How awful! Frankly I hope that the meteorologists are wrong. It happens!

ANNE: Je voudrais bien mais **ça m'étonnerait**.

I'd like that, but I'd be surprised.

Jugez de votre compréhension. *Check your comprehension. Write* T *(true) or* F *(false).*

1. _____ La météo annonce du temps chaud.

2. _____ Anne dit que tout le monde a l'air conditionné.

3. _____ Chris va souffrir de la chaleur à Paris.

4. _____ La Normandie est sur la mer Méditerranée.

5. _____ Anne dit que les météorologues se trompent toujours.

Improving your conversation

Dis donc

Use this expression to begin a discussion, but only in familiar situations.

> **Dis donc**, Rémy, tu as des nouvelles
> de Stéphane?

> *Hey, Rémy, do you have any news of
> Stéphane?*

C'est grave

Use this expression to indicate that something is serious. The opposite would be **Ce n'est pas grave** (*It's not serious / It's no big deal*).

> Il est malade et **c'est grave**.
> Elle a oublié de téléphoner mais **ce
> n'est pas grave**.

> *He is sick and **it's serious**.*
> *She forgot to call but **it's no big deal**.*

Pas drôle, ça!

Use this slightly sarcastic phrase to convey annoyance.

> Quoi? L'hôtel est fermé? **Pas drôle, ça!**

> *What? The hotel is closed? **That's not funny!***

Plus personne!

Use this double negative structure to declare that *there is nobody left.*

> Nous sommes en retard. **Plus
> personne** ici!

> *We're late. Everyone left! (**No one** here
> anymore!)*

Tu m'énerves!

Use this expression only with close friends and relatives to express irritation.

> Arrête de parler si fort! **Tu m'énerves.**

> *Stop talking so loud! **You're getting on
> my nerves.***

Veinard(e)!

Use this adjective in familiar settings to exclaim that a person is really lucky.

Veinard, tu as encore gagné.   *Lucky you*, *you won again.*

Franchement!

Use this adverb as an exclamation to show disapproval or dismay.

Tu n'as pas encore fini? **Franchement!**   *You haven't finished yet?* ***Why, really!***

Ça m'étonnerait!

Use this exclamation to show skepticism and doubt.

Tu dis que le restaurant sera fermé en   *You say that the restaurant will be closed*
pleine saison? **Ça m'étonnerait!**   *in high season?* ***I'd be surprised!***

Grammar note

Faire idioms

Most expressions describing the weather are **faire** idioms beginning with **Il fait** (*It is*), including the question **Quel temps fait-il?** (*What's the weather like?*):

Il fait beau	*It's nice*	**... chaud**	*hot*
... du soleil	*sunny*	**... mauvais**	*bad*
... frais	*cool*	**... nuageux** (*colloq.*)	*cloudy*
... froid	*cold*		

Notable exceptions are:

il grêle	*it hails / it's hailing*	**il pleut**	*it rains / it's raining*
il neige	*it snows / it's snowing*		

EXERCICE
4·5

Croire ou ne pas croire la météo? *To believe or not believe the weather report? Write the letter of the most appropriate completion on the line provided.*

1. _____ MARIETTE: Dis donc, Jacques, la météo annonce...

2. _____ JACQUES: ... il faut prendre les skis et partir tout de suite.

3. _____ MARIETTE: ... que les routes seront dangereuses?

4. _____ JACQUES: ... Nous serons seuls sur la route!

5. _____ MARIETTE: Pas drôle, ça!... tu sais.

a. Tu ne crois pas

b. Tant mieux! Quelle chance!

c. qu'il neige dans les Alpes depuis ce matin.

d. À mon avis,

e. me trouver coincée dans une tempête de neige.

f. Ça m'étonnerait, Mariette.

6. _____ JACQUES: ... quand on perd le sens de l'humour, Mariette.

7. _____ MARIETTE: Écoute! Moi, je ne voudrais pas...

8. _____ JACQUES: ... Ils n'ont pas toujours raison!

g. Tu m'énerves,

h. C'est grave

EXERCICE 4·6

Coincé en montagne. *Stuck in the mountains. Complete the following dialogue by choosing the most appropriate word or phrase from the list provided. Capitalize as necessary.*

zut	veinard	on dirait que
plaisanter	franchement	raison
neige	être de retour	

1. MARIETTE: Tu vois, Jacques, les routes sont couvertes de _____.

2. JACQUES: _____! Comment est-ce qu'on va rentrer?

3. MARIETTE: Tiens! _____ tu as perdu ton sens de l'humour, Jacques.

4. JACQUES: Je dois _____ au travail demain.

5. MARIETTE: _____! Tu vas avoir un jour de congé.

6. JACQUES: Arrête de _____, Mariette!

7. MARIETTE: Ça alors! C'était ton idée de venir. _____, tu m'énerves.

8. JACQUES: Tu as _____! Je m'excuse.

Dialogue 3

This time, Anne and Chris talk about an article Anne came across in the newspaper about the future of French transportation.

ANNE: Il y a un article super dans le journal sur l'avenir des transports en France.

There is a great article in the newspaper about the future of transportation in France.

CHRIS: Ça m'intéresse beaucoup! La production des voitures électriques augmente de plus en plus aux États-Unis. **Où en est-on** en France?

I'm very interested! The production of electric cars is increasing more and more in the United States. Where are they in France?

ANNE: On en fait. Mais un problème majeur, c'est de pouvoir recharger son véhicule rapidement et n'importe où. **On parle de** créer un réseau national de sites de recharge.

We make them. But a major problem is to be able to recharge your vehicle rapidly and from anywhere. They're talking about creating a national network of recharging sites.

CHRIS:	**Ce n'est pas évident, ça!**	*That's not easy!*
ANNE:	**Une autre idée qui circule**, c'est des batteries interchangeables.	*Another idea going around is interchangeable batteries.*
CHRIS:	Ça existe déjà, **il me semble**.	*That exists already, I think.*
ANNE:	**Je me demande** si on ne **fantasme** pas **à force de** vouloir rompre la dépendance pétrolière.	*I wonder if it's not wishful thinking because we want to be free from oil dependency.*
CHRIS:	Admets que tous les pays ont été **des accros** du pétrole pendant trop longtemps. Il est temps de **faire marche arrière**.	*Admit that we have all been dependent on oil for too long. It's time to go backward.*
ANNE:	Ou plutôt **marche avant**.	*Or rather forward.*
CHRIS:	J'ai entendu dire que certaines villes françaises ont déjà des bus hybrides. C'est vrai?	*I heard that some French cities already have hybrid buses. Is it true?*
ANNE:	**Bien sûr que** c'est vrai. Nous sommes très **écolo** en France. Si ça t'intéresse **tant que ça**, tu devrais aller à l'exposition qui aura lieu **à l'occasion de** la Fête des transports la semaine prochaine.	*Of course it's true. We are very ecologically minded in France. If you're that interested, you should go to the exposition taking place along with the Transportation Fair next week.*
CHRIS:	La fête des transports! **Décidément, vous autres Français**, vous avez des fêtes pour tout. **C'est tordant!**	*The transportation festival! Honestly, you French have festivals for everything. It's hilarious!*

**EXERCICE
4·7**

Jugez de votre compréhension. *Check your comprehension. Write* T *(true) or* F *(false).*

1. _____ La France ne fabrique pas de voitures électriques.

2. _____ Chris pense que les batteries interchangeables existent.

3. _____ Chris pense qu'il faut limiter l'utilisation du pétrole.

4. _____ Anne déclare que les Français veulent protéger l'environnement

5. _____ Anne conseille à Chris d'aller à une exposition pour s'informer sur les transports.

Improving your conversation
Où en est-on?

Ask this question to find out how a project is coming along.

Le gâteau n'est pas encore prêt? **Où en es-tu?**	*The cake isn't ready yet?* ***How far along are you?***

On parle de (d')...

Use this expression to report something you heard.

Il y a eu un accident. **On parle de** trois blessés.	*There has been an accident. **They're talking about** three injured people.*
Le temps est horrible en montagne. **On parle** d'avalanches.	*The weather is horrible in the mountains. **They're talking about** avalanches.*

Ce n'est pas évident, ça! / c'est pas évident, ça!

Use this phrase to convey that something is hard to conceive of. **C'est pas évident** is an abbreviated and more familiar form of **Ce n'est pas évident**. Note that the negative adverb **ne (n')** is often omitted in familiar language.

Tu dois finir ce travail ce soir? **C'est pas évident!**	*You have to finish this work tonight? **That's not / won't be easy!***

Une autre idée qui circule...

This phrase is used to talk about unconfirmed news.

Une autre idée qui circule est qu'on a commandé des bus hybrides.	***Another idea that's around** is that they've ordered hybrid buses.*

Il me semble que (qu')...

Use this phrase to express an opinion that you share.

Il me semble que nos amis sont en retard.	***It seems to me that** your friends are late.*
Il me semble que les Français ont beaucoup de fêtes.	***It looks like** the French have many celebrations.*

Je me demande...

Use this reflexive verb when you are wondering about something.

Je me demande quand les batteries interchangeables seront disponibles.	***I wonder** when interchangeable batteries will be available.*

On fantasme sur...

Use this verb when you want to convey the notion of *dreaming about something*, desirable but perhaps hard to obtain or outside the scope of reality.

Je suis très optimiste. **Je fantasme sur** un avenir de paix.	*I am very optimistic. **I dream about** a peaceful future.*

À force de (d')...

Use this prepositional phrase to link ideas of cause and effect. This phrase introduces the cause.

Elle a réussi à me persuader **à force de** me donner des exemples.	*She managed to persuade me **by** giving me examples.*
À force de persévérance, j'ai atteint mon but.	***By** persevering, I reached my goal.*

Un(e) accro

This noun is derived from the adjective **accroché(e)** (*attached to / hooked on to*). It is often used to describe people who are dependent and addicted.

C'est **un accro** du tabac!   *He is **addicted** to tobacco!*

Faire marche avant / marche arrière

Use this phrase to express *forward* or *backward* motion, literally or figuratively.

Faisons marche avant et parlons de l'avenir!   ***Let's move forward** and talk about the future!*

Tu es trop près de la rue. **Fais marche arrière!**   *You are too close to the street. **Back up!***

Bien sûr que (qu')...

Use this phrase to confirm something vehemently.

Bien sûr que je sais parler français!   ***Of course** I know how to speak French!*

Écolo

This abbreviated form of the adjective **écologique** is used to describe people who believe in promoting habits and processes that are good for the planet.

Il faut être **écolo** et recycler autant que possible.   *We must be **ecologically minded** and recycle as much as possible.*

Tant que ça

Use this phrase to add emphasis to what a person does or feels.

Si tu veux protéger l'écologie **tant que ça**, tu dois t'adhérer à une organisation «verte»!   *If you want to protect ecology **so much**, you have to join a "green" organization!*

Une personne qui travaille **tant que ça** doit gagner beaucoup.   *A person who works **that much** must earn a lot.*

À l'occasion de (d')...

Use this phrase to introduce any special occasion or moment.

À l'occasion de la sortie de son nouveau livre, elle en a autographié plusieurs.   ***When** her new book came out, she autographed several.*

À l'occasion de ton anniversaire, nous dînerons ensemble.   ***For** your birthday, we'll have dinner together.*

Décidément

Use this adverb as an exclamation to show a variety of emotions you want to emphasize.

Tu travailles encore? **Décidément!**   *Are you still working? **Honestly!***

Quelle corruption dans ce gouvernement! **Décidément!**   *What corruption in this government! **Honestly!***

Vous autres...

Use this all-encompassing phrase to address several people.

Vous ne faites jamais d'objections, **vous autres?**	*Don't **you (all)** ever object?*
Vous avez bien de la chance, **vous autres!**	*You are quite lucky, **you all!***

C'est tordant!

Use this exclamation to show how amused you are!

Tu es rouge comme une tomate! **C'est tordant!**	*You're red as a tomato! **It's hilarious!***

Les voitures du futur. *Cars of the future. Write the letter of the most appropriate completion on the line provided.*

1. _____ MARIETTE: On devrait acheter...

2. _____ JACQUES: Et pourquoi pas une voiture... ?

3. _____ MARIETTE: Il paraît qu'il faut souvent recharger...

4. _____ JACQUES: Oui, mais je pense que bientôt elles seront...

5. _____ MARIETTE: Ce serait bien, ça! Il faut être... !

6. _____ JACQUES: Je suis d'accord. Je ne veux pas...

a. les batteries.

b. interchangeables.

c. une voiture hybride.

d. écolo de nos jours.

e. être un accro du pétrole.

f. électrique

Les transports de demain. *Tomorrow's transportation. Complete the following dialogue by choosing the most appropriate word or phrase from the list provided. Capitalize as necessary.*

je me demande	évident	batteries
où en est-on	écologiques	qui circule
on parle	il paraît	tant que ça
décidément		

1. MARIETTE: Dis, Jacques, _____ avec le projet de bus hybrides?

2. JACQUES: _____ qu'il y en a déjà pas mal en France.

3. MARIETTE: _____ si notre ville va en avoir aussi.

4. JACQUES: C'est une idée _____! Espérons-le!

5. MARIETTE: Dans notre proche avenir, je vois des voitures et des bus

à _____!

6. JACQUES: Bien sûr qu'on aura des transports en commun _____! J'en suis sûr.

7. MARIETTE: _____! Nous sommes très optimistes!

8. JACQUES: Écoute, _____ même de sites de recharge partout dans le pays.

9. MARIETTE: Alors, ça, c'est pas _____. Mais il le faut évidemment!

10. JACQUES: Si nous voulons protéger l'environnement _____, c'est une bonne idée!

EXERCICE
4·10

Les dernières nouvelles. *The latest news. In this dialogue, Jacques and Mariette are watching a YouTube video on Jacques's iPod about the wedding of two celebrities. Write the dialogue using the English guidelines provided.*

Jacques tells Mariette to watch the short video he just found on line. He tells her that she will love it.

1. JACQUES: _____. _____!

Mariette asks what it is about.

2. MARIETTE: _____?

Jacques tells her it is the wedding of two celebrities (*you may use any real or imaginary names*).

3. JACQUES: _____.

Mariette comments that the bride is magnificent in white and that the groom is as handsome as a god.

4. MARIETTE: _____.

Jacques wonders how much such a wedding costs.

5. Jacques: _____.

Mariette says it costs more than he can imagine or afford.

6. MARIETTE: _____.

 **Watching sports events**

Dialogue 1

Didier invites his friend Chris to a soccer game. They make plans as to where and when to meet.

DIDIER: Allô, Chris. C'est Didier. Tu as envie d'aller à un match de foot demain?

Hello, Chris. This is Didier. Do you feel like going to a soccer game tomorrow?

CHRIS: Salut, Didier. Oui, **j'aimerais bien. Qui joue?**

Hi, Didier. Yes, I would like to. Who's playing?

DIDIER: Les Girondins de Bordeaux contre Paris-Saint-Germain. **C'est un match amical** entre des équipes régionales.

The Girondins from Bordeaux against Paris-Saint-Germain. It's a friendly match between regional teams.

CHRIS: **Je ne m'y connais pas très bien en foot.** Mais je crois que le club des Girondins a une bonne équipe, non?

I don't know much about soccer. But I believe that the Girondins Club has a good team, doesn't it?

DIDIER: Ils ont une très bonne saison. On verra comment ça se passera demain.

They're having a very good season. We'll see what happens tomorrow.

CHRIS: **Tu viens me chercher?** Je veux te présenter à ma tante et à mon oncle.

Are you picking me up? I would like to introduce you to my aunt and uncle.

DIDIER: D'accord. Je veux bien. Je serai chez toi vers onze heures.

OK. Gladly. I'll be at your place around eleven o'clock.

CHRIS: Tu déjeuneras avec nous alors?

Will you have lunch with us, then?

DIDIER: Je regrette, Chris, mais comme le match commence à quatorze heures précises, **il vaut mieux qu'**on achète une saucisse au stade.

I'm sorry, Chris, but since the game starts at exactly two P.M., we'd better buy a sausage at the stadium.

CHRIS: **Il faut si longtemps que ça** pour arriver au stade?

Does it take that long to get to the stadium?

DIDIER: **De chez toi**, oui, même en métro, c'est assez loin.

From your place, yes, even by subway, it's pretty far.

CHRIS: Bon, puisque je suis ton invité, je te fais entièrement confiance.

Well, since I'm your guest, I'll trust you completely.

DIDIER: Tu peux me **faire confiance!**
Rendez-vous chez toi demain!

CHRIS: Oui, merci, Didier. À demain,
vers onze heures chez moi. Salut.

You can trust me! We'll meet at your
place tomorrow!

Yes, thank you Didier. See you tomorrow,
around eleven o'clock at my place. Bye.

EXERCICE
5·1

Jugez de votre compréhension. *Check your comprehension. Write* T *(true) or* F *(false).*

1. _____ Chris s'y connaît bien en foot.

2. _____ Chris veut présenter son copain Didier à sa tante et à son oncle.

3. _____ Didier et Chris vont déjeuner au stade.

4. _____ La maison de Chris est loin du stade.

5. _____ Chris et Didier vont au match de foot aujourd'hui.

Improving your conversation
J'aimerais bien

This expression may be used whenever a person is glad to do something.

—Tu voudrais venir au barbecue de
Simon?
—Oui, **j'aimerais bien.**

—*Would you like to come to Simon's*
barbecue?
—*Yes, **I would like to**.*

Qui joue?

Sports fans frequently use this expression to find out what player or what team is playing in a given sport.

Il y a un match de tennis aujourd'hui
mais **qui joue?**

*There's a tennis game today but **who's**
playing?*

C'est un match amical

This is another phrase frequently heard in conversations about sports. It indicates that the game does not count toward a cup, a championship, or a tournament.

La saison de foot n'a pas encore
commencé mais il y a quelques
matches amicaux.

The soccer season has not started yet, but
*there are a few **friendly (out-of-season)***
games.

Je ne m'y connais pas en...

This phrase is useful in various contexts to express that one does not know much about a certain topic or field.

| Tu t'y **connais en** informatique? | *Do you know something about computers?* |
| Elle ne s'y **connaît pas du tout en** musique country. | *She does not know anything about country music.* |

Tu viens me chercher?

This expression is used, with the verb **venir** in the present tense, to ask people whether they are going to pick you up.

| Denise, **tu viens me chercher** ce soir? | *Denise, **are you picking me up** / **will you pick me up** tonight?* |

Il vaut mieux...

This impersonal expression to give advice is often followed by an infinitive, usually when it is obvious who the subject of the infinitive is or when the subject is people in general.

| Il va y avoir beaucoup de spectateurs. **Il vaut mieux** arriver tôt. | *There are going to be many spectators. **It's better** to arrive early.* |

This may apply to *us*, to *you*, or to *people* in general.

Il faut si longtemps que ça?

This expression is used to show surprise or verify that something actually takes or will take so long.

| Une heure pour aller au stade! **Il faut si longtemps que ça?** | *An hour to get to the stadium! **Does it takes that long?*** |

De chez moi/toi/lui/elle...

Use the prepositions **de** and **chez** consecutively when talking about *coming from* or *leaving from* someone's house. The combination is also used in prepositional phrases such as **près de** (*near*) or **loin de** (*far from*). Remember to use a stress pronoun if you want to replace the name of person whose house it is.

| J'arrive **de chez mes parents.** | *I'm arriving **from my parents' house.*** |
| J'habite **près de chez eux.** | *I live **near them.*** |

Faire confiance à...

This idiomatic **faire** expression is used to express that one trusts or has trust in someone or something.

| Elle est naïve. **Elle fait confiance à** tout le monde. | *She is naive. **She trusts** everyone.* |
| **Je te fais confiance,** mon petit Michel! | *I trust you, my dear Michel!* |

Grammar notes

The subjunctive mood

Remember that the *present subjunctive* and the *present indicative* of regular -er verbs are identical except in the **nous/vous** forms. Compare the present indicative and present subjunctive forms of the verb **arriver** (*to arrive*):

PRESENT INDICATIVE	PRESENT SUBJUNCTIVE
j'/il/elle/on arrive	j'/il/elle/on arrive
tu arrives	tu arrives
nous arrivons	nous arriv**ions**
vous arrivez	vous arriv**iez**
ils/elles arrivent	ils/elles arrivent

Il vaut mieux que **nous arrivions** en avance à l'aéroport.	*It's better if **we arrive** early at the airport.*
Il vaut mieux que **tu arrives** avant dix-huit heures.	*It's better if **you arrive** before six P.M.*

Il vaut mieux (*it's better*) is followed by **que** (**qu'**) and a verb conjugated in the subjunctive mood when there is a specific subject.

Il vaut mieux **que nous déjeunions**.	*We'd better **have lunch**.*
Il vaut mieux **qu'Alex reste à la maison**.	*It's better **that Alex stay home**.*

De (d')

The preposition **de** (**d'**) usually means *of* or *from* and must be contracted with the article **le** to produce **du** and with **les** to produce **des**. (**De** does not contract with **la** or with **l'**.)

L'heure **du** match est quinze heures.	*The time **of the** game is three P.M.*
Le club **des** Girondins est excellent.	*The Girondins' club is excellent.*
Le stade est **loin du** quartier de Chris.	*The stadium is **far from** Chris's neighborhood.*
Le stade est **près des** stations de métro.	*The stadium is **near** the subway stations.*

Comme, puisque (puisqu'), parce que (parce qu')

The conjunctions **comme**, **puisque** (**puisqu'**), and **parce que** (**parce qu'**) are used to establish a cause and effect relationship between events. They are all similar in meaning.

Comme c'est notre équipe nationale, il faut l'applaudir.	***As** it is our national team, we must cheer it on.*
Je vais venir chez toi **puisque** je ne suis pas loin.	*I'm going to come to your house **since** I'm not far.*
Je viens te chercher **parce que** tu ne connais pas le chemin.	*I'm coming to pick you up **because** you don't know the way.*

On va à un match de tennis? *Should we go to a tennis match? Write the letter of Jeanine's reply to Sophie on the line provided.*

1. _____ SOPHIE: Jeanine, tu veux venir avec moi à un match de tennis?

2. _____ SOPHIE: Serena Williams contre la championne belge.

3. _____ SOPHIE: À seize heures.

4. _____ SOPHIE: Oui, même plus tôt. Tu veux que je te cherche?

5. _____ SOPHIE: Alors, je serai chez toi à quatorze heures trente précises.

6. _____ SOPHIE: Bon. C'est d'accord. Rendez-vous chez toi demain!

a. Je serai prête! Tu peux me faire confiance.

b. À demain, Sophie!

c. Oui, s'il te plaît. Le stade est près de chez moi.

d. Alors, il faut y être vers quinze heures, non?

e. Oui, j'adore le tennis. Qui joue?

f. Elles sont super! Leur match est à quelle heure?

Olivier et Nicolas aiment le basket. *Olivier and Nicolas like basketball. Write Nicolas's replies to his friend Olivier on the lines provided.*

1. OLIVIER: Dis, Nicolas, tu as envie de regarder le match de basket à la télé avec moi?

NICOLAS: _____

(*Yes, of course. Who's playing?*)

2. OLIVIER: L'équipe nationale de France contre la Croatie.

NICOLAS: _____

(*Do you think the French team can win?*)

3. OLIVIER: C'est toujours possible. Nos joueurs sont assez bons!

NICOLAS: _____

(*Yes, but Croatia is really good.*)

4. OLIVIER: Écoute, tu viens chez moi vers dix heures.

NICOLAS: _____

(*OK. At what time is the game?*)

5. OLIVIER: À onze heures, mais il vaut mieux quand même venir vers dix heures!

   NICOLAS: _____

   (*Gladly! You can make breakfast.*)

6. OLIVIER: Comme tu veux. À demain!

   NICOLAS: _____

   (*I'll be there.*)

Dialogue 2

Anne and Didier are making plans to go to Chris's and watch a rugby game on TV.

ANNE: **Allô**, Didier. Salut, **mon petit** cousin. Ça va?

Hello, Didier. Hi, dear (little) cousin. Is everything OK?

DIDIER: Oui, **ma petite** cousine. Et toi?

Yes, dear (little) cousin. How about you?

ANNE: Bien, merci. Dis, je viens de parler à Chris. Il nous invite chez lui dimanche.

Fine, thanks. Hey, I just spoke to Chris. He's inviting us to his place on Sunday.

DIDIER: **Seulement si** c'est pour regarder le match de rugby à la télé.

Only if it's to watch the rugby game on TV.

ANNE: Justement. Pour lui, c'est intéressant puisque ça ressemble un peu au football américain.

That's it. For him, it's interesting since it kind of resembles American football.

DIDIER: Pas seulement pour lui. Tu sais que je suis un fana du rugby, moi.

Not just for him. You know that I'm a rugby fan.

ANNE: Oui, je sais. On apporte des chips, et Chris procure les boissons.

Yes, I know. We're bringing chips, and Chris is providing drinks.

DIDIER: On devrait faire aussi des saucisses, peut-être des merguez, tiens!

We should also make sausages, maybe merguez, OK!

ANNE: Pourquoi pas des brochettes à l'agneau **tant que tu y es**?

Why not lamb kebabs while you're at it?

DIDIER: Pour ça, on devrait inviter Alex, le spécialiste des grillades.

For that, we should invite Alex, the barbecue specialist.

ANNE: Puisqu'il adore le rugby, lui aussi, pourquoi pas?

Since he loves rugby too, why not?

DIDIER: Comme c'est ton idée, **c'est à toi de** rappeler Chris et de demander permission.

Since it's your idea, it's your job to call Chris back and ask permission.

ANNE: **Tu es gonflé, toi!**

You have some nerve!

DIDIER: Mais non, ma petite Anne. Tu es **simplement** meilleure que moi à ce genre de choses.

No, my dear Anne. You're just better than me at this type of thing.

Jugez de votre compréhension. *Check your comprehension. Write* T *(true) or* F *(false).*

1. _____ Chris, Didier et Anne vont regarder un match de rugby ensemble.

2. _____ Anne ne veut pas apporter de chips chez Chris.

3. _____ Anne veut inviter un autre copain chez Chris.

4. _____ Didier offre de téléphoner à Chris.

5. _____ Anne préfère inviter son copain chez elle.

Improving your conversation

Allô

Use this word when answering the phone or after initiating a call.

Allô, Pierre! C'est Gisèle à l'appareil.	*Hello, Pierre! It's Gisèle speaking.*

Mon petit... / ma petite...

The adjective **petit**(e), in addition to meaning *small*, is often used as a term of endearment.

Viens vite, **mon petit** Pierre!	*Come quickly, **dear** Pierre!*

Seulement si

This phrase indicates that a restriction is attached to an outcome or an effect. Note that the **si** becomes **s'** before **il** or **ils** (**s'il/s'ils**), but remains **si** before **elle** or **elles** (**si elle / si elles**).

On va célébrer mais **seulement s'**ils gagnent.	*We're going to celebrate, but **only if** they win.*

Tant que tu y es

This phrase serves as an excuse to ask someone to do something for you.

Ah! Tu es au marché? **Tant que tu y es**, apporte-moi des tomates!	*Oh! You're at the market? **While you're there**, bring me some tomatoes!*

C'est à toi de (d')...

This expression helps to indicate that it is someone's responsibility to do something. The appropriate stress pronoun must be used after **c'est à**.

C'est à moi de parler.	*It is **my turn to** speak.*
C'est à elles de faire la cuisine.	*It is **their turn to** do the cooking.*

Tu es gonflé(e)

This very familiar slang phrase serves to express how you feel about a person who is exasperatingly demanding or has a big ego.

Tu demandes encore de l'argent à ton père? **Tu es gonflée!**	*You're still asking your father for money?* ***You have nerve!***

Simplement

This adverb is often used before an adjective to emphasize the meaning of the adjective and express a strong emotion.

Il est **simplement** horrible, ce match.	*This game is **just** horrible.*

Grammar notes

On

The subject pronoun **on** (*one/they/people/we*) has a variety of translations, depending on the context, but is often used instead of the subject pronoun **nous** (*we*) in familiar conversation.

On apporte les chips.	*We're bringing the chips.*

Me (m') / te (t')

The pronouns **me** (**m'**) (*me / to me*) and **te** (**t'**) (familiar *you / to you*) are both used as direct and indirect object pronouns; they are placed before the verb, except in affirmative commands.

—Tu **m'**invites?	*—Are you inviting **me**?*
—Oui, je **t'**invite.	*—Yes, I'm inviting **you**.*

Nous and vous

Similarly, the pronouns **nous** (*us / to us*) and **vous** (formal or plural *you / to you*) are both used as direct and indirect object pronouns; they are also placed before the verb, except in affirmative commands:

—Tu **nous** rappelles?	*—Will you call **us** back?*
—Oui, je **vous** rappelle.	*—Yes, I'll call **you** back.*

Stress pronouns

Stress pronouns (**moi, toi, lui, elle, nous, vous, eux, elles**) are used to replace a person or the name of a person following prepositions such as **pour** (*for*) and **avec** (*with*).

Viens **avec moi**!	*Come **with me**!*
Ça, c'est **pour elle**.	*This is **for her**.*

Chez

The preposition **chez** (*at/to a person's place*) is also followed by a stress pronoun to replace the name of a person:

Viens **chez nous**!	*Come **to our house**.*
Je viens **chez vous**.	*I'm coming **to your place**.*

Qu'est-ce que ça veut dire? *What does that mean? Write the letter of the best translation on the line provided.*

1. _____ Ça, c'est une saucisse épicée.

2. _____ Va chez eux!

3. _____ Viens chez nous!

4. _____ Invite tout le monde tant que tu y es!

5. _____ Quelle heure est-il?

6. _____ Il est vingt heures.

a. What time is it?

b. Come to our house!

c. Go to their house!

d. This is a spicy sausage.

e. It's eight P.M.

f. Invite everybody while you're at it!

Alex's invite! *Alex invites himself over! Complete the dialogue with words or phrases from the list.*

à toi	toi	j'aimerais	simplement
Il faudrait	Tu crois	tant que tu y es	chez
heure	heures		

1. ALEX: Dis, Éva, on va chez _____?

2. ÉVA: D'accord, mais pas pour _____ regarder la télé.

3. ALEX: Non, _____ dire bonjour à tes parents.

4. ÉVA: Pas vrai? Tu veux dire bonjour à mes petits frères _____?

5. ALEX: _____ que je plaisante. J'aime bien tes parents. Ils sont cool!

6. ÉVA: Quelle _____ est-il?

7. ALEX: Il est dix-huit _____.

8. ÉVA: Alors, viens, on va _____ moi.

9. ALEX: _____ peut-être téléphoner chez toi?

10. ÉVA: C'est _____ de faire ça puisque c'est ton idée!

Dialogue 3

Anne calls Chris to see if she may invite a few friends to his party.

ANNE: Dis, Chris, **ça te dérangerait** si on invitait quelques copains pour voir le match de rugby chez toi?

Hey, Chris, would it bother you if we invited a few friends to watch the rugby game at your place?

CHRIS: **Ça dépend.** Combien de copains? *It depends. How many friends?*

ANNE: Deux ou trois, **ça irait?** *Two or three, would that be OK?*

CHRIS: **Ne quitte pas!** Je demande à ma tante. *Hold on! I'll ask my aunt.*

[Quelques secondes plus tard.] *[A few seconds later.]*

CHRIS: Ma tante dit que ça va **du moment que** chacun apporte quelque chose. *My aunt says it's OK as long as everyone brings something.*

ANNE: **Ne t'en fais pas**, Chris! **C'est** déjà **prévu!** *Don't worry, Chris! It's already arranged!*

CHRIS: Vous venez tous ensemble? Je ne les connais peut-être pas, tes copains. *Are you all coming together? I may not know them, your friends.*

ANNE: Oui, oui, Chris. On sera là **à l'heure**, ni **en retard**, ni **en avance** et tous ensemble! Et on aura **tout ce qu'il faudra**. *Yes, yes, Chris. We'll be there on time, neither early nor late and all together! And we'll have all that we need.*

CHRIS: Tant mieux! **Remarque que** ce ne sera pas grave si vous êtes en retard. Ne t'en fais pas pour ça! *Sounds great! Mind you, it won't be a problem if you're late. Don't worry about it!*

ANNE: Ce sera super-sympa! Merci, Chris, et remercie ta tante. Nous le ferons **d'ailleurs nous-mêmes**. *It'll be super nice! Thanks, Chris and thank your aunt. Anyway we'll do that ourselves.*

EXERCICE 5·7

Jugez de votre compréhension. *Check your comprehension. Write T (true) or F (false).*

1. _____ Anne voudrait inviter quelques copains chez Chris.

2. _____ La tante de Chris veut seulement deux invités.

3. _____ La tante de Chris veut préparer à manger.

4. _____ Anne veut tout organiser.

5. _____ Chris pense que Didier et Anne seront en retard.

Improving your conversation

Ça te dérangerait...

Use this expression to ask for a favor and, at the same time, apologize for imposing on the friend or relation you are addressing. Substitute the formal pronoun **vous** for **te (t')** with strangers or in any formal settings.

Ça te dérangerait si j'empruntais ta voiture? *Would it bother you if I borrowed your car?*

Madame, **ça vous dérangerait** de me donner l'addition? *Madam, would you mind giving me the check/bill?*

Ça dépend

Use this expression to express reservations and offer clarification.

—Tu as toujours faim à cette heure?
—Non, **ça dépend** des jours.

—*Are you always hungry at this time of day?*
—*No, **it depends** on the day.*

Ça irait?

This expression helps ascertain whether someone agrees with your plans.

Je pourrais arriver vers dix heures.
Ça irait?

I could arrive around ten o'clock.
Would that be OK?

Ne quitte pas! / ne quittez pas!

This expression is used whenever a person puts you on hold during a telephone conversation.

Ne quitte pas, Marie. J'ai quelqu'un sur l'autre ligne.
Un instant, madame. **Ne quittez pas.**

Hold on, *Marie. I have someone on the other line.*
*One moment, madam. **Stay on the line.***

Du moment que (qu')...

This versatile expression can be used to express a condition or a reservation.

Tes copains peuvent venir **du moment qu'**ils apportent quelque chose.
Je viendrai te chercher **du moment que** l'avion arrive à l'heure.

*Your friends can come **as long as** they bring something.*
*I'll come pick you up **provided** the plane is on time.*

Ne t'en fais pas! / ne vous en faites pas!

This expression is used to express that something is no big deal, nothing to worry about.

Si tu es en retard, **ne t'en fais pas**.
Ce n'est pas grave.

*If you're late, **don't worry** (**about it**).*
It's no big deal.

C'est prévu

Use this expression to confirm that you have planned something.

On célébrera sa fête d'anniversaire ici.
C'est prévu pour le quinze.

We'll celebrate her birthday here.
***It's planned** for the fifteenth.*

À l'heure / en retard / en avance

These adverbial phrases are frequently needed to indicate when someone or something happened.

Justin arrive toujours **en retard** à ses rendez-vous.
Il est poli d'être **à l'heure**.

*Justin always arrives **late** for his appointments.*
*It is polite to be **on time**.*

Remarque que (qu')...

This transitional phrase helps add a detail to elaborate on a statement or detract from it.

Tes copains sont très sympa. **Remarque que** toi aussi, tu es très sympa.

Nous avons de la chance d'avoir un si beau temps. **Remarque que** je vois quelques nuages paraître.

*Your friends are very nice. **Mind you**, you're also very nice.*

*We are lucky to have such beautiful weather. **Mind you**, I see a few clouds appearing.*

Tout ce qu'il faut

This expression helps express that something is just right, since you have everything you need.

Allons-y! J'ai **tout ce qu'il faut** pour le pique-nique.

*Let's go! I have **all we need** for the picnic.*

D'ailleurs

This versatile phrase may be used in different contexts and can be translated as *anyway* or *besides*.

Je n'ai pas envie de sortir. **D'ailleurs** toi, tu es fatigué aussi.

J'y serai à l'heure. **D'ailleurs**, est-ce que je ne suis pas toujours ponctuel?

*I don't feel like going out. **Anyway**, you're tired too.*

*I'll be there on time. **Besides**, aren't I always punctual?*

Nous-mêmes

A stress pronoun followed by the word -**même**(s) in the singular or plural points out that the subject himself/herself is involved.

Je veux faire ce travail **moi-même**.

Nous voulons répondre **nous-mêmes**.

*I want to do this work **myself**.*

*We want to answer **ourselves**.*

Grammar note

Irregular stems

Some common verbs have irregular stems in the future and present conditional.

aller	→	**ir-**	faire	→	**fer-**
avoir	→	**aur-**	falloir	→	**faudr-**
devoir	→	**devr-**	venir	→	**viendr-**

Review the endings of the future tense: **-ai, -as, -a, -ons, -ez, -ont.**

J'aurai les boissons.
Vous viendrez ensemble?
On devra arriver à l'heure.
Il faudra remercier Chris.

I will have the drinks.
You'll come together?
We'll have to arrive on time.
We'll have to thank Chris.

Review the endings of the present conditional: **je/j' -ais, tu -ais, il/elle/on -ait, nous -ions, vous -iez, ils/elles -aient.**

Elle voudrait m'inviter.
Il faudrait apporter quelque chose.
Je ferais ça moi-même.

She would like to invite me.
We/They/One should bring something.
I would do that myself.

Nous allons voir un match de foot à la télé. *We're going to watch a soccer game on TV. Complete the following lines of dialogue with words and phrases from the list provided to reconstitute the conversation between Maurice and Pascal. Capitalize as necessary.*

à demain   moi-même   remarque
regarder   c'est prévu   Il faudrait
d'ailleurs   un match amical   si tu veux
ne t'en fais pas

1. MAURICE: Dis, Pascal, Éva nous invite chez elle demain pour _____ le match de foot entre Grenoble et Strasbourg.

2. PASCAL: Ah oui. C'est _____ avant la vraie saison.

3. MAURICE: Oui, mais _____ que ce sont de très bonnes équipes.

4. PASCAL: Je sais. _____ Strasbourg est une de mes équipes favorites.

5. MAURICE: _____ que chacun apporte un peu de bouffe.

6. PASCAL: Oui, bien sûr! _____! Moi, j'apporte tout ce qu'il faut.

7. MAURICE: Ah non! J'insiste pour apporter les boissons _____.

8. PASCAL: Bon, _____.

9. MAURICE: Oui, je veux bien. _____.

10. PASCAL: D'accord. _____, mon petit pote! Salut.

On va tous ensemble à un match de basket. *We're going to a basketball game together. Write Daniel's replies to Martine's statements and questions according to the English guidelines in parentheses.*

1. MARTINE: Allô, Daniel, j'ai quatre billets pour un match de basket au stade Jean-Jaurès dimanche.

DANIEL: _____

(*Who's playing?*)

2. MARTINE: L'Espagne contre la France.

DANIEL: _____

(*Two excellent teams. Great!*)

3. MARTINE: J'invite aussi Maurice et Pascal.

DANIEL: _____, Martine?

(*OK. Do I pick you up?*)

4. MARTINE: Oui, viens me chercher vers dix heures.

   DANIEL: _____

   (*Don't worry. I'll be at your house on time.*)

5. MARTINE: Maurice et Pascal vont aussi venir ici et nous irons au stade ensemble.

   DANIEL: _____

   (*Oh! It's already planned, I see.*)

6. MARTINE: Bien sûr, mon petit Daniel. J'ai tout organisé.

   DANIEL: _____

   (*Thanks, Martine. See you tomorrow.*)

EXERCICE
5·10

Qui va gagner? *Who's going to win? In this dialogue, Jonathan and David are watching a soccer game on TV. Each has a favorite team. Write the dialogue using the English guidelines provided.*

1. Jonathan says that Montreal, his favorite soccer team, is going to win against Toronto. He is sure and certain.

   JONATHAN: _____

2. David objects that the Toronto team won its last three games and points out it is a great team.

   DAVID: _____

3. Jonathan comments that it is easy to win a friendly game.

   JONATHAN: _____

4. David tells Jonathan that he has a lot of nerve to say that. Even friendly games are important.

   DAVID: _____

5. Jonathan tells David not to worry. Even if Toronto loses, it doesn't mean it's a bad team.

   JONATHAN: _____

6. David tells Jonathan that if Toronto loses today, he (David) will have to buy (offrir) him a drink, but he doubts it / it would surprise him.

   DAVID: _____

7. Jonathan says that he is planning a barbecue anyway. So he's inviting David to celebrate either Toronto or Montreal's victory.

   JONATHAN: _____

8. David says he'll be there.

   DAVID: _____

Celebrating and having fun

Dialogue 1

Didier and his cousin Anne talk about the upcoming French national holiday, known as Bastille Day, which the French simply refer to as **le quatorze juillet**.

ANNE: Didier, qu'est-ce que tu fais pour le quatorze juillet?

Didier, what are you doing for the fourteenth of July?

DIDIER: Mes parents organisent une fête chez nous. D'ailleurs, tes parents et toi, vous êtes invités.

My parents are planning a party at our house. By the way, you and your parents are invited.

ANNE: **Ah bon?** Mes parents n'ont rien dit.

Really? My parents have not said a thing.

DIDIER: Maman vient d'envoyer les invitations. Vous recevrez bientôt la vôtre.

Mom just sent the invitations. You'll get yours soon.

ANNE: **Je me rappelle** la fête de l'an dernier chez vous. **On s'est amusés comme des fous.**

I remember last year's party at your house. We had a blast.

DIDIER: Oui. Je dois dire que mes parents savent organiser les fêtes.

Yes. I must say that my parents know how to put on parties.

ANNE: Et en plus, de chez vous, on peut bien voir les feux d'artifice.

And on top of that, from your place, we can easily see the fireworks.

DIDIER: C'est vrai. **C'était superbe. Je m'en souviens très bien.**

That's true. It was superb. I remember it very well.

ANNE: Est-ce que tes cousins italiens seront **de nouveau** là?

Will your Italian cousins be there again?

DIDIER: Ah oui! Papa a déjà invité toute sa famille italienne et ils ont accepté.

For sure! Dad already invited his whole Italian family, and they accepted.

ANNE: **Alors là, il y aura de l'ambiance!** **Je meurs d'impatience** de les revoir.

Well in that case, there will be (a great) atmosphere! I am dying to see them again.

DIDIER: Tu sais **qui d'autre va venir**? Chris avec sa tante et son oncle.

You know who else is going to come? Chris with his aunt and uncle.

ANNE: J'en suis ravie. Je les ai trouvés **drôlement** sympa quand on a fait le barbecue chez eux.

I'm delighted. I found them extremely nice when we had the barbecue at their place.

DIDIER: Et puis mes parents ont réinvité les musiciens de l'an dernier. **Ils ont eu bien du succès**, tu te rappelles?

And also my parents invited the musicians from last year again. They were quite a hit, do you remember?

ANNE:	**Et comment!** Tout le monde a dansé toute la soirée!	*You bet! Everybody danced all night!*
DIDIER:	Et **il y avait** de la musique pour tous les goûts!	*And there was music for every taste!*
ANNE:	J'espère seulement que mes parents ne voudront pas aller voir le défilé militaire le matin.	*I just hope that my parents won't want to go see the military parade in the morning.*
DIDIER:	Nous, on préfère le regarder à la télé.	*We prefer to watch it on TV.*
ANNE:	Veinard! Nous, **on est allés** voir le défilé chaque année jusqu'ici.	*Lucky you! Up till now, we've gone to see the parade every year.*

EXERCICE
6·1

Jugez de votre compréhension. *Check your comprehension. Write* T *(true) or* F *(false).*

1. _____ Les parents d'Anne organisent une fête pour le quatorze juillet.

2. _____ Didier dit que la fête de l'an dernier chez lui était très bien.

3. _____ Chris et sa famille sont invités à la fête.

4. _____ Les musiciens de la fête de l'an dernier vont revenir.

5. _____ Anne voudrait aller au défilé militaire avec ses parents.

Improving your conversation

Ah bon?

This expression is often used to express surprise or skepticism and to suggest a request for explanation.

—Ma sœur a un nouveau copain.	—*My sister has a new (boy)friend.*
—**Ah bon?** Je le connais?	—***Really?*** *Do I know him?*

—Je suis allé au musée d'Art moderne.	—*I went to the Museum of Modern Art.*
—**Ah bon?** Tu aimes l'art moderne?	—***Really?*** *You like modern art?*

Je me rappelle

This reflexive verb helps you talk about what you recall or remember.

Je me rappelle mes belles vacances en Normandie.	*I remember my beautiful vacation in Normandy.*

On s'est amusés comme des fous

This expression may be used to express *having a blast* or *thoroughly enjoying oneself.* The verb **s'amuser** means *to have fun* and **comme des fous** literally means *like mad people.*

Mes copains et moi, **on s'est amusés comme des fous** au club hier.	*My friends and I, **we had a blast** at the club yesterday.*

C'était superbe

Use this expression to convey your enthusiasm for a past event.

Je suis allé au concert hier soir. **C'était superbe.**	*I went to the concert last night. **It was superb.***

Je m'en souviens très bien

Use this expression when emphasizing how well you remember an event or thing previously mentioned (regardless of the gender and number of the noun).

—Tu te rappelles les feux d'artifice? —Oui, **je m'en souviens très bien.**	*—Do you remember the fireworks?* *—Yes, **I remember them well.***
—Tu te rappelles la fête? —Oui, **je m'en souviens très bien.**	*—Do you remember the party?* *—Yes, **I remember it very well.***

De nouveau

This expression is an emphatic **encore** or *once again*.

Tu as **de nouveau** oublié tes clés?	*Have you forgotten your keys **again**?*

Alors là...

Use this expression as an exclamation of surprise.

Ce film te plaît? **Alors là**, je suis surprise!	*You like this movie? **Well**, I am surprised!*

Il y aura de l'ambiance

This idiomatic expression includes the future tense of the verb **avoir** (*to have*) and predicts that there will be a great atmosphere or energy and liveliness at an event.

Nous aurons une grande fête chez moi et **il y aura de l'ambiance.**	*We will have a big party at my house and **there will be a great atmosphere / great energy**.*

Je meurs d'impatience

This idiomatic expression includes the verb **mourir** (*to die*) and conveys extreme impatience or anticipation for an event.

Je meurs d'impatience de revoir mon copain.	***I can't wait** to see my boyfriend again. (The longing is killing me.)*

Qui d'autre va venir?

Ask this question to find out who else is coming to a party or gathering.

Je suis content de venir à ta fête, mais **qui d'autre va venir?**	*I'm happy to come to your party, but **who else is going to come?***

Drôlement

This adverb (which literally means *funnily*), when placed before an adjective, has the meaning of *really* or *quite*.

Elle est **drôlement** sympa.   *She is **really** nice.*

Ils ont eu bien du succès

This idiomatic **avoir** expression is used here in the **passé composé** to express that someone or something was a "hit." (*They had quite a bit of success.*)

Les musiciens **ont eu bien du succès** hier soir.   *The musicians **were quite a hit** last night.*

Et comment!

This expression is used to agree enthusiastically.

—Tu as trouvé que l'ambiance était bonne?
—**Et comment!**

—*Did you think that the atmosphere was good?*
—***You bet! (And how!)***

Il y avait...

This is the expression **il y a** in the *imperfect* tense, meaning *there was*.

Il y avait un défilé ce matin.   ***There was** a parade this morning.*
Il y avait une fois un méchant loup.   ***Once upon a time, there was** a mean wolf.*

On est allés...

Here, the verb **aller** is conjugated in the **passé composé** and, as often happens in familiar conversation, the subject **on** is used instead of **nous**. Note that in writing the past participle **allé** agrees with the gender and number of the actual (plural) subject.

On est allés/allées chez Martine.   ***We went** to Martine's house/place.*

Grammar notes

Le/la nôtre and le/la vôtre

The possessive pronouns **nôtre** and **vôtre** are always preceded by the appropriate definite article (**le/la/les**) that reflects the gender and number of the noun replaced.

le nôtre / la nôtre / les nôtres   *ours*
le vôtre / la vôtre / les vôtres   *yours (formal or plural)*

Ta voiture est neuve; **la nôtre** est vieille.   *Your car is new; **ours** is old.*
Nos vacances sont courtes; **les vôtres** sont longues.   *Our vacation is short; **yours** is long.*

The passé composé

The **passé composé** of most verbs is formed by the conjugated auxiliary verb **avoir** plus a past participle:

J'ai passé mes vacances en France.   *I spent my vacation in France.*

The **passé composé** of some verbs of movement—**aller** is one example—requires the use of the auxiliary verb **être** plus a past participle, which agrees with the subject:

Elle est allée aux États-Unis l'an dernier.   *She went to the United States last year.*

The **passé composé** of reflexive verbs is also formed with the auxiliary verb **être** plus a past participle.

Note that, in familiar conversation, when the subject pronoun **on** is used for the pronoun **nous**, the past participle in writing has a masculine or feminine plural ending, depending on who is in the group.

On **s'est** amus**és**.   *We (males or mixed gender group) had fun.*
On **s'est** amus**ées**.   *We (females only) had fun.*

EXERCICE 6·2

Comment était la fête? *How was the party? Complete each sentence in the following dialogue with a word or phrase from the list provided. Capitalize as necessary.*

ah bon	des fous	et comment	une ambiance
rappelle	avait	était	
pense	du succès	vraiment	

1. SYLVIE: Comment _____ la fête hier soir, Pierre?

2. PIERRE: Super! On s'est amusés comme _____.

3. SYLVIE: Il y _____ des musiciens?

4. PIERRE: Oui, deux guitaristes _____ bien!

5. SYLVIE: Ils ont eu _____ alors?

6. PIERRE: _____!

7. SYLVIE: Je me _____ le groupe de musiciens de l'an dernier. Ils étaient très bien aussi.

8. PIERRE: _____? Ce n'était pas le même groupe?

9. SYLVIE: Je ne _____ pas.

10. PIERRE: En tout cas, il y avait _____ formidable!

On n'est pas d'accord. *We do not agree. Write Cédrick's replies to Martine's statements and questions according to the English guidelines in parentheses.*

1. MARTINE: Dis, Cédrick, tu trouves qu'elle était bien, la fête?

   CÉDRICK: _____

   (*It was great!*)

2. MARTINE: Ah bon? Vraiment?

   CÉDRICK: _____

   (*The food was excellent.*)

3. MARTINE: La musique t'a plu?

   CÉDRICK: _____?

   (*Yes, I liked it. And you?*)

4. MARTINE: J'ai trouvé les musiciens trop traditionnels.

   CÉDRICK: _____

   (*And yet, they were quite a success.*)

5. MARTINE: Pas pour moi, en tout cas.

   CÉDRICK: _____

   (*There was atmosphere, right?*)

6. MARTINE: Comme ci comme ça. Je suis allée à de meilleures fêtes que ça.

   CÉDRICK: _____

   (*Well, my friends and I, we had fun.*)

Dialogue 2

Chris and Anne are talking about yesterday's Bastille Day celebration at Didier's house.

ANNE: Dis, Chris, **comment ça t'a plu**, hier, la fête du quatorze juillet?

Hey, Chris, how did you like the fourteenth of July celebration yesterday?

CHRIS: C'était super! J'ai rencontré **plein de** gens.

It was great! I met lots of people.

ANNE: **Il y avait du monde.** Ça, c'est vrai.

There were lots of people. That's true.

CHRIS: J'ai rencontré le fameux oncle Sergio, par exemple.

I met the famous Uncle Sergio, for instance.

ANNE: Ah oui! **Une fois qu'**on le rencontre, on se souvient de l'oncle Sergio.	*Oh yes! Once you meet him, you remember Uncle Sergio.*
CHRIS: C'est vraiment **un personnage**. Quel comédien! Il racontait une blague après l'autre.	*He really is a character. What a comedian! He was telling one joke after another.*
ANNE: C'est toujours comme ça avec lui. Ses blagues sont **à mourir de rire**.	*It's always like that with him. His jokes are to die laughing.*
CHRIS: Et comment! Et de plus, ses filles sont charmantes.	*You bet! And in addition, his daughters are charming.*
ANNE: **Oui, elles sont bien.** Et les feux d'artifice? Ça t'a plu?	*Yes, they're great. What about the fireworks? Did you like that?*
CHRIS: Oui, bien sûr. C'était un beau spectacle. Mais, ça, j'ai l'habitude. C'est comme le quatre juillet aux États-Unis.	*Yes, of course. It was a nice show. But I am used to them. It's like the Fourth of July in the United States.*
ANNE: **Alors, qu'est-ce qui t'a le plus impressionné?**	*So, what impressed you the most?*
CHRIS: C'était l'ambiance. Remarque que j'ai aussi apprécié la musique, les hors-d'œuvre et le Champagne.	*It was the atmosphere. Mind you, I also appreciated the music, the hors d'oeuvres, and the champagne.*
ANNE: J'en suis ravie. Ton premier quatorze juillet en France. **Il fallait** que ce soit mémorable.	*I'm delighted. Your first Bastille Day in France. It had to be memorable.*

EXERCICE 6·4

Jugez de votre compréhension. *Check your comprehension. Write* T *(true) or* F *(false).*

1. _____ Il y avait du monde à la fête chez Didier.

2. _____ Chris est impressionné par l'oncle Sergio et par ses filles.

3. _____ Chris a admiré les feux d'artifice le plus.

4. _____ Chris n'a pas trop aimé les hors-d'œuvre.

5. _____ Anne voulait que son copain américain se rappelle la fête du quatorze juillet.

Improving your conversation
Comment ça t'a plu?

Use this question to find out how a person liked something.

Tu étais au concert. **Comment ça t'a plu?**	*You were at the concert. **How did you like it?***

Plein de (d')

This colloquial expression is frequently used instead of **beaucoup de (d')**. Note that, just like **beaucoup de (d')**, it is *invariable* in gender and number.

Tu as bu **plein de** Champagne.	*You drank **lots of** champagne.*
Nous avons entendu **plein d'**adorables chansons.	*We heard **lots of** adorable songs.*

Il y avait du monde

Use this idiomatic expression to express that there are or were many people present.

Il y avait du monde au magasin aujourd'hui.	*There were **many people** at the store today.*

Une fois que (qu')...

Use this phrase to express *once (that)* . . .

Une fois que tout le monde est arrivé, on a commandé.	***Once** everybody arrived, we ordered.*

Un personnage

Beware that this word usually means *a character*, as in a novel or play. It is not a cognate of English except when it refers to historical personages.

Mon **personnage** favori dans ce roman, c'est l'enfant.	*My favorite **character** in this novel is the child.*

Mourir de rire

The literal meaning of this idiomatic expression is *to die laughing*. Use it whenever something is really hilarious.

Quelle blague! C'est **à mourir de rire**.	*What a joke! It is **to die laughing**. (It's **hilarious**.)*

Oui, elles sont bien

The adverb **bien** (*invariable*) is often used as a descriptive adjective and can mean *fine* or *nice*.

Ta copine est **bien**.	*Your girlfriend is **nice**.*
Tes parents sont vraiment **bien**.	*Your parents are really **fine**.*

Alors, qu'est-ce qui t'a le plus impressionné(e)?

Use this question to ask friends what they found the most impressive.

Qu'est-ce qui t'a le plus impressionné en France, John?	*What impressed you the most in France, John?*

Il fallait...

This is the impersonal expression **il faut**, but in the imperfect tense. Remember that this expression may be followed by an infinitive *or* by the conjunction **que** (**qu'**) plus a subject and a verb in the subjunctive mood.

Il fallait écouter.	***It was necessary to*** *listen. /* ***We/They had to*** *listen.*
Il fallait que nous mangions.	***We had to*** *eat.*

Grammar notes
Être and avoir and the imparfait

The **imparfait** is generally used for descriptive verbs such as **être** (*to be*) and **avoir** (*to have*) and also to express ongoing and repeated actions in the past. To conjugate a verb in the **imparfait**, obtain the stem of the verb by dropping **-ons** from the **nous** form of the present tense; then add the following endings: **je/tu -ais, il/elle/on -ait, nous -ions, vous -iez, ils/elles -aient**.

The stem for the verb **être** is exceptional: **ét-**.

Quand il **était** jeune, il **avait** plein d'amis.	*When he **was** young, he **had** lots of friends.*
Il **n'étudiait pas** beaucoup, mais il **avait** de bonnes notes.	*He **did not study** a lot, but he **had** good grades.*
Ils **allaient** toujours au cinéma le samedi.	*They always **went** to the movies on Saturdays.*
Ils **organisaient** régulièrement des fêtes.	*They **would** regularly **organize** parties.*

The passé composé

The **passé composé** is used for actions that took place at a precise moment in the past. To conjugate a verb in the **passé composé**, use the appropriate auxiliary verb (**avoir** or **être**) in the present tense plus the past participle of the verb.

Remember that the past participle of a verb conjugated with **être** *must agree* in gender and number with the subject of the verb.

Elles **ont dormi** ici hier soir.	*They **slept** here last night.*
J'**ai rencontré** mon mari il y a deux ans.	*I **met** my husband two years ago.*
Il **est arrivé** le trois juin.	*He **arrived** on June third.*
Elles **sont rentrées** il y a deux jours.	*They (f.) **came/went home** two days ago.*

The imparfait with the passé composé to describe interrupted actions

Use both the **passé composé** and the **imparfait** in the same sentence when one action (**passé composé**) interrupted or was superimposed on another action that was already in progress (**imparfait**).

Ses parents **dormaient** quand il **est rentré**.	*His parents **were sleeping** when he **got home**.*
Il **était** à la piscine quand tout à coup, l'orage **a éclaté**.	*He **was** at the pool when suddenly the storm **broke out**.*

Jean et Martine se sont amusés! *Jean and Martine had fun! Write the letter of the most appropriate reply to Martine's comments and questions.*

1. _____ Dis, Jean, qu'est-ce qui t'a le plus impressionné hier?

2. _____ Ah oui, ça ne m'étonne pas. Il fait rire tout le monde.

3. _____ Des blagues à mourir de rire, n'est-ce pas?

4. _____ Qu'est-ce que tu penses de mes copines Célia et Aimie?

5. _____ Pas trop sérieuses, non?

6. _____ Tant mieux! J'en suis ravie.

a. Elles sont vraiment très bien, ces filles.

b. Non, une fois qu'on les connaît, elles sont même drôles.

c. Oui, d'ailleurs, je meurs d'impatience de les revoir.

d. C'était l'humour de ton copain Paul.

e. Exactement. Très drôles.

f. Oui, il racontait plein de blagues.

Une fête bien réussie! *A successful party! Write the letter of the correct English translation for each line of dialogue.*

1. FABIAN: _____ Dis, il y avait du monde hier à la fête.

2. NICKIE: _____ C'est vrai. Quelle ambiance, n'est-ce pas?

3. FABIAN: _____ Surtout avec ce personnage qui racontait des blagues. Quel comédien!

4. NICKIE: _____ Il anime n'importe quelle fête avec ses blagues.

5. FABIAN: _____ Elles étaient à mourir de rire.

6. NICKIE: _____ La musique m'a bien plu aussi.

7. FABIAN: _____ Moi aussi. Je me rappelle, l'an dernier, il y avait un groupe pas très bien.

8. NICKIE: _____ Je me rappelle aussi. Ils n'étaient pas très emballants.

9. FABIAN: _____ Bon, en tout cas, tout le monde s'est amusé hier. Une fête bien réussie!

10. NICKIE: _____ C'est sûr et certain.

a. *Well, in any case, everybody had fun yesterday. A successful party!*

b. *He livens up any party with his jokes.*

c. *That's true. What atmosphere, right?*

d. *I remember too. They weren't very exciting.*

e. *Hey, there were a lot of people at the party yesterday.*

f. *That's for sure.*

g. *Especially with that character who was telling jokes. What a comedian!*

h. *I also liked the music.*

i. *They were hysterically funny.*

j. *Me too. Last year, there was a group that was not so good.*

Dialogue 3

Chris and Anne talk about a French wedding that Chris just attended.

CHRIS: **J'ai assisté à** un mariage hier, Anne! C'était **fort** intéressant.

I attended a wedding yesterday, Anne! It was very interesting.

ANNE: Est-ce que c'était très différent d'un mariage aux États-Unis, par exemple?

Was it very different from a wedding in the United States, for example?

CHRIS: **Oui, plutôt.** La réception, les photos, le déjeuner ont tous eu lieu dans un grand jardin. Mais le mariage a été célébré dans une **toute vieille** église du village.

Yes, very (different). The reception, the photos, the lunch all took place in a large garden. But the wedding was celebrated in a very old village church.

ANNE: Je vois, un mariage à la campagne. Qui s'est marié, en fait?

I see, a wedding in the country. Who got married, by the way?

CHRIS: C'est la nièce de mon oncle français. Elle portait une robe couleur crème, très courte, très moderne, mais **pas de voile. Par contre,** elle portait un chapeau **assorti** à la robe.

My French uncle's niece. She was wearing a cream color dress, very short, very modern, but no veil. On the other hand, she was wearing a hat that matched her dress.

ANNE: **Une toilette** pas du tout traditionnelle alors. Et son fiancé?

So not at all a traditional outfit. What about her fiancé?

CHRIS: Alors lui, il portait un très beau et très léger costume en toile. **Ça tombait bien** parce qu'il faisait assez chaud.

As for him, he was wearing a very good-looking, very light linen suit. Just right because it was pretty hot.

ANNE: Et la cérémonie civile, tu y es allé?

What about the civil ceremony, did you go?

CHRIS: Non, **pas tout le monde** n'y est allé. Seulement les témoins.

No, not everybody went. Only the witnesses.

ANNE: Et les demoiselles d'honneur.

And the bridesmaids.

CHRIS: Non, elles sont restées, et il a fallu qu'elles m'expliquent qu'en France tout mariage est sanctionné par un contrat civil.

No, they stayed back, and they had to explain to me that in France every marriage is legalized by a civil contract.

ANNE: Ah oui, c'est vrai qu'aux États-Unis, un mariage religieux est tout à fait valide. **Pas en France.** Il faut signer le contrat de mariage à la mairie et **se faire donner** le fameux livret de famille.

Yes, it's true that in the United States, a religious wedding is entirely valid. Not in France. You have to sign the marriage contract at City Hall and obtain the famous family registry.

CHRIS: **Qu'est-ce que c'est que ça?**

What is that?

ANNE: C'est un document où ils vont **inscrire** tous **les renseignements** sur la filiation du couple marié, la date de leur mariage et **plus tard** la naissance des enfants.

It is a document where they'll record all the information about the family of the couple, the date of their marriage, and later on, the birth of their children.

CHRIS: **J'en apprends des choses auprès de toi!**

I'm learning so much with you!

Jugez de votre compréhension. *Check your comprehension. Write* T *(true) or* F *(false).*

1. _____ Chris était invité à un mariage en ville.

2. _____ Chris a accompagné les mariés à la mairie.

3. _____ Chris a beaucoup apprécié le lieu de la réception et du déjeuner.

4. _____ On a pris les photos de mariage à l'église.

5. _____ Chris apprend qu'une union civile est nécessaire en France.

Improving your conversation

Assister à...

Use this verbal expression to refer to *attendance at an event*. Do not use it when you mean attending school; use the verb **aller** for *going to school*.

Je vais **assister à** une conférence.	*I'm going to **attend** a lecture.*
Je vais au lycée. L'an prochain, **j'irai** à l'université.	***I'm going** to high school. Next year **I'll attend** the university.*

Fort

This adjective, which literally means *strong*, is sometimes used as an invariable adverb before an adjective as a synonym of the adverb **très** (*very*).

Le mariage a été **fort réussi**.	*The wedding was **very much a success**.*

Oui, plutôt

This familiar expression is frequently used to confirm a suggestion or answer a question in a positive, emphatic manner.

—Tu aimes le vin?	*—Do you like wine?*
—**Oui, plutôt.**	*—Yes, indeed. / Yes, I do.*

Tout vieux / toute vieille

This expression describes something or someone *very* old.

J'ai une **toute vieille** photo de grand-mère.	*I have a **very old** photo of Grandmother.*

Pas de (d') / pas

Pas de (d') is used to negate a noun. **Pas** alone can be used before other parts of speech such as prepositions or adverbs.

Pas sur le gazon, s'il vous plaît!	***Not** on the lawn, please!*
Pas tout le monde.	***Not** everyone.*

Pas en France.	*Not* in France.
Pas de chance aujourd'hui.	*No luck today.*
Pas de photos, s'il vous plaît!	*No photos, please!*

Par contre

Use this phrase to introduce a contradictory statement or the opposing side of an argument.

| Je n'ai pas très faim. **Par contre**, je prendrais bien un dessert. | *I'm not very hungry. **On the other hand**, I would gladly have a dessert.* |

Assorti(e) à...

Use this adjective for anything that *matches*.

| Il portait une cravate **assortie à** la robe de sa fiancée. | *He was wearing a tie **that matched** his fiancée's dress.* |
| Les serviettes **sont assorties à** la nappe. | *The napkins **match** the tablecloth.* |

Une toilette

In this context, **la toilette** describes one's attire.

| Ma **toilette** favorite est ce tailleur en soie. | *My favorite **outfit** is this silk suit.* |
| Je vais mettre ma plus jolie **toilette** ce soir. | *I am going to put on my prettiest **outfit** tonight.* |

Ça tombe bien

Use this idiomatic expression when exclaiming that something happened appropriately or at a propitious time.

| J'ai reçu mon passeport. **Ça tombe bien.** | *I received my passport. **How convenient. (Just in time.)*** |

Qu'est-ce que c'est que ça?

This question is used to ask what something is.

| —Tiens! Je vais te montrer mon livret de famille. | *—Look! I'm going to show you my family registry.* |
| —**Qu'est-ce que c'est que ça?** | *—**What is that?*** |

Inscrire

This term refers to recording or writing down official information.

| S'il vous plaît, **inscrivez** vos renseignements sur ce formulaire! | *Please **record** your information on this form!* |
| Les règlements sont **inscrits** sur ce panneau. | *The rules are **written** on this sign.* |

Le renseignement

Use this term to ask for any type of information.

Pardon, madame. J'ai besoin d'**un renseignement** concernant cette fiche.

*Excuse me, madam. I need **a piece of information** concerning this form.*

Plus tard

Use this phrase to convey *later on*.

Je t'appellerai **plus tard**.

*I'll call you **later**.*

En apprendre des choses

Use this expression when referring to lots of things to be learned or things already learned.

Avant de voyager dans un pays étranger, **il y a tellement de choses à apprendre**. **J'en ai appris des choses** aujourd'hui!

*Before traveling to a foreign country, **there are so many things to learn**. **I learned so much** today!*

EXERCICE 6·8

On se marie! *We're getting married! Write the letter of the most appropriate reply to Isabelle's comments and questions.*

1. _____ Dis, Jean, on se marie dans la toute vieille église du village?

2. _____ Je sais, et puis c'est si romantique et spirituel là-bas.

3. _____ Tu as raison. Il y a une liste d'attente.

4. _____ Qu'est-ce que tu penses de mes sœurs comme demoiselles d'honneur?

5. _____ C'est vrai qu'elles portent toujours les mêmes toilettes aux fêtes!

a. Justement! N'attendons pas!

b. Pourquoi pas. Elles sont adorables.

c. Oui, ça tombe bien. Elles porteront des robes assorties.

d. Oui, mes parents se sont mariés là aussi.

e. Je suis d'accord. Il faut s'inscrire bientôt.

EXERCICE 6·9

Les mariages à la campagne. *Weddings in the country. Complete each sentence of the following dialogue with the appropriate word or phrase from the list provided.*

Plus tard	célèbre	des choses
renseignements	Ça tombe bien	à la campagne
pas encore	plutôt	demoiselles d'honneur
fort		

1. JEAN: On pourrait se marier _____, Isabelle.

2. ISABELLE: Bien sûr, il y a un parc magnifique où on _____ des mariages près de notre église.

3. JEAN: Tu veux réserver les lieux tout de suite ou _____?

4. ISABELLE: Oui, _____ tout de suite! Il vaut mieux pour être sûrs de l'avoir.

5. JEAN: C'est _____ raisonnable. Allons-y!

6. ISABELLE: On demandera aussi les _____ nécessaires, combien ça coûte par exemple.

7. JEAN: C'est ça. Je pense qu'on en apprendra _____!

8. ISABELLE: _____ il faudra qu'on parle de ma toilette.

9. JEAN: Tu feras ça avec tes _____, non?

10. ISABELLE: J'ai rendez-vous avec elles aujourd'hui. _____!

**EXERCICE
6·10**

Une fête d'anniversaire amusante. *A fun birthday party. In this dialogue, Jean and Isabelle are at their friend Jordan's birthday party. Write the dialogue using the English guidelines provided.*

1. Jean tells Isabelle that he can't believe that their friend Jordan is already thirty years old.

   JEAN: _____

2. Isabelle agrees and adds that he is as old as they are.

   ISABELLE: _____

3. Jean comments on how great the Mexican food is and asks Isabelle what she thinks of it.

   JEAN: _____

4. Isabelle answers that she loves all of that. She says it was her idea.

   ISABELLE: _____

5. Jean tells her that it was the best idea she ever had and asks her if she made all the sombreros for decorations.

   JEAN: _____

6. Isabelle says that she simply suggested the Mexican theme for the party.

   ISABELLE: _____

7. Jean compliments Isabelle on the attire she's wearing today.

   JEAN: _____

8. Isabelle asks him why he is so impressed. He has seen her before in this dress with matching hat.

   ISABELLE: _____

Accomplishments ◆7◆

Dialogue 1

Didier, Marie-Josée, Chris, and Anne are chatting on the terrace of a café one afternoon in early September.

ANNE: **On ne t'a pas vue depuis** la fête du quatorze juillet, Marie-Josée.

We haven't seen you since the fourteenth of July celebration, Marie-Josée.

MARIE-JOSÉE: Je travaillais encore à ma thèse **à ce moment-là. Heureusement que** j'ai terminé.

I was still working at my thesis at that time. Fortunately I finished.

ANNE: **Ça s'est bien passé?**

Did it go well?

MARIE-JOSÉE: J'ai présenté ma thèse à un jury de quatre professeurs. C'était intimidant.

I presented my thesis to a jury of four professors. It was intimidating.

ANNE: Ils t'ont posé beaucoup de questions, je suppose.

They asked you a lot of questions, I suppose.

MARIE-JOSÉE: Oui, mais **je me suis bien défendue**. Je connaissais bien mon sujet.

Yes, but I did well. I knew my topic well.

ANNE: Tu as célébré **ta réussite**?

Did you celebrate your accomplishment?

MARIE-JOSÉE: **Tu parles!** Mes parents étaient si contents! Ils ont ouvert une bouteille de Champagne.

You bet! My parents were so happy! They opened a bottle of champagne.

DIDIER: Et moi donc, comme j'étais content et fier de toi, Marie-Josée!

And me, how happy and proud of you I was, Marie-Josée!

MARIE-JOSÉE: Tu étais soulagé, je crois. J'étais souvent stressée et pas de bonne compagnie.

You were relieved, I think. I was often stressed out and not good company.

ANNE: **Ça se comprend.** Tu travaillais si dur.

That's understandable. You were working so hard.

MARIE-JOSÉE: Il le fallait bien; ça valait la peine. J'ai mon diplôme!

That's how it had to be; it was worth it. I have my diploma!

CHRIS: **Félicitations**, Marie-Josée!

Congratulations, Marie-Josée!

Jugez de votre compréhension. *Check your comprehension. Write* T *(true) or* F *(false).*

1. _____ Marie-Josée a terminé son travail de thèse et a obtenu son diplôme.

2. _____ Les parents de Marie-Josée ont célébré la réussite de leur fille.

3. _____ Didier a travaillé dur pour obtenir son diplôme.

4. _____ Didier est soulagé maintenant qu'il a terminé sa thèse.

5. _____ Tout le monde est content pour Marie-Josée.

Improving your conversation

On ne t'a pas vu(e) depuis...

Use this expression to explain you have not seen someone for a while.

Gigi, je **ne t'ai pas vue depuis** la fin de l'année scolaire.	*Gigi, I **haven't seen you since** the end of the school year.*
Papi, les enfants **ne t'ont pas vu depuis** Noël.	*Grandpa, the children **haven't seen you** since Christmas.*

À ce moment-là...

Use this phrase to refer to a precise moment. It is often used with the **passé composé**.

La prof a donné un exemple, et **à ce moment-là**, j'ai compris.	*The professor gave an example, and **at that moment**, I understood.*
Le prof est arrivé, et **à ce moment-là**, tout le monde s'est arrêté de parler.	*The professor arrived, and **at that moment**, everyone stopped talking.*

Heureusement que (qu')...

This adverbial phrase introduces a clause that recounts a fortunate outcome.

L'examen était difficile. **Heureusement que** vous avez bien étudié.	*The exam was difficult. **Luckily** you studied well.*
Il croyait que son livre était perdu. **Heureusement qu**'il l'a retrouvé.	*He thought his book was lost. **Fortunately** he found it.*

Ça s'est bien passé?

Use this question to ask if an event had a happy outcome.

Tu avais un examen aujourd'hui. **Ça s'est bien passé?**	*You had an exam today. **Did it go well?***

Je me suis bien défendu(e)

This sentence is used to express a sense of accomplishment.

L'entretien était long et stressant, mais **je me suis bien défendu**.	*The interview was long and stressful, but **I did well**.*
Je lui ai posé des questions difficiles, mais **elle s'est bien défendue**.	*I asked her difficult questions, but **she did well**.*

La réussite

This word, which literally means *success*, is often used to express *accomplishment* as well.

Ses parents sont heureux de **sa réussite**.	*His/Her parents are happy about **his/ her success/accomplishment**.*

Tu parles!

This exclamatory phrase is used to confirm an assumption in a hyperbolic fashion.

—J'espère que tu as bien compris.	*—I hope that you understood.*
—**Tu parles!** Je comprends parfaitement.	*—**You bet!** I understand perfectly.*

Ça se comprend

This phrase is used to validate an assumption or defend an opinion.

Elle est fatiguée à force de travailler jour et nuit. **Ça se comprend.**	*She is tired from working day and night. **That's understandable.***
Ils pensent que ce film est idiot. **Ça se comprend.**	*They think that this movie is stupid. **It's understandable.***

Félicitations!

This word is used to congratulate or celebrate someone's accomplishments.

Vous êtes mariés depuis trente ans? **Félicitations!**	*You've been married for thirty years? **Congratulations!***
Vous avez votre diplôme? **Félicitations!**	*You have your diploma? **Congratulations!***

Grammar notes

Si

The adverb **si** used before an adjective means *so*.

Il est **si** poli.	*He is **so** polite.*
Elles sont **si** contentes.	*They are **so** happy.*

Falloir and valoir

The verbs **falloir** and **valoir** are frequently used in the **imparfait** (rather than the **passé composé**) because they indicate conditions rather than actions.

Il fallait faire attention pour ne pas tomber sur la glace.	*We (People) **had to** be careful not to fall on the ice.*

| Ça valait la peine d'attendre. Le spectacle était magnifique. | It was worth waiting for. The show was magnificent. |

Reflexive verbs

The past participle of a reflexive verb agrees with its preceding direct object. The preceding direct object is often the reflexive pronoun (which has the same gender and number as the subject pronoun).

| Elle **s'est** bien défend**ue**. | She did well. |
| **Ils se** sont bien défend**us**. | They did well. |

EXERCICE 7·2

Arielle a réussi à l'examen de maths. *Arielle passed the math exam. Complete the lines of dialogue between Arielle and Joëlle with appropriate words or phrases from the list.*

valait	depuis une semaine	parles
défendue	si	Ça s'est bien passé
tout ce que	fallait	Ça ne va pas
Félicitations		

1. JOËLLE: Bonjour Arielle. Tu n'as pas bonne mine. _____?

2. ARIELLE: Je viens de passer l'examen de maths le plus difficile de ma vie. C'était _____ dur!

3. JOËLLE: Ma pauvre Arielle. Il _____ étudier!

4. ARIELLE: C'est _____ j'ai fait toute la semaine!

5. JOËLLE: Ah bon? C'est pour ça qu'on ne t'a pas vu _____.

6. ARIELLE: Oui, remarque que je me suis bien _____ quand même!

7. JOËLLE: Tu as tes résultats? _____?

8. ARIELLE: J'ai une assez bonne note: quinze sur vingt. Ça _____ la peine d'étudier.

9. JOËLLE: _____, Arielle! Pour quelqu'un qui ne comprend pas bien les maths, c'est bien!

10. ARIELLE: Tu _____! Pour moi, c'est un grand succès.

EXERCICE 7·3

Jeu de synonymes. *Synonym game. Write the letter of the expression that is most synonymous on the line provided.*

1. _____ Ça se comprend!

2. _____ Heureusement!

a. J'ai réussi!

b. C'était un succès!

3. _____ Félicitations!   c. Et comment!

4. _____ Ça s'est bien passé!   d. C'est une chance!

5. _____ Je me suis bien défendu!   e. C'est normal!

6. _____ Tu parles!   f. Bravo!

Dialogue 2

Didier, Marie-Josée, Chris, and Anne continue their conversation. There is more good news.

MARIE-JOSÉE: Didier, toi aussi, tu as fait **quelque chose de** bien cet été.

And you, Didier, you did something neat this summer also.

ANNE: Ah oui? Qu'est-ce que tu as fait, **petit cachottier**?

Really? What did you do, you little rascal?

DIDIER: J'ai postulé pour un travail de recherche génétique, et **j'ai été accepté**. Je commence le premier octobre.

I applied for a job in genetic research, and I was accepted. I start on October first.

ANNE: Rien que de bonnes nouvelles! Hourra!

Nothing but good news! Hurrah!

MARIE-JOSÉE: Heureusement que son laboratoire est à Paris. Quelle chance!

Fortunately his lab is in Paris. What luck!

DIDIER: Ça me permet de continuer d'habiter avec mes parents. C'est bien parce que je suis fauché.

It lets me continue living with my parents. That's good because I'm broke.

ANNE: Alors, Marie-Josée et Didier, vous avez tous deux terminé vos vies d'étudiant.

So, Marie-Josée and Didier, you both finished your student lives.

MARIE-JOSÉE: Oui, c'est un peu triste **au fond. Je me sens** vieille.

Yes, it's a little sad after all. I feel old.

DIDIER: Dis, ne dramatise pas, **mon chou**!

Hey, don't dramatize, honey!

MARIE-JOSÉE: Je plaisante, voyons! Oh! Il est déjà dix-sept heures. Demande l'addition, Didier!

I'm only joking! Oh! It's already five P.M. Ask for the check, Didier!

EXERCICE 7·4

Jugez de votre compréhension. *Check your comprehension. Write* T *(true) or* F *(false).*

1. _____ Didier a travaillé pendant l'été.

2. _____ Didier a trouvé un emploi pendant l'été.

3. _____ Didier va travailler à Paris.

4. _____ Didier aime bien habiter avec ses parents.

5. _____ Didier a beaucoup d'argent.

Improving your conversation
Quelque chose de (d')...

Quelque chose de (d') is generally followed by the masculine singular form of an adjective. The expression **quelque chose de bien** is idiomatic because **bien** (*well*) is not an adjective, but an adverb.

J'ai **quelque chose d'intéressant** à vous raconter.	*I have **something interesting** to tell you.*
Elle porte **quelque chose de neuf** chaque jour.	*She wears **something new** every day.*
Elle a fait **quelque chose de bien**.	*She did **something good**.*

Petit cachottier / petite cachottière

This expression is used familiarly with a person you suspect is hiding something.

Dis-nous ce que tu as fait, **petit cachottier**!	*Tell us what you did, **you (secretive) little rascal**!*
Tu as bien gardé le secret, **petite cachottière**!	*You kept the secret, **you (secretive) little rascal**!*

J'ai été accepté(e)

Use this phrase to announce that you have been accepted at a school or university, for a job, or by any organization where you applied for membership.

J'ai été accepté(e) à ton club.	***I was accepted** at your club.*

Au fond...

Use this adverbial phrase to convey that you have thought deeply about something.

J'espère être acceptée, mais **au fond** ce n'est pas si important que ça.	*I hope to be accepted, but it's not so important **after all (upon due consideration)**.*

Je me sens...

This reflexive verb is used with an adjective to express how a person feels.

Je me sens triste aujourd'hui.	***I feel** sad today.*
Elle se sent heureuse.	***She feels** happy.*

Mon chou

This term of endearment, literally meaning *my cabbage* or *my cream puff* (as in **chou à la crème**), is used in the same fashion as the English word *honey* with a person (male or female) we are fond of.

Jacques, viens ici, **mon chou**.	*Jacques, come here, **honey/sweetie**!*
Éva, fais-moi la bise, **mon chou**!	*Éva, give me a kiss, **honey/sweetie**!*

Arielle va à l'université. *Arielle goes to the university. Complete Arielle's lines in French as indicated in parentheses.*

1. JOËLLE: Bonjour Arielle. Quoi de neuf?

   ARIELLE: _____!

   (*I feel so happy!*)

2. JOËLLE: Ah oui? Pourquoi?

   ARIELLE: _____.

   (*I was accepted at the University of Paris.*)

3. JOËLLE: Félicitations, Arielle! Je ne savais pas que c'était l'université de ton choix.

   ARIELLE: _____!

   (*It was my only choice, dear!*)

4. JOËLLE: Qu'est-ce qu'il fallait faire pour être admise?

   ARIELLE: _____.

   (*All I did was to pass the baccalauréat.*)

5. JOËLLE: Chapeau, Arielle! Ça c'est quelque chose!

   ARIELLE: _____!

   (*Yes, it was worth studying hard!*)

Joëlle est une petite cachottière. *Joëlle is secretive. Write the letter of the most appropriate reply to her comments and questions.*

1. _____ Moi aussi, j'ai de bonnes nouvelles.

2. _____ J'ai réussi au baccalauréat.

3. _____ Depuis le mois de juillet.

4. _____ Remarque qu'on ne s'est pas vues depuis quelques semaines.

5. _____ J'étais en vacances.

a. Oh! Petite cachottière! Tu n'as rien dit.

b. C'est vrai. Je ne savais pas où tu étais.

c. Ah oui? Qu'est-ce que c'est?

d. Sans blague! Depuis quand est-ce que tu le savais?

e. Mais, tu sais, au fond, je savais que tu allais réussir.

Dialogue 3

Chris and Anne continue their conversation after Didier and Marie-Josée have left.

ANNE: J'envie Marie-Josée et Didier. Ils ont vraiment bien réussi dans leurs études.

I envy Marie-Josée and Didier. They really succeeded in their studies.

CHRIS: Moi, je les admire et je suis content pour eux. Mais je ne les envie pas.

I admire them and I'm happy for them. But I don't envy them.

ANNE: Moi, tu comprends, je ne sais **pas encore** ce que je vais faire dans la vie. **Ça me travaille** un peu.

You see. I don't know yet what I'm going to do in life. It bugs me a little.

CHRIS: Tu trouveras ta vocation **un jour ou l'autre**.

You'll find your vocation one day.

ANNE: **À propos de** vocation, justement, **tout ce que j'ai** fait jusqu'à présent, c'était du travail volontaire!

Speaking about vocations, that's just it, all I've done up until now is volunteer work!

CHRIS: **Tu n'as pas à t'excuser**, Anne. Ça montre que tu es généreuse.

You don't have to apologize, Anne. It shows that you're generous.

ANNE: Tu sais, ça fait quatre ans que je travaille dans un dispensaire de la SPA.

You know, I've been working in an SPA clinic for four years.

CHRIS: Qu'est-ce que c'est que la SPA?

What is the SPA?

ANNE: Ah oui, pardon! C'est l'acronyme pour la Société Protectrice des Animaux, l'équivalent de votre *Humane Society.* J'y fais du **travail bénévole** quatre heures par semaine.

Yes, sorry! It's the acronym for Société Protectrice des Animaux, *the equivalent of your Humane Society. I volunteer there four hours a week.*

CHRIS: Maintenant je comprends pourquoi je t'ai trouvée sympathique dès que je t'ai rencontrée. **Le bénévolat** est fortement encouragé aux États-Unis aussi.

Now I understand why I found you so endearing as soon as I met you. Volunteer work is also strongly encouraged in the United States.

ANNE: **Pareil** en France. On vient de passer une nouvelle loi sur le travail civique. Mais, dis donc, **remettons cette discussion à plus tard** et demandons l'addition, Chris! Il est l'heure de partir si nous voulons assister à la séance de dix-huit heures.

Same thing in France. They just passed a new law on community work. But, hey, let's postpone this discussion and ask for the check, Chris! It's time to leave if we want to catch the six P.M. movie.

CHRIS: Tu as raison. **Monsieur, l'addition, s'il vous plaît!**

You're right. Sir, check, please!

EXERCICE
7·7

Jugez de votre compréhension. *Check your comprehension. Write* T *(true) or* F *(false).*

1. _____ Chris admire Marie-Josée et Didier.

2. _____ Anne ne sait pas comment elle va gagner sa vie.

3. _____ Anne n'aime pas les animaux.

4. _____ Chris pense qu'Anne devrait être plus généreuse et sympa.

5. _____ Chris comprend tout en français.

Improving your conversation

Pas encore

Even though the adverb **encore** means *still* or *again*, the phrase **pas encore** means *not yet*.

—Tu as fini tes études?　　　　　—*Have you finished your studies?*
—**Pas encore.**　　　　　　　　—***Not yet.***

Ça me travaille

Use this idiomatic expression to say that *something is bothering* or *worrying you*.

Je ne comprends vraiment pas cette　　*I don't really understand this lesson,*
leçon, et **ça me travaille.**　　　　　　　*and **it bothers/worries me**.*

Un jour ou l'autre

Use this phrase to express *someday* or *any day soon*.

Tu arrives toujours en retard. **Un jour**　　*You always arrive late. **Someday** you'll*
ou l'autre tu le regretteras.　　　　　　*regret it.*

À propos de (d')...

Use this prepositional phrase as a transition when you want to elaborate on a topic that was just mentioned.

Tu parlais de tes vacances. **À propos de**　　*You were talking about your vacation. **On the***
vacances, les miennes seront en juin.　　　***subject of** vacations, mine is in June.*

Tout ce que j'ai fait...

This phrase is used to express *all that I did*.

Lis mon essai. C'est **tout ce que j'ai fait,**　　*Read my essay. It's **all I did**, but it's good.*
mais c'est bon.

Tu n'as pas à t'excuser

Use this phrase to assure someone that no apology is necessary.

Tu n'as pas à t'excuser, Sophie. Ce　　***You don't have to apologize**, Sophie.*
n'était pas de ta faute.　　　　　　　　　　*It was not your fault.*

Le travail bénévole / le bénévolat

These expressions refer to *volunteer work*.

Le travail bénévole permet à tous de prouver leur engagement civique.

Volunteer work allows everyone to prove their community spirit.

Pareil...

This adjective is used to convey the idea that something is the same. Note that it is an abbreviated construction (**c'est pareil**).

Vous avez beaucoup de volontaires dans vos communautés? **Pareil** chez nous!

*You have many volunteers in your communities? **Same thing** here!*

Remettre une discussion à plus tard

This expression is used to ask for a discussion to be tabled or postponed.

Il vaut mieux **remettre cette discussion à plus tard**, car nous n'arriverons pas à une conclusion aujourd'hui.

*It's better **to table this discussion for later** because we will not reach a conclusion today.*

Monsieur, l'addition, s'il vous plaît!

This is the customary expression to ask for a bill or a check in a restaurant or café.

Madame/mademoiselle/monsieur, l'addition, s'il vous plaît!

Madam/Miss/Sir, check please!

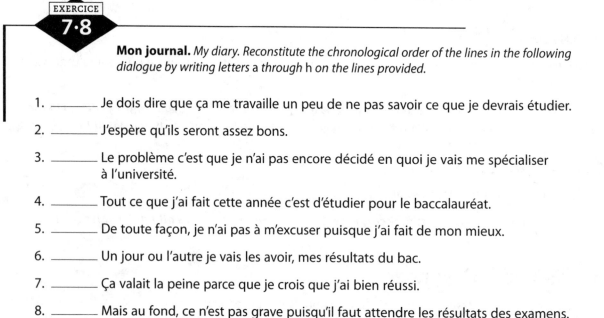

EXERCICE
7·8

Mon journal. *My diary. Reconstitute the chronological order of the lines in the following dialogue by writing letters* a *through* h *on the lines provided.*

1. _____ Je dois dire que ça me travaille un peu de ne pas savoir ce que je devrais étudier.

2. _____ J'espère qu'ils seront assez bons.

3. _____ Le problème c'est que je n'ai pas encore décidé en quoi je vais me spécialiser à l'université.

4. _____ Tout ce que j'ai fait cette année c'est d'étudier pour le baccalauréat.

5. _____ De toute façon, je n'ai pas à m'excuser puisque j'ai fait de mon mieux.

6. _____ Un jour ou l'autre je vais les avoir, mes résultats du bac.

7. _____ Ça valait la peine parce que je crois que j'ai bien réussi.

8. _____ Mais au fond, ce n'est pas grave puisqu'il faut attendre les résultats des examens.

Bénévolat ou travail non-payé? *Volunteer work or unpaid work? Write the letter of the most appropriate reply on the line provided.*

1. _____ Qu'est-ce que tu penses du travail bénévole?

2. _____ Et les gens qui travaillent gratuitement pour un futur employeur?

3. _____ Mais ce n'est pas pareil que travailler à la SPA!

4. _____ Le vrai bénévolat, c'est donner son temps et son labeur à la communauté.

5. _____ Bonne question! Les très jeunes et les personnes à la retraite, certainement.

6. _____ Je ne sais pas. Il y a des familles où tout le monde travaille dur pour gagner sa vie.

a. Remarque, le volontariat peut se faire en famille, non?

b. Bon. Remettons cette discussion fort intéressante à plus tard!

c. Si c'est dans leur propre intérêt, pourquoi pas?

d. Je pense que tout le monde devrait en faire.

e. Mais est-ce que tout le monde en est capable?

f. Tu as raison. Ça ne profite qu'à la personne elle-même et à l'employeur.

Grammar notes

Direct object pronouns

The direct object pronouns **le/la/l'/les** are used to replace both things and people.

Le film? Je **le** trouve bon.
La pièce? Je **la** trouve bonne.
Ta copine? Je **l'**aime bien.
Tes amis? Je **les** aime bien aussi.

*The movie? I find **it** good.*
*The play? I find **it** good.*
*Your girlfriend? I like **her**.*
*Your friends? I like **them** too.*

The direct object pronouns **me/te (t')/nous/vous** are only used to replace *people*.

Je **te/vous** cherche.
Tu **me/nous** cherches?

*I am picking **you** up.*
*Are you picking **me/us** up?*

In the case of verbs conjugated in the **passé composé** with **avoir**, the past participle agrees with the *preceding direct object* noun or pronoun.

La pièce? Je **l'**ai trouvé**e** bonne.
Les films? Je **les** ai trouvé**s** bons.

*The play? I found **it** good.*
*The movies? I found **them** good.*

Ça fait... que (qu')...

Ça fait... que (qu') + *present tense* is used to express that an action started in the past but is still going on in the present.

Ça fait un mois **que** je voyage.

*I have been traveling **for** a month.*

Quel genre de film voudrait-on voir? *What type of film would we like to see? Write the letter of the most appropriate reply on the line provided.*

1. _____ Ça fait longtemps qu'on n'a pas vu de film.

2. _____ Tu as envie de voir un film d'aventures?

3. _____ Tu as déjà vu *Avatar*?

4. _____ Il est justement à la télé ce soir.

5. _____ C'est un mélange de beaucoup de choses.

6. _____ Tu as apporté la pizza?

7. _____ Tu blagues, n'est-ce pas?

8. _____ Tu es un vrai comédien.

a. Non, je l'ai mangée.

b. Tu parles! Il faut s'amuser dans la vie.

c. Bon, je veux bien le regarder avec toi.

d. Mais oui, je plaisante. Ne t'en fais pas!

e. Pas encore.

f. Ça fait un mois, je crois.

g. Mais c'est un film d'aventures, non?

h. Oui, pourquoi pas? Du moment que ce n'est pas un film policier.

Dialogue 4

Chris and Anne continue the conversation after Didier and Marie-Josée have left.

ANNE: **Mince alors!** Pour un film de science-fiction, c'était plein de messages sur l'environnement!

Gee! For a science fiction movie, it was full of messages about the environment!

CHRIS: Oui, je suis d'accord. Ça m'a beaucoup plu. C'est si beau d'imaginer un monde où le respect et l'amour de la nature gagnent contre le matérialisme.

Yes, I agree. I liked it a lot. It is so beautiful to imagine a world in which respect and love of nature win over materialism.

ANNE: Tiens! **Tu as un côté** rêveur et romantique que je ne connaissais pas.

Wow! You have a dreamy and romantic side that I didn't know.

CHRIS: Ma petite Anne, je suis un peu obsessif **quand il s'agit de** l'environnement et de notre planète.

Dear Anne, I am a little obsessive when it comes to the environment and our planet.

ANNE: Tu as probablement raison! Qu'est-ce que tu fais, toi, personnellement?

You are probably right (to be that way). What do you do (about it), you, personally?

CHRIS: Quand j'étais au lycée, j'étais président du club de recyclage.

When I was in high school, I was president of the recycling club.

ANNE: Ah! **Chapeau!** C'est bien ça.

Kudos! That's neat.

CHRIS: Et l'an dernier, j'ai formé un club à l'université. Nous organisons des nettoyages de parc et nous publions des brochures avec des conseils utiles pour protéger l'environnement.

And last year, I formed a club at the university. We organize park clean-ups, and we publish brochures with useful advice on how to protect the environment.

ANNE: Quelle belle initiative, Chris! Est-ce que vous avez du succès?	*What a great undertaking, Chris! Are you having success?*
CHRIS: **Je pense que oui!** Nous faisons des rallyes et il y a plein de monde qui vient.	*I think so! We have rallies, and lots of people come.*
ANNE: Tant qu'il y a de la vie, il y a de l'espoir!	*As long as there's life, there's hope!*

EXERCICE 7·11

Jugez de votre compréhension. *Write T (true) or F (false).*

1. _____ Chris et Anne ont apprécié le film.

2. _____ Anne a trouvé que les messages dans le film n'étaient pas corrects.

3. _____ Anne ne savait pas que Chris peut être romantique.

4. _____ Chris est un activiste quand il s'agit de l'environnement.

5. _____ Anne est pessimiste quand il s'agit de l'environnement.

Improving your conversation

Mince (alors)!

This phrase expresses surprise.

Quel beau cadeau! **Mince alors!** Il devait être cher.	*What a beautiful gift! **Gee!** It had to be expensive!*

Un côté...

This phrase refers to an aspect of one's personality. It is followed by an adjective or a noun.

Même à l'âge adulte, elle a gardé **un côté** enfant.	*Even in adulthood, she kept **a** childlike **quality**.*
Il a **un côté** très excentrique.	*He has **a** very eccentric **streak**.*

Quand il s'agit de (d')...

This phrase is used to introduce a topic before elaborating on it.

Quand il s'agit de vacances, les Français préfèrent les pays chauds.	***When it comes to** vacations, the French prefer warm places.*

Chapeau!

Use this exclamation to show approval, admiration, appreciation, or respect.

Tu fais du volontariat depuis quatre ans? **Chapeau!**	*You've been doing volunteer work for four years? **Kudos! (I take my hat off to you!)***

Je pense que oui / je pense que non

Use one of these phrases to express an affirmative or negative opinion and to say that you *think so* or *do not think so*.

—Est-ce qu'ils vont réussir?   —*Are they going to succeed?*
—**Je pense que oui.**   —*I think so.*

—Il va neiger?   —*Is it going to snow?*
—**Je pense que non.**   —*I don't think so.*

Grammar note

Connaître and savoir

Using **connaître** and **savoir** in the **imparfait** (rather than the **passé composé**) is common because these verbs indicate states of mind.

Je ne **connaissais** pas cet aspect de ta personnalité.   *I did not **know** this aspect of your personality.*
Nous ne **savions** pas qu'il faisait une thèse.   *We didn't **know** that he was doing a thesis.*

EXERCICE
7·12

Théo et Chris l'an dernier à l'université. *Théo and Chris last year at the university.*
Complete Théo's replies to Chris according to the English guidelines in parentheses.

1. CHRIS: Dis, Théo, j'ai terminé la nouvelle brochure pour le rallye.

   THÉO: _____!

   (*Hats off to you! It's great!*)

2. CHRIS: Tu ne trouves pas les images un peu violentes?

   THÉO: _____!

   (*No, they are fine!*)

3. CHRIS: Tu sais, il y a toujours plein de gens qui ne sont pas pour la protection de l'environnement.

   THÉO: _____!

   (*When it comes to the environment, I'm pessimistic!*)

4. CHRIS: Alors, à ton avis, ça ne va pas choquer les gens.

   THÉO: _____!

   (*I don't think so!*)

5. CHRIS: Pourquoi est-ce que ça me travaille comme ça?

   THÉO: _____!

   (*Don't worry! It's really fine!*)

L'histoire de Chris. *Chris's story. Write the letter of the most appropriate completion for each sentence.*

1. _____ Quand j'étais à l'université...

2. _____ Dès que j'ai rencontré ma copine...

3. _____ J'organisais des rallyes...

4. _____ Je n'avais jamais d'argent...

5. _____ J'étudiais beaucoup...

6. _____ J'ai réussi...

7. _____ Mes parents étaient...

8. _____ Mon père m'a acheté une voiture.

a. je l'ai trouvée sympa.

b. Mince alors! Quelle surprise!

c. à tous mes examens.

d. si fiers de moi.

e. parce que je ne travaillais pas.

f. pour la protection de l'environnement.

g. pour avoir de bonnes notes.

h. je faisais beaucoup de volontariat.

Dialogue 5

Didier invites Marie-Josée to a party at his house to celebrate his mother's promotion.

DIDIER: Allô, Marie-Josée. J'ai d'excellentes nouvelles concernant maman!

Hello, Marie-Josée. I have excellent news concerning Mom.

MARIE-JOSÉE: Ah oui? **Attends que** je devine. Elle a gagné la loterie!

Yes? Let me guess. She won the lottery!

DIDIER: Mais non. Elle ne joue pas à la loterie. Non, elle a été **promue au poste** de directrice de son lycée.

Of course not. She doesn't play the lottery. No, she was promoted to the position of principal of her high school.

MARIE-JOSÉE: **Chouette!** Elle doit être heureuse comme tout.

Cool! She must be really happy.

DIDIER: Tu parles! Elle attendait l'annonce anxieusement depuis un mois. **Quel soulagement!**

You can say that again! She's been anxiously expecting the announcement for a month. What a relief!

MARIE-JOSÉE: Elle le mérite. Elle est si qualifiée dans l'enseignement! De plus, **elle avait l'ancienneté**, non?

She deserves it. She is so qualified in the teaching field! Plus, she had seniority, right?

DIDIER: Oui, mais il fallait quand même qu'elle reçoive une lettre officielle avant de **se réjouir**.

Yes, but she still had to wait for an official letter before celebrating.

MARIE-JOSÉE: Je comprends. Mais maintenant elle peut **se vanter**.

I understand. But now she can boast.

DIDIER: C'est pour ça que je téléphone. Papa et moi, nous invitons la famille et les amis à venir chez nous samedi pour la féliciter et pour célébrer sa promotion.

That's why I'm calling. Dad and I are inviting family and friends to come to our house Saturday to congratulate her and to celebrate her promotion.

MARIE-JOSÉE: Tu veux que j'apporte un plat?

Do you want me to bring a dish?

DIDIER: Non, non, papa a déjà **fait une commande** chez le traiteur du quartier! On va **faire la fête!**

No, no, Dad already placed an order with the neighborhood caterer (deli)! We're going to party!

EXERCICE
7·14

Jugez de votre compréhension. *Check your comprehension. Write* T *(true) or* F *(false).*

1. _____ La maman de Didier a obtenu le poste qu'elle désirait.

2. _____ Marie-Josée a gagné à la loterie.

3. _____ La maman de Didier travaille dans l'enseignement.

4. _____ Didier et son père vont organiser une fête au lycée.

5. _____ Didier accepte l'offre de Marie-Josée de contribuer à la fête.

Improving your conversation

Attends que (qu')...

Use this phrase to encourage patience or elicit curiosity. The verb following **que** (**qu'**) is in the subjunctive mood.

Attends que je vérifie que le taxi est arrivé!

Wait until I check that the taxi arrived!

Attends seulement **que** je t'attrape, petit coquin!

Just let me catch you, you little rascal!

Promu(e)

Use this adjective to refer to someone who has been promoted.

Il attend d'être **promu**. Il aura une augmentation de salaire.

He is waiting to be promoted. He will get a raise in salary.

Le poste

Use this term to refer to a professional or occupational position.

Tu as eu **le poste** de superviseur? Félicitations!

You got the position of supervisor? Congratulations!

Chouette!

Use this exclamation to show admiration or pleasure.

Tu as reçu ta promotion? **Chouette!** Je te félicite.

You got your promotion? Neat/Cool! I congratulate you.

Le soulagement

This term means *relief*, usually from a worry or concern.

Le vol va arriver à temps! Quel **soulagement**!	*The flight is going to arrive on time! What a **relief**!*

Avoir l'ancienneté

This term refers to *seniority* on a job or in a position.

M. Pointu va recevoir sa promotion. C'est normal parce qu'**il a l'ancienneté** dans l'entreprise.	*Mr. Pointu is going to receive his promotion. It's expected because **he has seniority** in the company.*

Se réjouir

Use this reflexive verb to express happiness or joy.

Je vais fêter mon anniversaire avec mes amis. **Je me réjouis!**	*I'm going to celebrate my birthday with my friends. **I'm so happy!***
Paul se réjouit d'avoir réussi à l'examen.	***Paul is happy** to have passed the exam.*

Se vanter

Use this reflexive verb to express the action of *bragging* or *boasting*.

Elle **se vante** toujours de ses exploits. C'est énervant!	*She always **brags** about her accomplishments. It's annoying!*

Faire une commande

This expression refers to *placing an order* with a business.

Je vais **faire une commande** à ma banque pour des chèques.	*I'm going to **place an order** at my bank for some checks.*

Faire la fête

This expression refers to *partying* or *having fun*.

Ce soir on va s'amuser et **faire la fête** avec nos copains.	*Tonight we are going to have fun and **party** with our friends.*

Grammar notes
Attendre que (qu')...

Attendre que (qu') is followed by a verb in the subjunctive mood.

On **attend qu'**il **soit** assez âgé pour lui acheter une voiture.	*We **are waiting** for him **to be** old enough to buy him a car.*

Avant de (d')...

The prepositional phrase **avant de (d')** is followed by an infinitive.

Avant de partir, mange quelque chose.   ***Before leaving**, eat something.*

Pour

The preposition **pour** followed by an infinitive is used to express *in order to*.

On sortira dîner **pour fêter** cette promotion.   *We'll go out for dinner (**in order) to celebrate** this promotion.*

EXERCICE
7·15

On attend la bonne nouvelle. *Waiting for good news. Put the following sentences in order by placing the letters* a *through* f *next to the statements.*

1. _____ Elle aura la nouvelle officielle demain.

2. _____ Son mari invitera la famille et les amis et fera une commande chez le traiteur.

3. _____ Mme Dupoint attend l'annonce de sa promotion.

4. _____ Quand elle sera officiellement promue, elle le dira d'abord à son mari.

5. _____ Tout le monde viendra féliciter Mme Dupoint et ils feront la fête.

6. _____ Mais avant de se réjouir, elle doit attendre et être sûre qu'elle aura le poste désiré.

EXERCICE
7·16

Chouette! *Cool! Fill in the blanks with the hints provided as Madame Dupoint tells her husband she's been promoted.*

1. MME DUPOINT: Chéri, j'ai une _____! (*good news*)

2. M. DUPOINT: C'est ce que _____ (*you've been waiting for*) depuis un mois?

3. MME DUPOINT: C'est ça. _____ (*I've been promoted*).

4. M. DUPOINT _____! (*What a relief*)

5. MME DUPOINT: Je me réjouis! _____. (*I have the position*)

6. M. DUPOINT: Eh bien. On va _____. (*place an order at the caterer*)

7. MME DUPOINT: Et on va inviter tous nos amis! Ça va être _____! (*cool*)

8. M. DUPOINT: _____, ma chérie. Tu le méritais! (*I congratulate you*)

9. MME DUPOINT: Je ne veux pas _____ mais c'est vrai. (*boast*)

10. M. DUPOINT: Nous pouvons tous deux _____. C'est aussi une belle augmentation de salaire. (*rejoice*)

EXERCICE 7·17

Félicitations! *Congratulations! In this dialogue, Nathalie tells her father that she passed her* **baccalauréat** *exam. Write the dialogue using the English guidelines provided.*

1. M. Boily asks Nathalie why she looks so happy.

   M. BOILY: _____

2. Nathalie asks her dad what important news she has been waiting for in the last month.

   NATHALIE: _____

3. Mr. Boily exclaims it's silly of him to ask. He guesses she is happy because she passed the baccalaureate exam.

   M. BOILY: _____

4. Nathalie expresses her relief. She passed.

   NATHALIE: _____

5. Mr. Boily congratulates her and tells her that now she deserves a nice, long vacation.

   M. BOILY: _____

6. Nathalie agrees and says that all she's been doing in the last year is studying.

   NATHALIE: _____

7. Mr. Boily adds that now he really can boast he has a very smart daughter.

   M. BOILY: _____

8. Nathalie says that when it comes to school, she always tries her best.

   NATHALIE: _____

·8· ◆ Making comparisons

Dialogue 1

Didier and Marie-Josée just bought new phones and are comparing them.

DIDIER: J'adore mon Smartphone. Je peux recevoir ou envoyer mes e-mails instantanément et lire mes pièces jointes, tout ça pour **un forfait** raisonnable.

I love my Smartphone. I can receive or send my e-mails instantly and read my attachments, all that at a reasonable rate.

MARIE-JOSÉE: Le mien aussi est très bien. Je peux jouer à des jeux vidéo, écouter de la musique et surfer le Net.

Mine is very good too. I can play video games, listen to music, and surf the Net.

DIDIER: **Tu t'en sers** comme moi pour gérer ton emploi du temps?

Do you use it like I do to manage your schedule?

MARIE-JOSÉE: Oui, bien sûr. C'est un outil professionnel **aussi bien qu'**un moyen de divertissement personnel.

Yes, of course. It's a professional tool as well as a means of personal entertainment.

DIDIER: J'ai acheté le mien à prix réduit parce que ce n'était pas le modèle le plus récent.

I bought mine at a reduced price because it wasn't the most recent model.

MARIE-JOSÉE: Eh bien, moi, je ne sais pas **si** c'était le dernier modèle **ou non** mais il était en promotion. Et actuellement tous les Smartphones sur le marché ont l'air de très bien **marcher**.

Well, I don't know whether it was the latest model or not, but it was on sale. And these days all the Smartphones on the market seem to work very well.

DIDIER: C'est vrai. Tu as un forfait?

That's true. Do you have a monthly contract?

MARIE-JOSÉE: Tu parles! Cinquante euros par mois.

Of course! Fifty euros a month.

DIDIER: Ça alors, tu paies **moins que** moi! Le mien est de soixante euros.

Darn, you pay less than me! Mine is sixty euros.

MARIE-JOSÉE: En effet, c'est **plus que** mon forfait. Tu as payé combien pour l'appareil même?

True, that's more than my package. How much did you pay for the phone itself?

DIDIER: Il était gratuit avec un abonnement de deux ans.

It was free with a two-year contract.

MARIE-JOSÉE: Ah! Il fallait que tu t'abonnes pour deux ans **alors que** moi, j'ai acheté mon appareil pour cent euros, mais je me suis abonnée aux services pour seulement six mois.

Oh! You had to subscribe for two years, while I bought my phone for a hundred euros, but I only subscribed to the services for six months.

DIDIER: **Tu as** probablement **bien fait**!

You probably did the right thing!

EXERCICE
8·1

Jugez de votre compréhension. *Check your comprehension. Write* T *(true) or* F *(false).*

1. _____ Didier pense qu'il paie un forfait raisonnable pour son abonnement.

2. _____ Marie-Josée paie plus que Didier pour son abonnement.

3. _____ Didier se sert de son Smartphone pour le travail.

4. _____ Marie-Josée se sert de son Smartphone pour travailler seulement.

5. _____ Didier n'a rien payé pour le téléphone, seulement pour l'abonnement.

Grammar note
Adverbs

Adverbs are frequently derived from the *feminine* form of the related adjective.

actuel (*m.*)	→	**actuelle** (*f.*)	→	**actuellement**	*currently*
seul (*m.*)	→	**seule** (*f.*)	→	**seulement**	*only*

For adjectives that are spelled the same in the masculine and feminine forms, add **-ment** to the adjective.

probable (*m., f.*)	→	**probable** (*m., f.*)	→	**probablement**	*probably*

Improving your conversation
Un forfait

Use this word to refer to any package deal, fixed price, or regular contract for services.

Ils ont trouvé **un forfait** voyage en dernière minute.

*They found a **fixed-price** travel **deal** at the last minute.*

Tu t'en sers?

Ask this question to verify whether someone is using a previously mentioned object or item.

—Je vois que tu as ton ordinateur. **Tu t'en sers** en ce moment?
—Oui, **je m'en sers**.

*—I see you have your computer. **Are you using it** at the moment?*
*—Yes, **I'm using it**.*

Aussi bien que (qu')...

Use this adverbial phrase to express *as well as*.

Mon téléphone marche **aussi bien que** le tien.	*My phone works **as well as** yours.*
Vous parlez **aussi bien qu'**eux.	*You speak **as well as** them (they do).*

Si

The word **si** has many functions in French. Here, it means *if* or *whether*:

Je ne sais pas **si** c'est un bon prix.	*I don't know **if** it's a good price.*
Dis-moi **si** tu penses que c'est une aubaine ou non.	*Tell me **whether** you think that it's a bargain or not.*

Ou non

Use this expression to emphasize affirmative and negative choices or opinions.

Tu peux le croire **ou non**.	*You can believe it **or not**.*

Marcher

Use the verb **marcher** to express if or how a mechanical device, an electronic device, a tool, or an appliance works.

La télé **ne marche pas**.	*The TV **doesn't work**.*
Le nouvel ordinateur **marche** mieux que l'ancien.	*The new computer **works** better than the old one.*

Moins/plus que (qu')...

Use one of these expressions in comparisons.

Il tape **moins** vite **que** toi.	*He types **less** fast **than** you (does not type as fast as you).*
J'ai **plus** de temps **qu'**elle pour le faire.	*I have **more** time **than** she (does) to do it.*

Alors que (qu')...

Use this conjunction to establish a contrast.

Je paie chaque mois, **alors que** toi, tu paies chaque semaine.	*I pay every month, **whereas** you pay every week.*

Tu as bien fait

Use this expression to show approval for a job or a deed well done.

Tu as acheté un nouveau mobile? **Tu as bien fait!**	*You bought a new cell phone. **Well done!***

Denis veut acheter un Smartphone. *Denis wants to buy a Smartphone. Complete each line of dialogue with an appropriate word or phrase from the list provided.*

profiter	marche	veux
réduit	un forfait	combien
des promotions	modèle	

1. DENIS: Je vais m'acheter un Smartphone. Tu _____ venir avec moi?

2. ARNAUD: D'accord. Moi, j'en ai acheté un il y a six mois à prix _____.

3. DENIS: Ah bon. Ce n'était probablement pas le dernier _____ à ce moment-là.

4. ARNAUD: Probablement pas, mais il _____ très bien.

5. DENIS: Et _____ tu paies pour les services?

6. ARNAUD: La compagnie qui m'a vendu mon Smartphone m'a offert _____ de cinquante euros par mois pour une gamme de services.

7. DENIS: Pas mal. Il y a _____ en ce moment pour les derniers modèles.

8. ARNAUD: Il faut en _____ alors. Allons-y!

Denis et Arnaud comparent leurs téléphones. *Denis and Arnaud compare their phones. Write the letter of Renaud's reply to each of Denis's statements on the line provided.*

1. _____ Un téléphone gratuit! C'est incroyable!

2. _____ Et le forfait de soixante euros est bien aussi.

3. _____ Mais je crois que j'ai plus de services que toi.

4. _____ Pas grave! Tu n'as pas de voiture.

5. _____ Bien sûr. Il le faut. Et la messagerie aussi.

a. Oui, le mien est de cinquante euros.

b. Tu parles! Je reçois des messages instantanés toute la journée!

c. Justement! Internet, par contre, je l'ai.

d. C'est vrai. Je n'ai pas le système de navigation sur le mien.

e. Le mien était gratuit aussi.

Dialogue 2

Anne and Marie-Josée have a casual chat about clothes.

ANNE: Quelle jolie robe, Marie-Josée! Tu viens de l'acheter? Elle est vraiment **du dernier style**.

What a pretty dress, Marie-Josée! Did you just buy it? It's really in style.

MARIE-JOSÉE: **C'est gentil de dire ça.** Je suis entrée dans cette boutique **haut de gamme** doutant de **pouvoir m'offrir quoi que ce soit**. Tu ne peux pas imaginer combien de temps j'ai mis pour la choisir.

It's nice of you to say that. I went into that high-end boutique doubting that I could afford anything. You can't imagine how much time I spent choosing it.

ANNE: Eh bien, ça valait la peine. Elle est tout à fait adorable. Elle était chère?

Well, it was worth it. It's just adorable. Was it expensive?

MARIE-JOSÉE: Tu sais, il me fallait quelques nouvelles **fringues**, et puisque c'est la fin de l'été, il y a beaucoup de soldes. Alors, j'en ai profité.

You know, I needed a few new clothes, and since it's the end of the summer, there are lots of sales. So I took advantage of them.

ANNE: Tu l'as eue à bon marché alors?

You got it at a good price then?

MARIE-JOSÉE: **Oh que oui**, ma chère! J'ai payé moins que la moitié du prix. J'en avais **tellement** envie! Le problème, évidemment, c'est que l'an prochain, cette robe sera de nouveau démodée.

You can say that again, my dear! I paid less than half the price. I wanted it so much! The problem, of course, is that next year, this dress will be out of style.

ANNE: C'est vrai. **Tu suis la mode de près**, toi?

That's true. Do you follow fashion closely?

MARIE-JOSÉE: Quand **j'ai les moyens**, oui! J'aime bien **être dans le coup** et porter des vêtements **du dernier cri**. Et puis je me lasse facilement de ce que je porte.

When I can afford it, yes! I like to be with it and wear the latest style clothes. Plus, I tire easily of whatever I'm wearing.

ANNE: Je te comprends. **C'est pareil pour moi.** J'achèterais volontiers de nouveaux habits chaque mois **si je le pouvais**.

I understand what you're saying. It's the same for me. I'd happily buy new clothes every month if I could.

MARIE-JOSÉE: J'ai remarqué que tu es toujours vêtue **de façon** très unique.

I noticed you're always dressed in a very unique style.

ANNE: **Faute de** pouvoir acheter tout ce qui me plaît, il faut bien que je crée ma propre mode.

Since I can't buy everything I like, I have to create my own fashion.

MARIE-JOSÉE: Génial! J'aimerais bien être aussi originale que toi.

Amazing! I'd love to be as original as you.

ANNE: Et moi, j'aimerais être plus raisonnable et ne pas **tellement me tracasser question de** vêtements!

And I would love to be more reasonable and not worry so much about clothes!

Jugez de votre compréhension. *Check your comprehension. Write* T *(true) or* F *(false).*

1. _____ Marie-Josée achète toujours des vêtements chers.

2. _____ Marie-Josée a acheté sa robe dans une boutique haut de gamme.

3. _____ Marie-Josée et Anne suivent la mode de près.

4. _____ Marie-Josée aime changer de vêtements souvent.

5. _____ Anne est ingénieuse et sait créer son propre style de vêtements.

Improving your conversation

Du dernier style / du dernier cri

Use this expression to describe the *latest fashion* in clothes.

Ils portent toujours des vêtements **du dernier style**.	*They always wear **the latest fashion** in clothes.*

C'est gentil de dire ça

Use this sentence to acknowledge a compliment rather than or in addition to saying **Merci**. It allows the speaker to remain humble while accepting the compliment.

—Quel bel ensemble!	*—What a beautiful outfit!*
—**C'est gentil de dire ça.**	*—**It's nice of you to say that.***

Haut de gamme

Use this phrase to describe anything that is high end, upmarket, or "classy."

Pour une fois, j'ai acheté un téléphone **haut de gamme**.	*For once, I bought a **high-end** phone.*

Pouvoir s'offrir quoi que ce soit

Use this expression to express the concept of being able to afford something.

Je ne sais pas si **je peux m'offrir quoi que ce soit** ici.	*I don't know if **I can afford anything** here.*

Les fringues (f. pl.)

This familiar term is often used for *clothing,* instead of **les habits** or **les vêtements**.

Je vais donner mes vieilles **fringues** à l'Armée du Salut.	*I'm going to give my old **clothes** to the Salvation Army.*

Oh que oui! / oh que non!

Use one of these expressions for an emphatic *yes* or *no*.

—Il y a des soldes en ce moment?	—*Are there sales on at the moment?*
—**Oh que oui!**	—***Yes, there are! / There certainly are!***
—Tu ne veux pas cette chemise marron?	—*Don't you want this brown shirt?*
—**Oh que non!**	—***No, I certainly don't!***

Tellement

This adverb is used before an adjective to express *so much*. **Tellement de (d')** is used before a noun to express *so much* or *so many*.

On paie **tellement** plus cher quand c'est le dernier cri.	*You pay **so much** more when it is the latest style.*
Tu es **tellement** bien habillé, Marc!	*You are **so** well dressed, Marc!*
Ne dépense pas **tellement d'**argent!	*Don't spend **so much** money!*
Elle achète **tellement de** vêtements!	*She buys **so many** clothes!*

Suivre la mode de près

Use this expression when talking about people who follow fashion closely and passionately.

C'est une passionnée de la mode.	*She is passionate about fashion.*
Elle la suit de très près.	***She follows it very closely.***

Avoir les moyens

Use this expression when talking about having the means or being able to afford things.

Tu as les moyens d'acheter cette robe Dior? Chapeau!	***You can afford** to buy this Dior dress? My compliments!*

Être dans le coup

Use this expression to describe people or things who are seen as following the latest trends.

Cette dame de cinquante ans **est dans le coup**.	*This fifty-year-old woman **is hip / cool / with it**.*
Regarde, nos chaussures sont du dernier cri. **Nous sommes dans le coup!**	*Look, our shoes are the latest style. **We're trendy!***

C'est pareil pour moi

Use this emphatic expression to state that you feel or act the same way as someone else.

Tu n'aimes pas cette mode. **C'est pareil pour moi.**	*You don't like this fashion. **I feel the same (way)**.*
Tu respectes l'originalité! Eh bien! **C'est pareil pour moi.**	*You respect originality! Well! **It's the same with me. / I do too.***

De façon...

This expression plus an adjective make up an adverbial expression that describes how something is or was done.

Tu agis **de façon arrogante**! | *You're acting **arrogantly**!*
La vendeuse m'a servi **de façon** très **courtoise**. | *The saleswoman served me very **courteously**.*

Faute de (d')...

Use this expression before a noun or an infinitive to introduce the reason for a negative result.

Faute d'argent, je ne peux rien acheter. | ***For lack of money**, I can't buy anything.*
Faute d'avoir gagné quelque chose le mois dernier, il est fauché. | ***Since he didn't earn** something/anything last month, he is broke.*

Se tracasser

Use this reflexive verb instead of the verb **s'inquiéter** (*to worry*), especially when speaking familiarly.

Cette jupe est encore jolie. Je ne devrais pas **me tracasser**. | *This skirt is still pretty. I shouldn't **worry**.*

Une question de (d')... / question de (d')...

Use this phrase before a noun or an infinitive to introduce a topic or a reason.

Je ne peux pas venir ce soir. C'est **une question de** temps. | *I can't come tonight. It's **a question of** time.*
Ce n'est pas toujours **question de** savoir choisir ce qui te va. | *It's not always **a matter of** knowing how to choose what suits you.*

Grammar notes

The **imparfait** tense

Use the **imparfait** after **si** (in the **si** clause) when the result (stated or implied) is in the conditional mood.

Si j'avais les moyens, **j'achèterais** de nouveaux habits. | ***If I had** the means, **I would buy** new clothes.*
Si seulement **j'osais**! | ***If** only **I dared**!*

Comparisons

In comparisons, place the two parts of the expressions **aussi... que...** (*as...as...*), **moins... que...** (*less...than...*), **plus... que...** (*more...than...*) around the adverb or adjective used in the comparison.

Cette robe est **moins chère que** l'autre. | *This dress is **less expensive than** the other.*
Ton pantalon est **aussi démodé que** le mien. | *Your pants are **as out of style as** mine.*
Tu parles **plus couramment que** moi. | *You speak **more fluently than** me (I do).*

Est-ce que je suis dans le coup? *Am I in style? Write Marc-Antoine's replies to Sophie's comments and questions on the lines provided according to the English guidelines in parentheses.*

1. SOPHIE: Dis, Marc, tu penses que cette robe est démodée?

   MARC-ANTOINE: _____

   (Yes, it certainly is, my dear Sophie!)

2. SOPHIE: C'est bien ce que je pensais! Tu sais comme je suis la mode!

   MARC-ANTOINE: _____

   (Yes, but don't worry. You can buy a new dress.)

3. SOPHIE: Pas vraiment! Question d'argent, tu vois.

   MARC-ANTOINE: _____

   (You are so original with your clothes. Create a new style!)

4. SOPHIE: Oui, c'est toujours une question d'imagination. C'est vrai, ça.

   MARC-ANTOINE: _____

   (One has to have the means to follow fashion closely.)

5. SOPHIE: Oui, les vêtements du dernier cri coûtent généralement un peu plus cher, surtout pour les femmes.

   MARC-ANTOINE: _____

   (It's the same for us men.)

6. SOPHIE: Bien sûr que oui. Tu as raison! Toi, tu es toujours dans le coup!

   MARC-ANTOINE: _____

   (It's nice of you to say that.)

7. SOPHIE: Si seulement on pouvait s'offrir quoi que ce soit!

   MARC-ANTOINE: _____

   (I feel the same way.)

8. SOPHIE: Allons voir ensemble si je peux m'offrir une nouvelle robe!

   MARC-ANTOINE: _____

   (In the high-end stores?)

Sophie s'achète une nouvelle robe. *Sophie buys herself a new dress. Choose the most appropriate reply that Sophie would give to Marc-Antoine in the following dialogue, and write the corresponding letter on the line provided.*

1. _____ Regarde cette robe! Elle est super!

2. _____ Elle n'est pas tellement chère!

3. _____ Tu peux te l'offrir, alors.

4. _____ Génial! Tu vas l'essayer pour voir si elle te va bien?

5. _____ Vas-y! Et prends ton temps! Je t'attends.

6. _____ Bien sûr que non! Seulement toi. Tu es ma meilleure copine!

a. Bien sûr que oui. Il faut qu'elle m'aille parfaitement.

b. Tu traites tous tes amis d'une façon si gentille?

c. C'est gentil de dire ça.

d. Elle est très belle mais combien coûte-t-elle?

e. C'est vrai. Seulement quarante euros.

f. Oui, je crois que j'en ai les moyens.

Dialogue 3

Anne and Didier try to help Marie-Josée find a studio or an apartment for rent in town. They compare the studio they saw earlier in the day with the apartment they are visiting.

ANNE: J'adore cet appartement-ci. Il est plus spacieux et ensoleillé que **celui qu'on a vu** avant.

I love this apartment. It is more spacious and sunny than the one we saw before.

MARIE-JOSÉE: Je suis d'accord. Mais je me demande s'il n'est pas un peu grand pour moi seule.

I agree. But I wonder if it's not too big for me alone.

ANNE: **Qu'est-ce que tu veux dire** «trop grand»? Il y a une chambre à coucher, un salon, une cuisine et une salle de bains! C'est parfait!

What do you mean "too big"? There's a bedroom, a living room, a kitchen, and a bathroom! It's perfect!

MARIE-JOSÉE: Oui, mais je cherchais un studio parce que je n'aurai pas le temps de nettoyer, tu sais, et parce que ça me suffira amplement.

Yes, but I was looking for a studio because I won't have time to clean, you know, and because it will be quite enough.

ANNE: **Pense à** tes amis. **Je compte** passer le week-end chez toi quelquefois.

Think about your friends. I plan to spend the weekend at your place sometimes.

DIDIER: Je ne savais pas que tu te cherchais une seconde résidence, Anne! Moi, je pense que l'autre appartement est aussi confortable que celui-ci et il est plus proche du lieu de travail de Marie-Josée.

Anne, I didn't know you were looking for a second home! I think that the other apartment is as comfortable as this one and is closer to Marie-Josée's work.

Marie-Josée: Remarque que tu seras la bienvenue au studio, Anne, **pourvu que** tu veuilles bien dormir sur un matelas pneumatique!	*Mind you, you'll be welcome at the studio, Anne, provided you're willing to sleep on an air mattress!*
Anne: Bon, mais **sans blague**, qu'est-ce que tu penses, Marie-Josée?	*OK, but seriously, what do you think, Marie-Josée?*
Marie-Josée: Le studio de ce matin est disponible immédiatement. Il est aussi mignon et aussi propre que cet appartement. **De plus**, le loyer est moins élevé. Je dois **tenir compte** de ça.	*This morning's studio is available immediately. It's just as cute and clean as this apartment. Plus, the rent is not as high. I have to take that into account.*
Didier: J'ai l'impression que **tu as pris ta décision**, Marie-Josée.	*I have the feeling that you've made your decision, Marie-Josée.*
Marie-Josée: Mission accomplie! Allons voir le propriétaire et signer le contrat!	*Mission accomplished! Let's go see the owner and sign the contract!*

EXERCICE 8·7

Jugez de votre compréhension. *Check your comprehension. Write* T *(true) or* F *(false).*

1. _____ Anne préfère l'appartement mais Marie-Josée préfère le studio.

2. _____ Le studio est moins propre que l'appartement.

3. _____ Le studio est plus proche du lieu de travail de Marie-Josée.

4. _____ Le loyer de l'appartement est moins élevé que celui du studio.

5. _____ L'appartement est aussi ensoleillé que le studio.

Improving your conversation

Celui qu'on a vu

Use this phrase to refer back to someone or something you saw. Note that **celui** *must agree* in gender and number (**celui, celle, ceux, celles**) with the person(s) or item(s) it replaces.

Nous avons vu deux jolies chambres. **Celle qu'on a vue** en dernier était la plus jolie.	*We saw two pretty rooms. **The one we saw** last was the prettiest.*

Qu'est-ce que tu veux dire? / Qu'est-ce que vous voulez dire?

Ask this question when you do not understand and need to clarify something.

Je ne comprends pas pourquoi tu dis ça. **Qu'est-ce que tu veux dire?**	*I don't understand why you say that. **What do you mean?***

Pense à / pensez à...

Use this verb in the literal sense of *think about* or as a rhetorical device to point something out.

Pense à nous quand tu seras de retour chez toi!	*Think about us when you're back home!*
Pense à ce que tu ferais sans moi!	*Think about what you would do without me!*

Je compte...

Use this verb followed by an infinitive when you want to convey the idea of planning to do something.

Je compte aller en France.	*I intend to go to France.*
Tu comptes louer une chambre?	*Do you plan to rent a room?*

Pourvu que (qu')...

This conjunction is used to set limits and conditions. It is followed by a verb in the subjunctive mood.

Tu peux sortir **pourvu que** tes devoirs **soient** finis.	*You can go out **provided** your homework **is** finished.*

Sans blague

This phrase is used to point out or question the seriousness or authenticity of a statement.

Je cherche un nouvel appartement. **Sans blague!**	*I'm looking for a new apartment. **No kidding! / I'm serious!***
Tu as les moyens de payer comptant. **Sans blague?**	*You can afford to pay in full. **You're not kidding?***

De plus...

Use this transitional phrase whenever you introduce more evidence to support a statement.

La maison est grande. **De plus**, elle est bien située.	*The house is big. **In addition**, it is well located.*

Tenir compte de (d')

Use this expression to refer to what needs to be considered.

Vous devez **tenir compte du** prix de la maison.	*You must **consider the** price of the house.*

Prendre une décision

Use this expression to refer to a decision-making process

Prends une décision! J'attends.	*Make a decision! I'm waiting.*

Grammar notes
Demonstrative adjectives

Demonstrative adjectives (**ce, cet, cette, ces**) agree in gender and number with the noun they precede. Remember that there are two *masculine singular* forms: **ce** (before a consonant) and **cet** (before a vowel sound).

Ce studio est beau.	*This studio is beautiful.*
Cet appartment est petit.	*This apartment is small.*
Cette chambre est grande.	*This room is big.*
Ces lieux sont connus.	*These sites are known.*

Demonstrative pronouns

Demonstrative pronouns (**celui, celle, ceux, celles**) agree in gender and number with the nouns they replace. They are always followed by **-ci** or **-là** (to compare real or imagined distance), a relative pronoun (**que/qu', qui**, or **dont**), or **de (d')**.

Regarde ces studios! **Celui-ci** est propre mais **celui-là** est sale. **Ceux** de ce matin étaient plus grands.	*Look at these studios. **This one** is clean, but **that one** is dirty. **The ones from** this morning were bigger.*
Regarde ces deux robes! **Celle-ci** est à la mode. **Celle-là** est démodée. **Celles** d'avant étaient moins chères.	*Look at these two dresses! **This one** is in style. **That one** is out of style. **The ones from** before were less expensive.*

EXERCICE
8·8

Faites des comparaisons! *Make comparisons! Write the following sentences in French.*

1. This room is bigger than the other one.

   _____

2. These kitchens are smaller than the other ones.

   _____

3. Look (familiar) at these apartments! This one is beautiful. That one is awful.

   _____

4. What do you think of these houses? This one is available immediately. That one is not available at the moment.

   _____

5. The price of this house is not as high as the price of the one we saw this morning.

   _____

6. I like these two studios. This one is as comfortable as that one.

   _____

7. How about the rent? This rent is higher than that one.

_____

8. I want this studio. It is cuter than the one from before.

_____

EXERCICE
8·9

François trouve le studio idéal. _François finds the ideal studio. Choose the most appropriate reply Sophie would give to François in the following dialogue, and write the corresponding letter on the line provided._

1. _____ Regarde ce studio! Il est super!

2. _____ Oh que oui! Il est plus spacieux.

3. _____ Bien sûr qu'il est propre. De plus, il est bien situé.

4. _____ Je l'adore. J'ai pris ma décision.

5. _____ Il n'est pas très élevé. J'ai les moyens.

6. _____ Pourvu que papa m'aide!

7. _____ Qu'est-ce que tu veux dire, Sophie?

a. Tu es assez grand pour payer ton loyer! Voilà ce que je veux dire!

b. Tu le trouves plus agréable que l'autre?

c. Attends! Pense au loyer!

d. Sans blague! Tu comptes demander de l'argent à tes parents?

e. D'accord. Mais est-il plus propre?

f. Si tu peux te l'offrir, alors pourquoi pas?

g. C'est vrai que ton travail est tout près d'ici.

Dialogue 4

Chloé confides in Anne about a new friend she just met. She obviously has a huge crush on him.

CHLOÉ: C'est le meilleur jour de ma vie. J'ai un nouveau copain. C'est le garçon le plus gentil, le plus intelligent et le plus beau que j'aie jamais rencontré.

ANNE: Oh là là! **Ne charrie pas!**

CHLOÉ: Non, mais je t'assure. Je n'ai jamais éprouvé de sentiments aussi forts. **J'ai le cœur qui bat la chamade** chaque fois que je le vois.

ANNE: Tu te rappelles ton Sergio que tu as rencontré l'an dernier? C'était aussi le plus beau, le plus mignon, le plus amusant, le plus romantique. Il était **à croquer**! Ce n'est qu'un vieil ami maintenant.

It's the best day of my life. I have a new boyfriend. He is the nicest, the most intelligent, and the most handsome boy I ever met.

Oh! Don't exaggerate!

No, I assure you. I have never felt such strong feelings. My heart beats wildly every time I see him.

Do you remember your Sergio you met last year? He was also the most handsome, the cutest, the most fun, the most romantic. He was good enough to eat! Now he's just an old friend.

CHLOÉ: **Ça, aujourd'hui c'était quelque chose!** Celui-ci est le plus beau de tous les garçons que tu puisses imaginer.	*That was another thing entirely! I was younger, less mature. This one is the handsomest of all the boys you could possibly imagine.*
ANNE: Et toi, tu es la plus belle de toutes les filles qu'il puisse imaginer!	*And you are the most beautiful of all the girls he could possibly imagine!*
CHLOÉ: **J'espère bien.** Tu n'as aucune idée comme on s'entend et comme on s'aime! C'est le plus beau jour de ma vie!	*I sure hope so. You have no idea how (well) we get along and how much we love each other! It's the most beautiful day of my life!*
ANNE: Quoi! C'est aujourd'hui que tu l'as rencontré? **Il ne manquait plus que ça!** Nouvel ami, nouvel amour, tout en un jour! Veinarde!	*What! You just met him today? That's all I needed to hear! New friend, new love, all in one day! You lucky duck!*

Jugez de votre compréhension. *Check your comprehension. Write* T *(true) or* F *(false).*

1. _____ C'est la première fois que Chloé rencontre un garçon qu'elle aime beaucoup.

2. _____ Chloé a des sentiments très forts pour son nouvel ami.

3. _____ Chloé connaît son nouvel ami depuis deux jours.

4. _____ Anne pense que Chloé exagère ses sentiments.

5. _____ Les derniers mots d'Anne sont ironiques.

Improving your conversation

Ne charrie pas!

Use this familiar expression as an alternative for **N'exagère pas!** (*Don't exaggerate!*)

Tu as déjà mangé la moitié du poulet. **Ne charrie pas!**	*You already ate half the chicken.* ***Don't overdo it!***
Tu veux revoir ce film pour la troisième fois? **Ne charrie pas**, dis!	*You want to see that movie again for the third time? Hey,* ***enough already!***

J'ai le cœur qui bat la chamade

This idiomatic expression, which literally talks about one's heart beating as wildly as the sound of a drum, is used to depict extreme emotion.

Quand je vois un bel homme, **mon cœur bat la chamade**.	*When I see a handsome man, my heart races.*

À croquer...

This phrase, which depicts something delicious to eat, is often used figuratively for something or someone irresistible.

Regarde ce tailleur printanier! Il est **à croquer**, tu ne trouves pas?
Ce bébé est **à croquer**!

*Look at this spring suit! It is **adorable (delicious)**, don't you think?*
*This baby is **so cute I could eat it up**!*

Ça c'était quelque chose!

Use this expression to emphasize your surprise or admiration after witnessing a special event.

J'ai assisté à un concert hier soir et je t'assure que **ça c'était quelque chose!**

*I attended a concert last night, and I assure you that **it was something else**!*

J'espère bien

Use this expression to emphasize your expectations.

Tu penses que les hommes vont arriver en smoking? **J'espère bien.**

*You think the men are going to arrive in tuxedos? **I do hope so.***

Il ne manquait plus que ça

This impersonal expression is used to show exasperation.

Il faut que tu retournes au travail à cette heure? Zut! **Il ne manquait plus que ça!**
Il faisait déjà froid mais il paraît qu'il va geler cette nuit. **Il ne manquait plus que ça.**

*You have to go back to work at this time of day? Darn it! **That's all you/we needed**!*
*It was already cold, but it seems that it's going to freeze tonight. **That's all we needed.***

Grammar notes

Beau, nouveau, and vieux

The adjectives **beau**, **nouveau**, and **vieux** each have two masculine singular forms, one used before a consonant and another used before a vowel sound. Look at the examples below:

J'ai un **nouveau** CD.
J'ai un **nouvel** album.
C'est un **beau** bouquet.
C'est un **bel** arbre.
Voilà un **vieux** monsieur.
Voilà un **vieil** homme.

*I have a **new** CD.*
*I have a **new** album.*
*This is a **beautiful** bouquet.*
*This is a **beautiful** tree.*
*There is an **old** gentleman.*
*There is an **old** man.*

Superlatives

To express a superlative idea, use **le plus / la plus / les plus** before the adjective-noun phrase, for adjectives that *precede* the noun.

C'est **le plus beau jour** de ma vie.

*It's **the most beautiful day** of my life.*

Another way to express a superlative idea is to use **le plus / la plus / les plus** and an adjective *after* the French noun it describes. Note that two definite articles are used in this construction.

C'est **le film le plus amusant** de tous ceux que j'aie vus dernièrement.
*It's **the most amusing film** of all those I've seen lately.*

Superlative structures are followed by a verb in the *subjunctive* mood (present or past) when the idea expressed is personal, subjective, or related to an opinion.

C'est **le plus beau garçon que je connaisse**.
*This (He) is **the most handsome boy I know**.*

The past subjunctive

The past subjunctive, like the **passé composé**, is a compound tense. It consists of the auxiliary verb (**avoir** or **être**) conjugated in the present subjunctive followed by the past participle of the verb.

C'est **la dame la plus polie que j'aie jamais rencontrée**.
*This (She) is **the most polite woman I have ever met**.*

Reciprocal actions

Reflexive verbs can be used to express reciprocal actions.

Nous **nous aimons**.
*We **love each other**.*

Ils **s'entendent** (bien).
*They **get along** (well).*

EXERCICE 8·11

Trouvez les traductions appropriées pour les superlatifs suivants. *Find the appropriate English translations for the following superlatives. Write the letter of the appropriate match on the line provided.*

1. _____ la plus grande chambre
2. _____ les amis les plus gentils
3. _____ la personne la plus amusante
4. _____ le propriétaire le plus strict
5. _____ le loyer le plus élevé
6. _____ les parents les plus aimables
7. _____ les plus vieux endroits
8. _____ la chambre la plus ensoleillée
9. _____ les nouvelles les plus tordantes
10. _____ les plus beaux hommes

a. *the most lovable parents*
b. *the highest rent*
c. *the sunniest room*
d. *the oldest places*
e. *the nicest friends*
f. *the most hilarious news*
g. *the most handsome men*
h. *the most amusing person*
i. *the largest room*
j. *the strictest landlord*

Créez votre partenaire idéal! *Create your ideal partner! Identify the best qualities you would want in a partner by checking them off. Eliminate the ones that do not make sense for you.*

1. _____ C'est le plus bel homme. C'est la plus belle femme.

2. _____ C'est l'homme le plus intelligent. C'est la femme la plus intelligente.

3. _____ C'est l'homme le plus sarcastique. C'est la femme la plus sarcastique.

4. _____ C'est l'homme le plus fort. C'est la femme la plus forte.

5. _____ C'est l'homme le plus romantique. C'est la femme la plus romantique.

6. _____ C'est l'homme le plus riche. C'est la femme la plus riche.

7. _____ C'est le plus vieil homme. C'est la plus vieille femme.

8. _____ C'est l'homme le plus élégant. C'est la femme la plus élégante.

Le coup de foudre! *Love at first sight! Complete the sentences with the most appropriate word or phrase from the list. Capitalize as necessary.*

à croquer	j'espère bien	épouser
il ne manquait plus	ne charrie pas	le cœur

1. J'ai rencontré la femme de ma vie! Je veux l'_____.

2. Dis, _____!

3. Quelle belle fille! J'ai _____ qui bat la chamade.

4. Dis donc, tu lui as parlé au moins? _____.

5. Non, pas encore. Mais elle est vraiment charmante. _____!

6. Alors tu ne lui as même pas parlé! _____ que ça! Calme-toi!

Tu as vu? *Did you see? In this dialogue, Sophie and Pascal are admiring the neighbor's new car. Write the dialogue using the English guidelines provided.*

1. PASCAL: _____!

(Pascal asks Sophie to come see their neighbor's new sports car.)

2. SOPHIE: _____!

(Sophie tells him she is coming. Then she exclaims what a marvel it is.)

3. PASCAL: _____.

(Pascal says he likes that car a lot. He believes it is an electric car.)

4. SOPHIE: _____.

(Sophie comments that the neighbor always has beautiful sports cars. But this one is the most impressive one of them all.)

5. PASCAL: _____?

(Pascal asks Sophie whether she does not think that this car looks a lot like his Smartcar.)

6. SOPHIE: _____.

(Sophie answers that Pascal's Smartcar is as small as this one, but that's all they have in common.)

7. PASCAL: _____.

(Pascal agrees that his Smartcar is not as plush [**luxueuse**] as this car, but it's just as cute.)

8. SOPHIE: _____

(Sophie tells Pascal not to worry. She teases him that perhaps he doesn't have the most beautiful car in the world, but he has the most beautiful wife, doesn't he?)

Asking for help

9

Dialogue 1

Chris wants to buy a few books before returning home. He was advised to go to the Fnac (a French chain that has a huge inventory of books, music, and videos).

CHRIS: **Excusez-moi**, mademoiselle, je cherche **le rayon** des romans francophones du vingtième et vingt-et-unième siècles.

Excuse me, miss, I'm looking for the section for twentieth and twenty-first century Francophone novels.

LA VENDEUSE: Vous avez les romans français modernes là-bas **à gauche**, monsieur. Les prix Goncourt des dernières années sont ici, sur ces étagères-là.

You have modern French novels over there to the left, sir. The Goncourt prize winners of the past few years are here, on these shelves.

CHRIS: Est-ce qu'il y a une section pour les romans africains? Et pour les romans canadiens?

Is there a section for African novels? And how about Canadian novels?

LA VENDEUSE: Oui, ils sont **en haut au deuxième étage à droite** contre le mur. Vous voyez le panneau?

Yes, they're upstairs on the third floor against the wall. Do you see the sign?

CHRIS: Oui, je le vois. **Je vous remercie**, mademoiselle.

Yes, I see it. Thank you, miss.

LA VENDEUSE: S'il y a des titres ou des auteurs particuliers que vous voulez, je peux faire une recherche rapide et vous dire ce que nous avons et où ils sont.

If there are specific titles or authors you want, I can make a quick search and tell you what we have and where they are.

CHRIS: Non, je préfère flâner dans le magasin et voir de moi-même. Mais **merci bien**.

No, I prefer roaming the store to see for myself. But thank you.

LA VENDEUSE: **Je vous en prie**, monsieur. Quand vous serez prêt, vous trouverez les caisses **en bas** au **rez-de-chaussée**.

You're welcome, sir. When you're ready, you'll find the cashiers downstairs on the ground floor.

Jugez de votre compréhension. *Check your comprehension. Write* T *(true) or* F *(false).*

1. _____ Chris préfère les vieux romans.

2. _____ Chris aime seulement les romans français.

3. _____ La vendeuse de la Fnac est polie et serviable.

4. _____ Chris veut trouver ses livres lui-même.

5. _____ Les livres de la Fnac sont gratuits.

Improving your conversation

Excusez-moi

This expression may be used not only to excuse oneself, but also to catch someone's attention.

Excusez-moi de vous déranger, madame.	***I'm sorry** to bother you, madam.*
Excusez-moi, monsieur, je cherche un dictionnaire.	***Excuse me**, sir. I'm looking for a dictionary.*

Le rayon

This word may be used in supermarkets, department stores, and bookstores to designate a specialized department.

Où est **le rayon** des livres de cuisine?	*Where is the cookbook **department**?*

À gauche / à droite

These phrases are useful in many contexts to give directions.

Le rayon de la musique pop est là-bas **à droite**.	*The pop music department is over there **on the right**.*
Les meilleurs livres de l'année sont exposés à l'entrée du magasin, là-bas **à gauche**.	*The best books of the year are displayed at the entrance of the store, over there **on the left**.*

En haut / en bas

These phrases also serve to give directions.

Les guides touristiques sont **en haut** ou **en bas**?	*Are the tourist guides **upstairs** or **downstairs**?*

Le deuxième étage / le rez-de-chaussée

Note that a store or other building in France has a **rez-de-chaussée**, which is the street- or ground-level floor (usually called *first floor* in the United States), a **premier étage** which is a *second floor* in the United States, and so on.

Nous sommes au **premier étage**.	*We're on the **second floor**.*
Il faut monter au **deuxième étage**.	*You have to go up to the **third floor**.*

Je vous remercie / merci bien

Use either of these expressions to thank a salesperson. Remember to use a title whenever you address someone in a business setting.

Je **vous remercie**, mademoiselle.	*Thank you, miss.*
Ah oui, je vois. **Merci bien**, mademoiselle.	*Oh yes, I see. **Thank you**, miss.*

Je vous en prie

This expression is a bit more formal than the customary **de rien** or **il n'y a pas de quoi** (for *you're welcome*) and should always be accompanied by the appropriate title of the person you are addressing.

—Merci bien.	*—Thank you.*
—**Je vous en prie**, monsieur.	*—**You're welcome**, sir.*

EXERCICE 9·2

Denise fait des achats. *Denise is shopping. Write the following dialogue in French.*

1. DENISE: _____

   (*Excuse me, madam, I'm looking for the ladies' clothing department.*)

2. LA VENDEUSE: _____

   (*That department is downstairs, miss.*)

3. DENISE: _____

   (*Are we on the second floor?*)

4. LA VENDEUSE: _____

   (*Yes, miss.*)

5. DENISE: _____

   (*I thank you, madam.*)

6. LA VENDEUSE: _____

   (*You're welcome, miss.*)

Dialogue 2

This morning, Chris met Anne at the Louvre. After visiting the museum and stopping at the gift shop, they went to a bistro.

CHRIS: Décidément, Anne, on ne peut pas **se lasser** du Louvre. La Joconde **me manquera** quand je rentrerai aux États-Unis!

No doubt about it, Anne, you never get tired of the Louvre. I'll miss the Mona Lisa when I go back to the United States!

ANNE: Il faudra revenir quand tu le pourras. En tout cas, tu as acheté quelques souvenirs.

You'll just have to come back when you can. In any case, you bought a few souvenirs.

CHRIS: Oui, j'ai acheté des reproductions de tableaux du Louvre qui me plaisent beaucoup.

Yes, I bought reproductions of the Louvre paintings that I like a lot.

ANNE: C'est pour décorer ta chambre à l'université quand tu rentreras?

Is it / Are they to decorate your room at the university when you get back?

CHRIS: Certaines, oui. D'autres seront **sans doute** des cadeaux.

Some, yes, others will no doubt be gifts.

LE SERVEUR: Bonjour, mademoiselle, monsieur. Que puis-je vous servir?

Hello, miss, sir. What may I serve you?

ANNE: Pour moi, une eau minérale et une salade niçoise. **J'ai une faim de loup**.

For me, a mineral water and a salade niçoise. I'm starving.

CHRIS: Tu as faim et tu ne veux qu'une salade? Prends encore quelque chose!

You're hungry and you only want a salad? Have something else!

ANNE: **Tu sais ce que c'est**, une salade niçoise, Chris? Avec des légumes, des œufs, du thon et tout ça. C'est **rassasiant comme tout**.

Do you know what a salade niçoise is, Chris? With vegetables, eggs, tuna, and all that. It's really filling.

CHRIS: Ah! **Je t'ai encore eue**, ma petite! Bon, pour moi, un steak au poivre avec des frites, s'il vous plaît.

Ah! Got you again, sweetie! All right, for me, a pepper steak with fries, please.

LE SERVEUR: Parfaitement. Et comme boissson, monsieur?

Certainly. And to drink, sir?

CHRIS: Un coca, s'il vous plaît.

A coke, please.

LE SERVEUR: Bien, **je reviens tout de suite**.

Fine, I'll be right back.

ANNE: **Petit blagueur!** Tu me manqueras dès que tu seras parti.

Little joker! I'll miss you as soon as you leave.

EXERCICE 9·3

Jugez de votre compréhension. *Check your comprehension. Write* T *(true) or* F *(false).*

1. _____ Chris a acheté des affiches à la boutique du Louvre.

2. _____ Ce sont des cadeaux pour Chris et Anne.

3. _____ Anne n'a pas très faim.

4. _____ Chris aime beaucoup plaisanter.

5. _____ Le serveur n'est pas patient avec ses clients.

Improving your conversation

Se lasser de (d')...

This reflexive verb is used to express that *you are tired of* or *bored with* something.

Je me lasse de toujours lire les mêmes nouvelles.	*I get tired of always reading the same news.*

... me manquera / ... me manqueront

Use this expression to say that *you will miss something or someone*. Remember that what or whom you will miss is always the *subject* of the verb in a sentence with the verb **manquer**.

La cuisine française **me manquera**.	*I will miss French cooking.*
Mes amis **me manqueront**.	*I will miss my friends.*

Sans doute

This adverbial expression is used to express a distinct probability.

Il a **sans doute** acheté quelque chose de cher.	*He probably bought something expensive.*

Avoir une faim de loup

This idiomatic **avoir** expression is used to stress how hungry you are, that is, *hungry as a wolf*.

Quand je fais du sport toute la journée, **j'ai** toujours **une faim de loup**.	*When I exercise all day, I am always hungry as a wolf.*

Rassasiant(e)/rassasié(e)

Use the first adjective to talk about *how filling a dish is* and the second to say *how filled up you are*.

Le bœuf bourguignon est un plat **rassasiant**.	*Beef bourguignon is a filling dish.*
Je ne peux plus manger. Je suis **rassasié(e)**.	*I can't eat any more. I'm full / I've had enough.*

Comme tout

Use this phrase to stress (*really*) what someone or something is like.

Il est gentil **comme tout**.	*He is really nice.*
Ce plat est délicieux **comme tout**.	*This dish is really delicious.*

Je t'ai eu(e)

This familiar expression should only be used with friends after you have tricked them.

Tu as cru mon histoire. **Je t'ai eu**, John!	*You believed my story. **I got you**, John!*
Je t'ai bien eue, Mireille! Poisson d'avril!	***I got you**, Mireille! April Fool's!*

Je reviens tout de suite

This expression is frequently used to say that you will be back promptly.

Je **reviens tout de suite** avec votre addition, monsieur.	***I'll be right back** with your check, sir.*

Petit blagueur / petite blagueuse

This familiar expression can be used to chide friends and family members.

Tu m'as joué un bon tour, **petite blagueuse**.	*You played a good trick on me, **little joker**.*

Grammar notes

The future tense

Contrary to English usage, the future tense in French must follow the conjunctions **quand**, **lorsque**, **dès que**, and **aussitôt que** when you want to refer to a future event.

Dès que tu finiras de lire ce poème, explique-le-moi!	***As soon as you finish** reading this poem, explain it to me!*
Quand ils recevront les bonnes nouvelles, ils seront contents.	***When they receive** the good news, they will be happy.*

The **futur antérieur**

Use the **futur antérieur** tense (made up of the forms of **avoir** or **être** in the future tense plus a past participle) after **quand, lorsque, dès que**, and **aussitôt que** when the action introduced will take place in the future, but will be finished *before* the other action in the sentence.

Aussitôt qu'il aura fini ce devoir, il pourra sortir.	***As soon as he finishes** this assignment, he will be able to go out.*

Ne... que (qu')...

Use **ne... que (qu')...** to express *only*.

Elle **ne** lit **que** des magazines de mode en ce moment.	*She reads **only** fashion magazines at the moment.*

Du, de la, de l', and des

Use the partitive articles **du**, **de la**, **de l'**, and **des** to express undefined quantities (English *some*) even if *some* is omitted or implied in English.

Tu voudrais **du** pain de seigle?	*Would you like (**some**) rye bread?*
Je prends **des** frites.	*I'm having (**some**) fries.*

EXERCICE
9·4

Au rayon de maquillage. *In the cosmetics department. Complete each line of the following dialogue with an appropriate word or phrase from the choices given.*

lasses	faim	le rayon
blagues	quelque chose	t'ai eue
comme tout	reviens	

1. SUZE: Je vais aux toilettes, Sandrine. Je _____ tout de suite.

2. SANDRINE: D'accord. Je serai ici dans _____ du maquillage.

3. SUZE: Encore, Sandrine. Tu fais toujours ça. Tu ne te _____ pas d'acheter du rouge à lèvres et du rimmel?

4. SANDRINE: Jamais. C'est amusant _____.

5. SUZE: Me voilà, Sandrine. Dis, on va manger quelque chose? J'ai une _____ de loup.

6. SANDRINE: Je veux bien mais je veux acheter _____ de plus.

7. SUZE: Tu _____, Sandrine. Je veux vraiment manger quelque chose.

8. SANDRINE: Je _____, ma petite. Allons-y!

EXERCICE
9·5

Que faire d'abord? *What should we do first? Write the letter of the most appropriate completion for each line of dialogue.*

1. NICOLAS: _____ Appelle-moi...

2. MARC: _____ Où est-ce que...

3. NICOLAS: _____ Je vais au rayon des sports...

4. MARC: _____ Tu ne veux pas m'aider...

5. NICOLAS: _____ Avec plaisir, mais il me faut...

6. MARC: _____ Dès que nous aurons trouvé mon pull...

a. des balles de tennis aujourd'hui.

b. on ira au rayon des sports.

c. quand tu seras prêt, Marc.

d. pour acheter des balles de tennis.

e. à choisir un pull?

f. tu vas?

Dialogue 3

Anne is taking Chris to a big department store. He is looking for a gift for his mom.

CHRIS: C'est gentil **de ta part**, Anne, de m'accompagner. J'ai besoin de toi pour trouver le cadeau parfait pour ma mère.

It's nice of you, Anne, to accompany me. I need you to find the perfect gift for my mother.

ANNE: Tu n'as rien trouvé dans la boutique du Louvre? Ça m'étonne. J'y ai vu de très beaux foulards et sacs à main.

You haven't found anything in the Louvre boutique? That's surprising. I saw some very beautiful scarves and purses.

CHRIS: Eh bien, tu vois, je ne les ai pas remarqués.

Well, you see, I didn't notice them.

ANNE: Bon. Où veux-tu commencer?

All right. Where do you want to start?

CHRIS: Eh bien, les foulards, c'est une bonne idée. Ça ne pèse pas lourd dans la valise.

Well, scarves, that's a good idea. That doesn't weigh much in the suitcase.

ANNE: Nous sommes au **bon** étage alors. Madame, s'il vous plaît, les foulards, **c'est où**?

We're on the right floor then. Madam, please, the scarves, where are they?

LA VENDEUSE: **Suivez-moi.** Le rayon est au bout de ce couloir. C'est pour vous, mademoiselle?

Follow me. The department is at the end of this hallway. Is it for you, miss?

CHRIS: **En fait**, c'est pour ma mère.

Actually, it's for my mother.

LA VENDEUSE: Vous connaissez son goût en couleurs?

Do you know her taste in colors?

CHRIS: **Euh!** Je pense que je saurai quand je verrai.

Ehm! I think I'll know when I see.

ANNE: Si par hasard, **ça ne lui va pas** ou si ça ne lui plaît pas, Chris, tu pourras toujours me l'envoyer.

If, by chance, it doesn't suit her or if she doesn't like it, Chris, you can send it back to me.

EXERCICE 9·6

Jugez de votre compréhension. *Check your comprehension. Write* T *(true) or* F *(false).*

1. _____ Chris a vu de beaux foulards au Louvre.

2. _____ Anne veut bien accompagner Chris aux Galeries Lafayette.

3. _____ Anne et Chris sont au bon étage pour trouver les foulards.

4. _____ La vendeuse n'est pas serviable.

5. _____ Chris sait quelles couleurs sa mère aime bien.

Improving your conversation

De ma/ta part

Use one of these phrases to indicate the originator of an act or a communication.

Dis-lui bonjour **de ma part**.	*Say hello to him/her **from me**.*
C'est gentil **de ta part** de m'inviter.	*It is nice **of you** to invite me.*

Bon(ne)/mauvais(e)

Use the adjective **bon(ne)** before a noun to indicate that it is the *right* one and the adjective **mauvais(e)** to indicate the *wrong* one.

C'est la **bonne** direction.	*This is the **right** direction.*
Il a donné la **mauvaise** réponse.	*He gave the **wrong** answer.*

C'est où?

Use this informal question whenever you are looking for something.

La pharmacie, **c'est où**?	***Where's** the pharmacy?*
Les articles de toilette, **c'est où**?	***Where are** the toiletries?*

Suivez-moi

This expression is used by someone who offers to lead you to a location.

Vous cherchez l'ascenseur? **Suivez-moi.**	*You're looking for the elevator? **Follow me.***

En fait

Use this short transitional phrase to express the English word *actually*.

Je cherchais un cadeau pour ma mère, mais **en fait** je n'ai rien trouvé.	*I was looking for a gift for my mother, but **actually** I didn't find anything.*
Tu crois que je suis français? Non, **en fait**, je suis américain.	*You think I'm French? No, **actually**, I'm American.*

Euh!

Expect to hear this interjection frequently in the speech of native French speakers. It shows hesitation.

—Où est le rayon des appareils ménagers?	*—Where is the home appliance department?*
—**Euh...**	*—Ehm / Let's see . . .*

Ça lui va

This phrase is used to say that something fits a person or looks good on the person.

Marie-Laure porte un béret. **Ça lui va!** Tu ne trouves pas?	*Marie-Laure is wearing a beret. **It looks good on her!** Don't you think?*
François ne devrait pas acheter ce pull. **Ça ne lui va pas.** Il est bien trop grand pour lui.	*François should not buy this sweater. **It doesn't fit him.** It's much too big for him.*

Grammar notes

Y

Use the pronoun **y** to replace **à** + *a thing* or *a prepositional phrase* indicating a location. Remember that, except for commands, object pronouns are placed before the conjugated verb and before the auxiliary verb in the **passé composé** and other compound tenses.

—Il répond bien **à la question**? —*Does he answer **the question** well?*
—Oui, il **y** répond bien. —*Yes, he answers **it** well.*

—Tu es allé **dans cette boutique**? —*Did you go **to this boutique**?*
—Oui, j'**y** suis allé. —*Yes, I went **there**.*

De or des?

In formal language, use **de** (**d'**) instead of **des** before a *plural* adjective that *precedes* the noun, such as **beaux/belles, nouveaux/nouvelles, vieux/vieilles, grand(e)s, petit(e)s**, etc.

Il y a **des sacs à main élégants** dans cette boutique. *There are **elegant purses** in this boutique.*

Il y a **de beaux sacs** ici. *There are **beautiful purses** here.*

EXERCICE 9·7

Luc et Marc se mettent d'accord. *Luc and Marc are in agreement. Complete the following dialogue according to the English guidelines in parentheses.*

1. LUC: _____ de vouloir faire du shopping tout seul. (*It's not very nice*)

2. MARC: Euh! _____. C'est pour ça. (*But I'm in a hurry*)

3. LUC: Qu'est-ce qu'_____, Marc? (*do you need*)

4. MARC: _____. (*I need new sweaters and new shirts*)

5. LUC: Moi, _____ du gel après-rasoir et de l'eau de Cologne. (*I need*)

6. MARC: Bon, je viens et _____ tes articles de toilette, on ira faire mes achats. (*as soon as we have*)

7. LUC: Voilà, mon pote. Ça, _____. (*it's nice of you*)

8. MARC: _____? (*Where is it?*)

9. LUC: Pardon, monsieur, le rayon des articles de toilette, _____? (*is it on this floor*)

10. LE VENDEUR: Oui, _____, monsieur. (*Follow me*)

Dialogue 4

After Anne left, Chris walked around the **quartier** (*neighborhood*) and is now looking for a subway station to go back home. He first stops a woman and then a man to get directions.

CHRIS: Pardon, madame, **pouvez-vous m'indiquer** la station de métro la plus proche?

Pardon me, madam, can you show me the nearest subway station?

UNE DAME: Désolée, je suis pressée!

Sorry! I'm in a hurry!

CHRIS: Pardon, monsieur, **excusez-moi de vous déranger**. Je cherche une station de métro.

Excuse me for the interruption, sir. I'm looking for a subway station.

UN MONSIEUR: Où allez-vous, monsieur?

Where are you going, sir?

CHRIS: **Il me faut** la ligne Orange direction Défense.

I need the Orange line going to the Défense.

UN MONSIEUR: Bon, alors, je vous conseille d'aller tout droit jusqu'à la Madeleine. Vous trouverez une station devant l'église.

All right, then I advise you to go straight ahead up to the Madeleine (church). You'll find a station in front of the church.

CHRIS: Merci, monsieur. **Vous êtes très aimable.**

Thank you, sir. You're very kind.

Chris is now in front of the church of the Madeleine, and since he is in a hurry, he asks a policeman where the station is exactly.

CHRIS: **Monsieur l'agent**, s'il vous plaît, **pouvez-vous me dire** où est la station de métro?

Officer, can you please tell me where the subway station is?

L'AGENT: **Avec plaisir**, jeune homme. Traversez la place! La station est au coin de ces deux rues.

My pleasure, young man. Go across the square! The station is at the corner of those two streets.

CHRIS: Merci beaucoup, **monsieur l'agent**.

Thank you very much, officer.

EXERCICE 9·8

Jugez de votre compréhension. *Check your comprehension. Write* T *(true) or* F *(false).*

1. _____ Une dame aide Chris à trouver sa station.

2. _____ Un monsieur trop pressé ne peut pas aider Chris.

3. _____ Chris sait quelle ligne de métro il veut prendre.

4. _____ Chris prend la mauvaise route pour aller à la Madeleine.

5. _____ Chris demande de l'aide à un agent de police.

Improving your conversation

Pouvez-vous m'indiquer... ? / Pouvez-vous me dire... ?

Use one of these expressions when you are asking a passerby for directions.

Pouvez-vous m'indiquer où se trouve
la rue Jean-Jaurès?

*Can you tell me where Jean-Jaurès
Street is?*

Excusez-moi de vous déranger

Use this expression as a lead-in when you have to ask a passerby for directions. This shows that you acknowledge that you may be imposing upon someone and that his or her help will be appreciated.

Excusez-moi de vous déranger, mais
pouvez-vous me dire où sont les
toilettes?

*I apologize for interrupting you, but can
you tell me where the bathroom is?*

Il me faut

This idiomatic impersonal expression followed by a noun, is used to express that you need something. Remember to use the appropriate object pronoun (**me** [**m'**], **te** [**t'**], etc.) before the verb to indicate who needs something.

Il me faut un taxi.
Il te faut quelque chose?

I need a taxi.
Do you need something?

Vous êtes très aimable

Use this sentence in addition to **merci** to thank people emphatically for any help they give you.

Oui, c'est exactement ce que je cherche.
Merci, **vous êtes très aimable**.

Yes, it is exactly what I'm looking for.
Thank you, you're very kind.

Monsieur l'agent

Use this title when addressing a police officer.

Pardon, **monsieur l'agent**. Je cherche un
bureau de police.

*Excuse me, officer. I'm looking for a
police station.*

Avec (grand) plaisir

This phrase is used to confirm that a service is being rendered or an invitation is accepted with (great) pleasure.

Je suis invité chez toi? D'accord, je
viendrai **avec plaisir**.

*I am invited to your house? OK, I'll come
with pleasure. / I'll gladly come.*

Corinne est un peu perdue. *Corinne is a little lost. Complete each line of dialogue with an appropriate word from the list.*

plaisir	droite	mauvaise
déranger	mademoiselle	monsieur

1. CORINNE: Bonjour, _____ l'agent. Pouvez-vous me dire où se trouve la rue Victor Hugo?

2. L'AGENT: Avec _____, mademoiselle. Allez tout droit et vous la trouverez à deux rues d'ici.

3. CORINNE: Excusez-moi encore de vous _____, mais ce sera à droite ou à gauche?

4. L'AGENT: Ce sera à _____, mademoiselle, après la station de métro.

5. CORINNE: Alors, en fait, j'allais dans la _____ direction.

6. L'AGENT: Euh! Oui, _____. Je pense que oui.

Dialogue 5

Chris goes to a **syndicat d'initiative** (*tourist office*) to inquire about the latest ecological tourist trend in Paris: bicycle tours around the city.

L'EMPLOYÉE: Bonjour, monsieur. **Puis-je vous aider?**

Hello, sir. May I help you?

CHRIS: Oui, bonjour, madame. Je voudrais des renseignements sur **les tours** de Paris à bicyclette.

Yes, hello, madam. I would like some information regarding bicycle tours of Paris.

L'EMPLOYÉE: Certainement, monsieur. Nous avons plusieurs options. Voulez-vous regarder ces brochures et me dire ce qui vous intéresse?

Certainly, sir. Do you want to look at these brochures and tell me what interests you?

CHRIS: Je les ai déjà regardées et je peux vous dire que **je préférerais la balade à vélo** dans Paris accompagnée d'**un guide-interprète** expérimenté.

I've already looked at them, and I can tell you that I'd like the bike tour of Paris with an experienced guide-interpreter.

L'EMPLOYÉE: Très bien, monsieur. Vous paraissez informé. Vous voulez partir du Pont-Neuf ou plutôt de la place de la Concorde?

Very well, sir. You seem informed. Do you want to leave from the Pont-Neuf or rather from the Place de la Concorde?

CHRIS: Je préfère la place de la Concorde si c'est le même prix.

I prefer the Place de la Concorde if it's the same price.

L'EMPLOYÉE: C'est le même prix **d'où que vous partiez.** Et le **forfait comprend** la visite guidée des quartiers et des monuments cités dans la brochure.

It's the same price no matter where you leave from. And the set price includes the guided tour of the neighborhoods and the monuments mentioned in the brochure.

CHRIS: **C'est bien ce qu'il me semblait.** *That's what I thought. Good, that's fine.*
Bon, ça va. Je vais réserver une *I'm going to reserve a bicycle for Tuesday*
bicyclette pour le tour de mardi matin, *morning's tour, please.*
s'il vous plaît.

EXERCICE
9·10

Jugez de votre compréhension. *Check your comprehension. Write* T *(true) or* F *(false).*

1. _____ Chris est bien informé sur les tours de Paris à bicyclette.

2. _____ Chris veut commencer son tour au Pont-Neuf.

3. _____ Le tour qui part du Pont-Neuf est plus cher.

4. _____ Le tour est limité à un seul quartier.

5. _____ Le tour est guidé.

Improving your conversation

Puis-je vous aider?

You will hear this formal expression when someone sees that you are puzzled or need help. You may also use it when you are in a position to help someone else.

Que désirez-vous, monsieur? **Puis-je** *What would you like, sir?* **May I help you?**
vous aider?

Un tour

This term refers to *a tour* such as the visit of a museum or any other tourist site, but it also refers to *a ride* such as a car, bicycle, motorcycle, or bus ride.

Je voudrais m'inscrire pour **un tour** *I would like to sign up for **a guided tour***
guidé du château. *of the castle.*
Nous allons **faire un tour en voiture** à *We are going **to drive around** in the*
la campagne. *countryside.*

La balade à vélo / à bicyclette

This colloquial expression refers to a bicycle ride. The word **balade** is also used for any other type of ride, walk, or outing undertaken for leisure.

Une **balade à vélo** à travers le parc me *A **bike ride** across the park will do*
fera du bien. *me good.*
Tu as envie de **faire une balade à pied** *Do you feel like **going for a walk** up to*
jusqu'au marché aux fleurs? *the flower market?*

Le guide-interprète

This term refers to a bilingual or multilingual guide who guides a group of tourists and describes historic or important sites.

Nous préférerions **un guide-interprète** pour faire la visite de ce musée.

*We would prefer **a guide-interpreter** to visit this museum.*

D'où que vous partiez

This expression is used to convey that it does not matter what the point of departure is.

D'où que vous partiez, vous visiterez les mêmes monuments.

***No matter where you leave from**, you will visit the same monuments.*

Un forfait

This term describes a set price for a service (other than a restaurant [**prix fixe**]), such as the price for phone service or package deals for vacations.

Je paie **un forfait** pour mon service téléphonique international.

*I pay a **set price** for my international phone provider.*

Nous essayons de trouver les meilleurs **forfaits** pour des croisières.

*We are trying to find the best **package deals** for cruises.*

Comprendre/compris

This verb is used to convey that something is *included*.

Le tour **comprend** la visite de trois monuments historiques et la location du vélo.

*The tour **includes** the visit of three historical monuments and the bike rental.*

Le total de la note **comprend** la taxe.

*The total on the bill **includes** the tax.*

Dans les restaurants français, le service est **compris**.

*In French restaurants, service is **included**.*

C'est bien ce qu'il me semblait

This phrase is used to confirm that reality is in line with your expectations or impressions.

Tu as payé très cher ces vacances. **C'est bien ce qu'il me semblait!**

*You paid a lot for this vacation. **Just as I thought!***

Grammar note
Préférer and related verbs

The verb **préférer** is a stem-changing verb. The -é- in the second syllable of the infinitive verb changes to -è- in all forms of the present tense *except* in the **nous/vous** forms:

je/il/elle/on préfère	vous préférez
tu préfères	ils/elles préfèrent
nous préférons	

Préférer and verbs like **préférer**, such as **répéter** (*to repeat*), **célébrer** (*to celebrate*), **considérer** (*to consider*), and **protéger** (*to protect*), do *not* have a stem change in the **futur simple** tense or the **présent du conditionnel**.

FUTUR	CONDITIONNEL
je préférerai	je préférerais
tu préféreras	tu préférerais
il/elle/on préférera	il/elle/on préférerait
nous préférerons	nous préférerions
vous préférerez	vous préféreriez
ils/elles préféreront	ils/elles préféreraient

EXERCICE
9·11

Un tour en autobus ou à vélo? *A tour by bus or by bike? Complete each line of dialogue with an appropriate word from the list. Capitalize as necessary.*

comprend	ne trouves pas	c'est bien
à vélo	d'où que	guide-interprète
balades	forfait	

1. CORINNE: Dis, Jean-Pierre. J'ai envie de faire un de ces tours _____.
C'est bon pour la santé et pour l'environnement.

2. JEAN-PIERRE: On a déjà fait tellement de _____ à pied. Tu ne veux pas plutôt faire un tour en autobus aujourd'hui?

3. CORINNE: Franchement non! Il fait trop beau. D'après cette brochure, il y a un tour qui

_____ le prix de la location de bicyclette et la visite guidée

de deux monuments.

4. JEAN-PIERRE: C'est un _____ qui coûte combien?

5. CORINNE: Alors, _____ nous partions, ce sera quarante euros pour un tour de quatre heures.

6. JEAN-PIERRE: Par personne? Tu _____ ça un peu cher?

7. CORINNE: Oui, naturellement, par personne! Mais les services du _____ sont compris!

8. JEAN-PIERRE: C'est quand même plus cher qu'un tour en bus. _____ ce qu'il me semblait! Il faut payer plus cher pour être écolo!

Dans un syndicat d'initiative. *In a tourist office. You are in an information office looking for things to do while visiting Paris. Complete your lines of dialogue* (**vous**) *according to the English guidelines in parentheses.*

1. L'EMPLOYÉ: Bonjour, mademoiselle. Puis-je vous aider?

   VOUS: Bonjour, monsieur. _____.
   (*I would like some information regarding tours of Paris, please.*)

2. L'EMPLOYÉ: Volontiers. Regardez ces brochures. Il y a beaucoup d'options.

   VOUS: _____. (*I would prefer some walking tours.*)

3. L'EMPLOYÉ: Je vous recommande la balade à pied dans un quartier de votre choix.

   VOUS: _____? (*How about bike tours?*)

4. L'EMPLOYÉ: Je vous les recommande aussi. Il y en a partout en ville. D'où préféreriez-vous partir?

   VOUS: _____, n'est-ce pas?
   (*No matter where we leave from, it is the same price*)

5. L'EMPLOYÉ: Oui, parfaitement! Je vous conseille la formule-forfait où tout est compris!

   VOUS: _____! Je vais m'inscrire alors. (*That's what I thought!*)

J'ai besoin d'un petit service. *I need a little help. In this dialogue, Mark needs help finding a book. Write the dialogue using the English guidelines provided.*

1. Mark asks a saleswoman to help him locate a cookbook.

   MARK: _____

2. The saleswoman tells him the cookbook section is upstairs on the first floor.

   LA VENDEUSE: _____

3. Mark is now upstairs and asks a salesman where the cookbook department is.

   MARK: _____

4. The salesman asks him what kind of cookbook he is looking for.

   LE VENDEUR: _____

5. Mark explains that he is looking for books by Julia Child.

   MARK: _____

6. The salesman explains that there are two cookbook sections in the bookstore; the French cooking section on this floor and another international cooking section on the third floor.

   LE VENDEUR: _____

7. Mark thanks the salesman and asks him if he could show him exactly where.

   MARK: _____

8. The salesman agrees and offers to accompany him to the right department.

   LE VENDEUR: _____

Departures

10

Dialogue 1

Chris is making preparations to return to the United States and is discussing his plans with Anne.

CHRIS: Bon, ça y est, Anne. J'ai confirmé ma réservation pour le vol du retour. **C'est un peu bizarre** que je me sente heureux et triste à la fois.

Well, that's it, Anne. I confirmed my return flight reservation. It's a little weird that I feel happy and sad at the same time.

ANNE: **Bien entendu!** Ça fait trois mois que **tu vis** en France. **Il est** d'ailleurs **extraordinaire que** tu te sois si bien adapté.

Of course! You've lived in France for three months. By the way, it's amazing that you adapted so well.

CHRIS: C'était facile. Je n'**ai** jamais **eu le mal du pays**, tu sais. Probablement parce que j'ai été **accueilli** par ma tante et mon oncle et parce que, grâce à Didier, j'ai tout de suite rencontré des gens sympa comme toi.

It was easy. I never felt homesick, you know. Probably because I was hosted by my aunt and uncle and because, thanks to Didier, I met friendly people like you right away.

ANNE: Oui, nous t'avons tous adopté. Tu vas vraiment nous manquer. Par contre, ta famille et tes copains **aux USA** seront contents de te **retrouver**.

Yes, we all adopted you. We'll really miss you. On the other hand, your family and friends in the USA will be happy to get you back.

CHRIS: C'est pourquoi je me sens déchiré. Je serais prêt à rester ici **beaucoup plus longtemps. Je suis** tout à fait **à l'aise**. Mais je suis prêt aussi à reprendre mes activités **auprès des miens**.

That's why I feel torn. I'd be ready to stay here much longer. I'm completely comfortable. But I'm also ready to pick up my activities with my friends and family.

ANNE: De toute façon, tu reviendras puisque tu as tant d'amis ici. En attendant, on gardera le contact. **Vive** Internet!

Anyway, you will come back since you have so many friends here. Meanwhile, we'll stay in contact. Yay for the Internet!

CHRIS: **Tu peux en être sûr!** Tu voudrais qu'on **fasse des projets** pour l'été prochain? Peut-être un voyage en train à travers l'Europe?

You can be sure of that! Would you like us to make plans for next summer? Maybe a train trip across Europe?

ANNE: **C'est tout à fait faisable, ça! J'ai hâte que** ce soit de nouveau **les grandes vacances**!

That's totally feasible! I can't wait until next summer vacation!

Jugez de votre compréhension. *Check your comprehension. Write* T *(true) or* F *(false).*

1. _____ Chris va passer une année en France.

2. _____ Chris a le mal de son pays.

3. _____ Chris a rencontré beaucoup d'amis en France.

4. _____ Anne ne comprend pas les sentiments de Chris.

5. _____ Anne est d'accord pour faire des projets de vacances avec Chris.

Improving your conversation

C'est un peu bizarre

This expression is used to describe something that seems a little weird.

Ces couleurs ne vont pas bien ensemble. **C'est un peu bizarre.**	*These colors don't go well together.* ***It's a little weird.***
Tu n'as pas lu ce livre? L'intrigue **est un peu bizarre.**	*You didn't read this book? The plot* ***is a little bizarre.***

Bien entendu!

This phrase is synonymous with **Bien sûr!** It is used to confirm or agree.

—Tu viens ce soir?	*—Are you coming tonight?*
—**Bien entendu!**	*—Of course!*

Vivre

This verb can be used in place of **habiter** (*to live, reside*), but it usually connotes a more permanent type of living, as **vivre** literally means *to exist*.

Quand on gagne bien sa vie, on **vit** bien.	*When you earn a good living, you* ***live*** *well.*
Mes parents **vivent** en Floride pendant l'hiver.	*My parents* ***live*** *in Florida during the winter.*

C'est / il est extraordinaire que (qu')...

This impersonal expression may begin with **c'est**, which gives it a familiar tone, or with **il est** for a more formal tone. It is followed by a verb in the subjunctive.

C'est extraordinaire que tu n'**aies** aucun accent en français.	***It's extraordinary that*** *you* ***have*** *no accent in French.*
Il est extraordinaire que la politique de ce pays **soit** si différente.	***It is extraordinary that*** *the politics of this country* ***are*** *so different.*

Avoir le mal du pays

This idiomatic **avoir** expression is used to refer to the homesickness one feels when away from one's own country.

Pendant sa première année à l'université de Paris, Audrey **a eu le mal du pays**.

*During her first year at the University of Paris, Audrey **was homesick**.*

Note that the expression includes the word **pays** (*country*); it is used exclusively for homesickness for one's country. Use the verb **manquer** (*to miss*) to refer to homesickness related to friends and family.

Ma famille / mon foyer **me manque**.

*I **miss** my family / my home.*

Accueillir

This verb refers to *welcoming* or *hosting*. Its past participle, **accueilli**, is used as an adjective to express that someone is welcome or well received.

Nous allons **accueillir** nos cousins canadiens cet été.
Nous sommes toujours si bien **accueillis** chez eux.

*We are going **to host** our Canadian cousins this summer.*
*We are always so well **received** at their home.*

Les USA / aux USA

This acronym is often used (with the French pronunciation of the letters) instead of the full name, **les États-Unis** (*the United States*).

J'ai visité **les USA**.
Nous allons **aux USA** cet été.

*I visited **the U.S.***
*We are going to **the U.S.** this summer.*

Retrouver

The literal meaning of this verb is to find something that has been lost. It also refers to meeting people whom you have met before.

J'ai retrouvé la clé que j'avais perdue.
Je vais **retrouver** mes copains au café du coin.

*I **found** the key I had lost.*
*I'm going **to meet** my friends at the corner café.*

Beaucoup plus longtemps

Use this phrase to emphasize how much longer something lasts (than expected).

Je connais Pierre depuis **beaucoup plus longtemps** que sa femme même.

*I have known Pierre for **much longer** than his wife even.*

Vive... !

Use this subjunctive form of the verb **vivre** before a noun to celebrate or express a strong desire for something. Formerly used in the cheer **Vive le roi!** (*Long live the king!*), it is now used for anything you want to prolong, wish for, or cheer on.

Vivent les vacances!	*Yay to vacation!*
Vive la technologie!	*Long live technology!*
Vive l'équipe de football!	*Cheers to the soccer team!*

Être à l'aise

This expression is used when referring to people's comfort. The French adjective **confortable** is used only to describe things.

Ce fauteuil est très **confortable**. Je suis **à l'aise** dedans.	*This armchair is **comfortable**. I am **comfortable** in it.*

Auprès des miens

Les miens refers to *my own people* (including my friends, my family, or my loved ones).

Je me sens toujours bien **auprès des miens**.	*I always feel good **near/with my loved ones**.*

En être sûr(e)

This expression conveys *certainty*.

Mes copains sont les meilleurs au monde. **J'en suis sûr.**	*My friends are the best in the world. **I'm sure (of it)**.*

Faire des projets

This expression refers to making plans (not necessarily projects).

Il n'est jamais trop tôt pour **faire des projets** de vacances.	*It's never too early **to make** vacation **plans**.*

C'est tout à fait faisable, ça

Use this expression to confirm that something can be done or is possible.

Organiser une sortie pour ce week-end, **c'est tout à fait faisable**.	*Planning an outing for this weekend **is quite feasible**.*

Avoir hâte que (qu')...

This idiomatic **avoir** expression is useful to express anticipation or expectation of an event or special occasion you can hardly wait for.

J'ai hâte d'être de retour à la maison.	*I **can't wait** to be back home.*
Tu as sans doute **hâte d'**avoir ton diplôme.	*You're probably **eager to** have/get your degree.*

Les grandes vacances

This phrase refers to summer vacation in the context of the standard school year.

Nos grandes vacances commencent en juin.	*Our **summer vacation** starts in June.*

Grammar notes

The subjunctive mood

Impersonal expressions that *do not* express certainty and others that express opinions or value judgments are followed by a verb in the *subjunctive mood* when that verb has a different subject from the one in the main clause.

C'est / Il est un peu bizarre que tu **fasses** tout ton travail le week-end.	*It is a bit strange that you do all your work on the weekend.*
C'est / Il est extraordinaire que vous **ayez** tant de congés payés.	*It is extraordinary that you have so much paid vacation.*

Verbs of wishing, wanting, and feeling are also followed by a verb in the subjunctive mood when that verb has a different subject from the one in the main clause.

Tu voudrais sans doute **que je vienne.**	*You probably would like me to come.*
Nous voulons que vous soyez là à l'heure.	*We want you to be there on time.*
Mes parents ont hâte que je finisse mes études.	*My parents look forward to my finishing my studies.*

Some high-frequency verbs such as **être**, **avoir**, **faire**, and **venir** have irregular conjugations in the present subjunctive:

être	*to be*	je/tu sois, il/elle/on soit, nous soyons, vous soyez, ils/elles soient
avoir	*to have*	j'aie, tu aies, il/elle/on ait, nous ayons, vous ayez, ils/elles aient
faire	*to do/make*	je/il/elle/on fasse, tu fasses, nous fassions, vous fassiez, ils/elles fassent
venir	*to come*	je/il/elle/on vienne, tu viennes, nous venions, vous veniez, ils/elles viennent

Note that English translations of French subjunctive verbs vary; in English, they can be indicative, subjunctive, an infinitive, or contain the auxiliary verb *may*.

Il vaudrait mieux que nous **soyons** à l'heure pour le vol.	*It would be better if we **were** on time for the flight.*
Il faut qu'elle **fasse** les courses avant de partir.	*She has **to do** the shopping before leaving.*
Il est possible qu'ils **viennent** aujourd'hui.	*It is possible that they **may come** today.*
Je veux que tu **aies** assez d'euros pour ton voyage.	*I want you **to have** enough euros for your trip.*

Vivre

The verb **vivre** has an irregular present indicative conjugation, as follows: **je/tu vis, il/elle/on vit, nous vivons, vous vivez, ils/elles vivent**.

Nous **vivons** dans un pays démocratique.	*We **live** in a democratic country.*
Ma sœur **vit** en France en ce moment.	*My sister **lives** in France at the moment.*

Possessive pronouns

Possessive pronouns used to express *mine* or *yours* (familiar) and *his* or *hers* agree in gender and number with the noun they replace, and are as follows:

le mien / la mienne	**les miens / les miennes**	*mine*
le tien / la tienne	**les tiens / les tiennes**	*yours* (*familiar*)
le sien / la sienne	**les siens / les siennes**	*his/hers*

Jacques et moi avons tous deux des chiens. **Le sien** est un caniche et **le mien** est un berger allemand.	*Jacques and I both have dogs. **His** is a poodle and **mine** is a German shepherd.*
Regarde nos robes! **La tienne** est cool, mais **la mienne** est vieux-jeu.	*Look at our dresses. Yours is cool, but **mine** is old fashioned.*
Je vais acheter de nouveaux vêtements à Jean. **Les siens** sont usés.	*I'm going to buy some new clothes for Jean. **His** are worn out.*

EXERCICE
10·2

Nathalie et Noah se disent au revoir. *Nathalie and Noah say good-bye. Complete each line of the following dialogue with the appropriate word or phrase from the list. Capitalize as necessary.*

miens	pays	accueillir
la tienne	retrouver	bien entendu
hâte	plus longtemps	dommage
manquer		

1. NATHALIE: Il est _____ que tu doives déjà partir.

2. NOAH: C'était gentil à ta famille de m'_____.

3. NATHALIE: Ça nous a fait grand plaisir. _____, tu reviendras nous voir.

4. NOAH: Oui, c'est sûr. Mais il est temps que je rentre auprès des _____.

5. NATHALIE: Je sais. Mais tu vas nous _____.

6. NOAH: L'année prochaine, il faudra que je reste beaucoup _____.

7. NATHALIE: Tu n'auras pas le mal du _____?

8. NOAH: Franchement, je ne pense pas. J'aime ma famille, mais j'aime bien _____ aussi.

9. NATHALIE: Bon, eh bien, j'aurai _____ que l'année scolaire soit terminée.

10. NOAH: Moi aussi. Maintenant va _____ ta famille et tes copains! Au revoir. À l'an prochain!

Noah est parti. *Noah has left. Write in French.*

1. NATHALIE: _____ (*That's it. Noah left for the USA.*)

   MAMAN: C'est extraordinaire qu'il se soit si bien adapté ici.

2. NATHALIE: _____ (*He was really comfortable with us. It's true.*)

   MAMAN: Pourtant ça doit être difficile de vivre dans un pays étranger, loin de sa famille.

3. NATHALIE: _____ (*Of course, but he was quite welcome in our family.*)

   MAMAN: En tout cas, il sera de retour un jour ou l'autre.

4. NATHALIE: _____ (*I am sure of it.*)

   MAMAN: Vive l'amitié franco-américaine!

5. NATHALIE: _____ (*And long live summer vacations!*)

Dialogue 2

Anne confides in Marie-Josée that she is beginning to realize how much she will miss Chris.

ANNE: **Vivement la rentrée des classes!** J'ai besoin de **me changer les idées**.

I can't wait for classes to start again! I need to take my mind off things.

MARIE-JOSÉE: Comment? Ce n'est pas du tout typique de toi, cette **humeur**. Qu'est-ce qui se passe?

What? That's not at all typical of you, this mood. What's going on?

ANNE: **Je fais une petite déprime**, je dois **le reconnaître**.

I am a little depressed, I must admit.

MARIE-JOSÉE: Est-ce que ce serait le départ de notre ami Chris, **par hasard**?

Would it be the departure of our friend Chris, by any chance?

ANNE: Eh bien, oui. On a passé beaucoup de temps ensemble, tu sais. **Je l'aime bien.**

Well, yes. We spent a lot of time together, you know. I like him.

MARIE-JOSÉE: Tu l'aimes bien!? **C'est peu dire**, si tu en fais une dépression.

You like him?! That's an understatement, if you're depressed over him.

ANNE: **C'est un peu fort** quand même, une dépression! **Je dirais plutôt** un mauvais moment quoi. Ça passera!

A depression is a little strong actually! I would rather call it a tough moment. It will pass!

MARIE-JOSÉE: Et lui, est-ce qu'il est triste de partir? Où est-ce que vous en êtes exactement au point de vue relation?

And him, is he sad to leave? Where exactly in your relationship are you?

ANNE: C'est difficile à dire. **On s'entend bien**, on a des sentiments **l'un pour l'autre. Mais en fin de compte**, on n'en est pas au point où on entrevoit un avenir en commun, tu vois.

That's difficult to say. We get along well, we have feelings for each other. But in the end, we aren't at the point where you foresee a common future, you see.

EXERCICE 10·4

Jugez de votre compréhension. *Check your comprehension. Write* T *(true) or* F *(false).*

1. _____ Anne est plutôt triste.

2. _____ Anne est souvent de mauvaise humeur.

3. _____ Anne veut se marier avec Chris.

4. _____ Anne dit qu'elle adore Chris.

5. _____ Marie-Josée est déprimée parce que Chris rentre aux USA.

Improving your conversation

Vivement...

This adverb is used to express one's expectation and anticipation of a special moment or event.

Vivement le week-end! Je suis fatigué.
Vivement l'arrivée de l'avion. On pourra se lever.

Let it be the weekend! I am tired.
We can't wait for the plane to arrive. We'll be able to get up.

La rentrée (des classes)

This phrase means *the first day back at school.* The noun **la rentrée**, related to the verb **rentrer** (*to come back / to go back*), is often used instead of the entire phrase **la rentrée des classes**.

Quelle est la date de **la rentrée** cette année?

*What is the date of **the first day of school** this year?*

Se changer les idées

This expression refers to changing your focus when it has become burdensome or uncomfortable.

Je vais faire un voyage pour **me changer les idées** car ce travail est épuisant.
Il faut sortir avec des amis pour **se changer les idées** quand on s'ennuie.

*I'm going on a trip to **get my mind off things** because this work is exhausting.*
*You have to go out with friends to **cheer yourself up** when you're bored.*

L'humeur (f.)

This term refers to one's *mood*.

Tu es d'une **humeur** bizarre aujourd'hui.	*You're in a strange **mood** today.*

Faire une déprime

This expression refers to *being in a state of depression*.

Je vais **faire une déprime** si je ne réussis pas à cet examen.	*I am going **to be depressed** if I don't pass this exam.*

Le reconnaître

Use this expression *to admit* or *confess* something.

Je suis de très mauvaise humeur. **Je le reconnais.**	*I'm in a very bad mood. **I confess.***
Tu as tort. **Reconnais-le!**	*You're wrong. **Admit it!***

Par hasard

This adverbial phrase refers to something that happens *haphazardly* or *by chance*.

Nous avons rencontré un autre Américain tout à fait **par hasard**.	*We met another American **quite by chance**.*
Tu aurais un billet de métro **par hasard**?	*Would you have a subway ticket **by any chance**?*

Je l'aime bien

The verb **aimer** can be interpreted as *to love* or *to like*. However, the verb **aimer** accompanied by the adverb **bien** can only mean *to like*.

J'aime bien le chocolat noir.	***I like** dark chocolate.*
Nous aimons bien nos profs.	***We like** our teachers/professors.*

C'est peu dire

This phrase conveys an *understatement*; that is, the reality is much stronger.

Je n'aime pas ce livre, et **c'est peu dire**.	*I don't like this book, and **that's an understatement**.*

C'est un peu fort

This expression is used to object to an exaggeration.

Tu dis qu'elle est malhonnête. **C'est un peu fort.**	*You say she is dishonest. **That's somewhat exaggerated**.*

Je dirais plutôt que (qu')...

Use this phrase to express a personal opinion that differs slightly from someone else's assumption.

Vous pensez que cette histoire est vraie! **Je dirais plutôt qu'**elle est vraisemblable.	*You think this story is true! **Rather I would say** it is likely.*

S'entendre (avec)

This reflexive verb is used to express *getting along with* others.

Elle **s'entend** très bien **avec** son frère.	*She **gets along** very well **with** her brother.*
Les partenaires dans cette société ne **s'entendent** pas.	*The partners in this company do not **get along**.*

L'un pour l'autre

Use this phrase, which literally means *one for the other*, to express reciprocity.

Ces deux amoureux sont faits **l'un pour l'autre**.	*These two lovers are made **for each other**.*
Ils ont du respect **l'un pour l'autre**.	*They have **mutual** respect.*

Mais en fin de compte

Use this phrase to introduce a contradiction, an opposing viewpoint, or an objection.

Ils ont l'air réservé, **mais en fin de compte** ils sont aimables.	*They look reserved, **but actually** they are friendly.*
La tâche était difficile, **mais en fin de compte** nous l'avons achevée.	*The task was difficult, **but in the end** we accomplished it.*

EXERCICE
10·5

Il l'aime ou il l'aime bien? *Does he love her or does he like her? Find the most appropriate completion for each sentence to reconstitute the dialogue between two friends. Write the letter of the completion in the space provided.*

1. MARC: _____ Vivement les vacances de Noël!　　　a. vraiment bien.

2. LUC: _____ Tu devrais partir en Espagne et...　　　b. vous vous aimez beaucoup.

3. MARC: _____ Je voudrais que Céline...　　　c. l'un pour l'autre.

4. LUC: _____ Tu lui as demandé... ?　　　d. si elle voulait venir avec toi?

5. MARC: _____ Pas encore mais...　　　e. je vais le faire.

6. LUC: _____ Vous deux, vous êtes faits...　　　f. En fin de compte, tu arrives à le dire.

7. MARC: _____ C'est vrai qu'on s'entend...　　　g. Je suis très fatigué.

8. LUC: _____ C'est peu dire. Admets que...　　　h. Voilà. Je l'adore.

9. MARC: _____ Je le reconnais.　　　i. te changer les idées.

10. LUC: _____ Félicitations!　　　j. m'accompagne.

Céline acceptera-t-elle de partir en vacances avec Marc? *Will Céline agree to go on vacation with Marc? Complete each sentence with an appropriate word or phrase from the list to reconstitute the following dialogue.*

Vivement	faire une déprime	peu dire
la rentrée des classes	par hasard	En fin de compte
dans un endroit tropical	humeur	

1. MARC: Dis, Céline. On a tellement travaillé depuis _____!

2. CÉLINE: Je sais, Marc. _____ les vacances!

3. MARC: Tu n'as pas envie de passer quelques jours _____?

4. CÉLINE: Tu ne vas pas me demander de t'accompagner en vacances, _____?

5. MARC: Eh bien, si. Si je continue comme ça, je vais _____.

6. CÉLINE: Tu seras de meilleure _____ si j'accepte?

7. MARC: Tu parles! C'est _____. Je serai aux anges.

8. CÉLINE: Eh bien. C'est décidé! On part ensemble! _____, ce sera bon pour moi et pour toi.

Dialogue 3

Chris shares his thoughts about starting an online blog for people who want to know more about French culture.

CHRIS: J'ai une idée sensationnelle, Anne. Je vais **lancer un blog**, tu sais, une sorte de journal de réflexions personnelles sur la culture française.

I have a great idea, Anne. I'm going to start a blog, you know, sort of a journal of personal reflections on French culture.

ANNE: **Qu'à cela ne tienne!** Tu es déjà **passionné** par un projet que tu feras après que tu seras rentré chez toi!

Fine! (in a sarcastic tone) You're already into a project that you'll do after you're back home!

CHRIS: Quel enthousiasme! Tu ne vas pas bien, Anne?

What enthusiasm! Aren't you feeling well, Anne?

ANNE: Non, excuse-moi. **J'ai le cafard.** En fait, c'est une bonne idée. Je suis sûre que tu auras **des adhérents.** Mais pourquoi pas simplement Facebook?

No, excuse me. I'm feeling down. In fact, it's a good idea. I am sure that you'll have subscribers. But why not simply Facebook?

CHRIS: Je ne sais pas. J'ai envie d'avoir mon propre blog. Mais pourquoi as-tu le cafard, toi qui es toujours **de si bonne humeur**?

I don't know. I feel like having my own blog. But why are you feeling down, when you're always in such good mood?

ANNE: Écoute, on est tous un peu tristes que tu partes bientôt. Moi surtout, je me sens abandonnée...	*Listen, we're all a little sad that you're leaving soon. I especially feel abandoned . . . .*
CHRIS: Alors, c'est ça? Eh bien, **rassure-toi que** moi aussi, **ça m'embête**, l'idée qu'on va être séparés.	*So that's it? Well, let me tell you the idea that we're going to be apart upsets me too.*
ANNE: Tu n'en as pas trop l'air.	*You don't look like it.*
CHRIS: Si! Je voulais te demander s'il te serait possible de me **rejoindre** chez moi en novembre. Mes parents sont d'accord.	*Yes, I am. I wanted to ask you to join me at my house in November. My parents agree / are in on it.*
ANNE: C'est vrai? J'en serais ravie!	*Really? I would love it!*
CHRIS: Tu pourras fêter le Thanksgiving avec nous. C'est une grande fête de famille. Et après avoir mangé la dinde traditionnelle, **on bloguera** ensemble, toi et moi!	*You can celebrate Thanksgiving with us. It's a big family holiday. And after eating the traditional turkey, we will blog together, you and I!*

EXERCICE 10·7

Jugez de votre compréhension. *Check your comprehension. Write* T *(true) or* F *(false).*

1. _____ Chris veut publier ses réflexions sur la France sur Internet.

2. _____ Anne est tout de suite très contente pour Chris.

3. _____ Chris annonce une bonne nouvelle à Anne.

4. _____ Anne ne veut pas aller aux USA.

5. _____ Chris taquine Anne à la fin de leur conversation.

Improve your conversation

Lancer un blog

This expression, like a number of terms related to modern communication, has adopted an English word, *blog*.

Je vais **lancer un blog** où j'exprimerai mes opinions sur la politique.	*I'm going **to start a blog** where I'll express my opinions on politics.*

Qu'à cela ne tienne!

This idiomatic expression shows the reluctant acceptance of things as they are.

Tu es de nouveau en retard. **Qu'à cela ne tienne!**	*You're late again. **Oh, well!***

Passionné(e)

This adjective is used to emphasize the intensity of someone's interest in a hobby, a job, or a sport.

Mes copains sont des **passionnés** du rugby.	*My friends are (huge) rugby **fans**.*
Maman est **passionnée** par son nouveau travail.	*Mom is **crazy** about her new job.*

J'ai le cafard

This colloquial expression describes *feeling "down" or "blue."*

J'ai le cafard après avoir rompu avec mon copain.	*I'm **feeling down** after breaking up with my boyfriend.*

Les adhérents

This term describes people (the members) who join a group, such as a club or a website.

Le site Facebook a des millions d'**adhérents**.	*The Facebook site has millions of **members**.*

Être de bonne/mauvaise humeur

These expressions refer to the *mood* someone is in.

Je suis de bonne humeur car j'ai eu de bonnes nouvelles.	*I'm **in a good mood** because I got some good news.*
Papa est de mauvaise humeur car sa voiture ne marche pas.	*Dad is **in a bad mood** because his car isn't running.*

Rassure-toi / rassurez-vous (que [qu']...)

Use this reflexive verb to reassure someone or to calm someone down. In a sentence, it is followed by the indicative mood.

Rassure-toi! Je serai de retour.	***Don't worry!** I'll be back.*
Rassurez-vous que cela se passera bien!	***Be (Rest) assured that** everything will be fine!*

Ça m'embête que (qu')...

Use this colloquial phrase to describe being *annoyed* or *irritated*. In a sentence, it is followed by the subjunctive mood.

Ça m'embête que tu **sois** si pessimiste.	***It annoys me that** you **are** so pessimistic.*

Rejoindre

Use this verb as one of several options to express *to meet (up with someone)*. Other synonyms are **rencontrer** and **retrouver**. Note, however, that **retrouver** and **rejoindre** connote meeting someone again or by appointment (that is, not for the first time).

Je vais **te rejoindre** au café à sept heures.	*I'm going **to meet you** at the café at seven o'clock.*

Bloguer

Use this French verb (derived from English) to refer to *blogging*.

Pierre passe toutes ses soirées à **bloguer**.   *Pierre spends all his evenings **blogging**.*

Grammar notes

Après que (qu')...

The conjunction **après que** is followed by the **futur simple** when the action of the subordinate clause (that is, following **après que**), takes place in a parallel future (contrary to English, which uses the present tense in that clause).

Après que tu **auras** ton diplôme, tu **pourras** gagner de l'argent.   *After (When) you **have** your diploma, you **will be able** to earn money.*

However, **après que** is followed by the **futur antérieur** (future perfect) when a future action takes place *before* another future action stated in the sentence.

Après que tu **auras fini** ce travail, on **pourra** sortir.   *After (When) you **have finished** this work, we **will be able** to go out.*

When the subject in the main clause and the subordinate clause is the *same*, the *past infinitive* construction is used with **après**. It consists of the auxiliary verb (**avoir** or **être**) in the infinitive form, plus a past participle.

Après avoir dormi, elle était reposée.   *After she slept, she was rested.*
Après être arrivés, ils ont ouvert leurs valises.   *After they arrived, they opened their bags.*

De (d')

Adjectives expressing feelings can be followed by the preposition **de (d')** plus an infinitive. Note that each of these example sentences has one subject only.

Ils sont **heureux d'avoir** de gentils voisins.   *They are **happy to have** nice neighbors.*
Elle est **ravie de savoir** parler anglais si bien.   *She is **delighted to be able** to speak English so well.*

EXERCICE 10·8

Fabian a créé un blog. *Fabian created a blog. Complete each sentence in the following dialogue with a word or phrase from the list provided.*

les passionnés	mes adhérents	Qu'à cela ne tienne
Ça m'embête	D'accord	commenter
ton blog	Rassure-toi	lancer
un commentaire		

1. NICOLAS: J'ai vu _____, Fabian. Il est vraiment bien. Chapeau!

2. FABIAN: Tu m'as laissé _____?

3. NICOLAS: Ah non. Je ne voulais pas être le premier à _____.

4. FABIAN: Pourquoi pas? Ça me ferait plaisir de te compter parmi

   _____.

5. NICOLAS: _____. La prochaine fois, je t'écrirai un billet.

6. FABIAN: _____ que tu sois le seul de mes amis à connaître
   mon blog.

7. NICOLAS: _____, Fabian. Je suis sûr que beaucoup de gens vont
   le trouver fort intéressant, ton blog.

8. FABIAN: Après avoir passé des heures et des jours à le _____, ce
   serait bien!

9. NICOLAS: Il faut que tu attendes un peu que _____ du rugby te
   trouvent, tu sais.

10. FABIAN: _____! Je dois patienter, tu as raison.

EXERCICE
10·9

Le club-cinéma de Fabian. *Fabian's film club. Write the letter of the most appropriate completion of each sentence on the line provided.*

1. _____ Fabian est absolument...

2. _____ Il va rejoindre les adhérents de son club...

3. _____ Après avoir vu la comédie,...

4. _____ Fabian aussi se sentira content...

5. _____ Une fois, les membres du club ont regardé...

6. _____ Après, tout le monde avait... Pas drôle, ça.

a. car il pourra discuter de ce film drôle avec eux.

b. le cafard.

c. passionné par les films français.

d. une histoire de suicide.

e. tout le monde sera de bonne humeur.

f. pour voir un nouveau film.

Dialogue 4

Anne, Chloé, Marie-Josée, and Didier give a farewell party for their friend Chris.

DIDIER: Alors, **c'est quand, le grand moment**?

So, when is the big moment?

CHRIS: Lundi prochain, j'ai un vol direct à partir de Charles de Gaulle à dix heures.

Next Monday, I have a direct flight from Charles de Gaulle at ten o'clock.

CHLOÉ: **À ta santé**, Chris! Reviens bientôt!

To your (good) health, Chris! Come back soon!

ANNE: Oui, **à la tienne**, Chris! **Je te souhaite un bon voyage.**	*Yes, cheers to you, Chris! I wish you a good trip.*
DIDIER: Je bois à ta santé, mon ami.	*I drink to your health, my friend.*
CHRIS: Vous êtes tous trop sympa. Je vous remercie **sincèrement** pour votre amitié. En réfléchissant bien, je devrais peut-être prolonger mon séjour. Est-ce que vous me feriez une autre fête comme ça?	*You are all too kind. I sincerely thank you for your friendship. Now that I think of it, maybe I should extend my stay. Would you put on another party like this for me?*
MARIE-JOSÉE: **Pas bête, cette idée.** Sans vouloir **carrément** changer de sujet, je dois quand même dire qu'on gardera un bon souvenir de toi et qu'on visitera ton blog pour voir si tu y parles de nous.	*Not a bad idea. Not that I want to change the subject abruptly, I must say though we'll keep good memories of you, and we'll visit your blog to see if you talk about us there.*
CHRIS: Je serais heureux que vous y laissiez **des commentaires. Comme ça**, vous ajouteriez **votre grain de sel** à ma perspective.	*I would be happy if you left your comments. That way, you would add your two cents to my perspective.*
DIDIER: En tout cas, continue de nous **donner de tes nouvelles** par e-mail, **d'accord.**	*In any case, keep in touch by e-mail, OK?*
CHRIS: **C'est entendu!**	*You can count on it!*

EXERCICE 10·10

Jugez de votre compréhension. *Check your comprehension. Write* T *(true) or* F *(false).*

1. _____ Chris va partir aujourd'hui.

2. _____ Ses amis ont préparé une fête en son honneur.

3. _____ Chris veut rester en contact électroniquement avec ses copains.

4. _____ Marie-Josée ne veut pas que Chris mentionne ses copains sur son blog.

5. _____ Chris et Didier vont continuer de s'envoyer des e-mails.

Improve your conversation

C'est quand, le grand moment?

This colloquial interrogative structure is used to ask when the big moment is. It is also used with other interrogative adverbs such as **où** (*where*) and **quoi** (*what*).

Tu vas te marier! **C'est quand, le grand moment?**	*You're going to get married!* **When is the big occasion?**
C'est où, la fête?	**Where is** *the party?*
C'est quoi, ce machin?	**What is** *this thing?*

À ta santé! / à la tienne!

Use this phrase to make a toast to someone's health.

Bon anniversaire, Patrick. **À ta santé!**   *Happy birthday, Patrick. **To your health!***

Souhaiter un bon voyage à...

Use this expression or its abbreviated version, which is also used in English (**Bon voyage!**), to wish someone a good trip.

Je te souhaite un bon voyage, Emma.   *I wish you a good trip, Emma.*
Nous vous souhaitons un excellent   *We wish you an excellent trip, dear friends.*
voyage, chers amis.

Sincèrement

Use this adverb to emphasize how sincerely or wholeheartedly you mean something.

Je te dis **sincèrement** que tu charmes   *I tell you **sincerely** that you charm*
tout le monde.   *everybody.*

Pas bête, cette idée

Use this phrase as a euphemism, to downplay the expression **Quelle bonne idée!** Both express approval or admiration for an idea.

Tu as cherché des billets d'avion à prix   *You looked for plane tickets at a reduced*
réduit sur Internet? **Pas bête, cette**   *price on the Internet? **Not a bad idea!***
idée!

Carrément

Use this adverb to emphasize the meaning of an adjective.

Cette personne est **carrément** géniale.   *This person is a **real** genius.*
Cette nouvelle invention est **carrément**   *This new invention is **clearly** revolutionary.*
révolutionnaire.

Des commentaires (*m. pl.*)

Use this phrase to refer to the comments you may leave on blogs.

J'essaie de contribuer à ce blog en laissant   *I try to contribute to this blog by leaving*
des commentaires pour le blogueur.   ***comments** for the blogger.*

Comme ça

Use this all-purpose phrase to make a transition or to establish a causal relationship.

Alors, **comme ça**, tu reviendras dans   *So, **really**, you'll come back in a few weeks.*
quelques semaines.
Il a fini tous ses devoirs. **Comme ça**, il   *He finished all his homework. **That way**, he*
pourra se détendre ce week-end.   *will be able to relax this weekend.*

Mettre son grain de sel

This phrase, which literally means putting in one's grain of salt, refers to contributing an idea.

Dis-moi ce que tu penses. **Mets-y ton grain de sel**, va!	*Tell me what you think. **Add your two cents**, go on!*

Donner de ses nouvelles

Use this expression to refer to keeping in touch with or hearing from someone.

Ne vous en faites pas, les amis, **je vous donnerai de mes nouvelles** souvent.	*Don't worry, friends, **I'll keep in touch** often.*

D'accord

Use this phrase to convey agreement or approval.

Tu veux acheter les billets de concert? Bon, **d'accord**.	*You want to buy the concert tickets? **OK***
Tu restes à la maison pour te reposer? **D'accord**, je comprends.	*You're staying home to rest? **OK**, I understand.*

C'est entendu

Use this expression as a synonym for **Bien entendu!** (*Of course!*), in order to accept or firmly agree to something.

Tu veux que j'y sois à dix-huit heures? **C'est entendu!** Compte sur moi!	*You want me to be there at six P.M.? **Understood.** Count on me!*

Grammar notes

En

The *present participle* (**-ant** form) of a verb following the preposition **en** expresses the simultaneity of two actions performed by the same subject.

En allant au marché, j'ai vu un accident.	***While going** to the market, I saw an accident.*
Il a fait un geste de la main pour dire au revoir **en partant**.	***While leaving**, he waved his hand to say good-bye.*
En écoutant bien, j'ai fini par comprendre.	***Listening well (carefully)**, I finally understood.*

Pour and sans

Prepositions such as **pour** (*in order to*) or **sans** (*without*) may be followed by verbs in the infinitive.

Il faut avoir l'esprit ouvert **pour apprécier** les différences culturelles.	*One must have an open mind (**in order**) **to** appreciate cultural differences.*
Sans savoir pourquoi, j'ai pleuré.	***Without knowing** why, I cried.*

René part en voyage. *René is leaving on a trip. Complete each line of the following dialogue with the appropriate word or phrase from the list. Capitalize as needed.*

e-mails   carrément   comme ça
d'accord   nouvelles   un bon voyage
à ta santé   s'ouvrir l'esprit

1. ALEXA: En venant ici, j'ai beaucoup réfléchi. Tu n'oublieras pas de donner de

   tes _____?

2. RENÉ: Bien sûr. Je t'enverrai plein d'_____.

3. ALEXA: _____! Je veux bien te croire.

4. RENÉ: Il faut bien voyager de temps en temps pour _____

5. ALEXA: Je sais mais c'est _____ embêtant que tu partes pour si longtemps!

6. RENÉ: Dis, tu vas me souhaiter _____?

7. ALEXA: Oui, donne-moi un verre de vin que je trinque _____.

8. RENÉ: Voilà! C'est mieux _____.

EXERCICE
10·12

Il va où? *Where is he going? Complete the following dialogue in French according to the English guidelines in parentheses. Use familiar structures to ask questions such as* **Tu l'aimes?** *or* **Est-ce que tu l'aimes?**

1. NATHALIE: _____? (*Where is he going, René?*)

   ALEXA: Il va passer trois mois aux États-Unis chez son correspondant.

2. NATHALIE: _____? (*Are you feeling sad?*)

   ALEXA: Oui, j'ai le cafard. C'est long, trois mois!

3. NATHALIE: _____? (*Couldn't you add your two cents when he made his decision?*)

   ALEXA: Non, parce que je suis sincèrement contente pour lui, tu vois.

4. NATHALIE: _____ (*So that's how it is!*)

   ALEXA: Vivent les voyages!

5. NATHALIE: _____ (*You are really crazy!*)

Les adieux de Nina et d'Henri. *Nina's and Henri's good-byes. In this dialogue, Nina is getting ready to study abroad for a year and says good-bye to her boyfriend Henri. Write the dialogue using the English guidelines provided.*

1. Nina tells Henri that she is both impatient to start her year abroad and sad to leave him.

   NINA: _____

2. Henri shows understanding and tells her that he will miss her a lot also.

   HENRI: _____

3. Nina says that in any case, they will stay in touch via e-mail.

   NINA: _____

4. Henri suggests Nina buy a webcam for her computer; that way they could communicate via Skype and see each other.

   HENRI: _____

5. Nina thinks that's not a bad idea at all. But she adds that she may not look that good on his computer screen.

   NINA: _____

6. Henri tells her not to worry. He will only invite two or three of his buddies to see her.

   HENRI: _____

7. Nina thanks him jokingly. Then she asks him jokingly what he would think if she put his worst picture on Facebook?

   NINA: _____

Answer key

1 Meeting people

1·1   1. F   2. F   3. F   4. T   5. F

1·2   1. Salut/Ça   2. Pas/toi   3. bien/sais/suis   4. même   5. Je pige

1·3   1. vous   2. elle   3. Toi   4. moi   5. lui

1·4   1. T   2. F   3. F   4. T   5. T

1·5   1. suis/aides   2. adore/écrire   3. sais/traduis   4. s'appelle/est   5. est/parle
     6. voudrais/connaître   7. vois/comptes   8. aide

1·6   1. Moi   2. toi   3. toi/toi   4. toi   5. moi

1·7   1. Tu travailles. Tu es en train de travailler.   2. Nous envoyons une lettre. Nous sommes en train d'envoyer une lettre.   3. Ils traduisent un article. Ils sont en train de traduire un article.   4. Vous lisez un mél. Vous êtes en train de lire un mél.   5. On présente un ami. On est en train de présenter un ami.   6. Elle corrige une faute. Elle est en train de corriger une faute.

1·8   1. T   2. T   3. F   4. F   5. T

1·9   1. d   2. f   3. g   4. e   5. h   6. b   7. c   8. a

1·10   1. T   2. T   3. F   4. T   5. T

1·11   1. je peux   2. prendre   3. peut-être une autre fois   4. je peux   5. habite   6. ça se fait

1·12   1. Bonjour/Enchanté   2. monsieur / l'ami   3. madame / Je m'appelle   4. là/voilà
     5. pote/va   6. Très

1·13   1. F   2. T   3. T   4. F   5. T

1·14   1. sa   2. son   3. sa   4. son   5. ses   6. ses   7. C'est le père de Didier.   8. Il est enchanté de faire la connaissance de Chris.   9. C'est sa mère. 10. Elle est affectueuse. 11. C'est sa sœur.   12. Elle est mariée.

1·15   1. Bonjour, Chris. Comment allez-vous?   2. Bien, merci. Je suis ravi de faire votre connaissance.   3. C'est bien vous, l'ami anglais de Didier?   4. Pas exactement. Je suis son copain américain.   5. Excusez-moi. Je sais bien que vous êtes son copain américain.
     6. Comme c'est samedi aujourd'hui, nous avons tous deux un peu de temps libre.
     7. C'est bien. Le samedi, la famille dîne toujours ensemble et on voulait tous vous rencontrer.

2 Making conversation and making plans

2·1   1. T   2. T   3. F   4. T   5. F

2·2   1. vous   2. moi   3. m'appelle   4. J'ai entendu parler   5. aux États-Unis
     6. c'est vrai   7. exactement   8. au Colorado   9. plaît   10. Qu'est-ce qui
     11. grandes villes   12. des copains   13. j'avais envie

2·3   1. T   2. F   3. T   4. F   5. T

2·4	1. b 2. f 3. h 4. d 5. g 6. a 7. e 8. c
2·5	1. T 2. T 3. F 4. F 5. T
2·6	1. a 2. d 3. e 4. b 5. f 6. c 7. a 8. d 9. f 10. b 11. e 12. c
2·7	1. F 2. T 3. F 4. T 5. F
2·8	1. a 2. e 3. g 4. f 5. b 6. h 7. c 8. d
2·9	1. profite 2. suis 3. me promener 4. quitter 5. me baigner 6. me bronzer 7. lire 8. me suffit 9. Et puis 10. tout seul
2·10	1. T 2. T 3. F 4. F 5. T
2·11	1. prêt 2. d'accord 3. Mais non, voyons 4. Ce qui est intéressant 5. C'est parce que 6. C'est gentil 7. Alors 8. si tu veux 9. Il y a mille choses à faire 10. Dommage
2·12	1. F 2. T 3. T 4. F 5. T
2·13	1. a 2. e 3. f 4. b 5. d 6. c
2·14	1. Je vais te chercher. 2. N'importe quand. 3. Volontiers. 4. C'est au sujet de Facebook. / Il s'agit de Facebook. Ça m'intéresse. 5. Le sujet est bon, mais le film? On verra. 6. Écoute, je serai chez toi à six heures.
2·15	1. Je suis un cours d'histoire de l'art le mercredi avec le professeur Pouce. 2. Quelle surprise! Moi aussi, je suis un cours d'histoire de l'art avec le professeur Pouce mais le lundi. 3. Mon cours n'est qu'une introduction, et le tien? 4. Mon cours est un cours de seconde année et je l'adore. 5. Tu vas régulièrement visiter les musées alors? 6. Tu penses bien! Je passe tout mon temps libre dans les musées et les galeries d'art. Tu veux me rejoindre demain à une exposition d'art moderne? 7. Volontiers! À quelle heure? 8. N'importe quand après dix-neuf heures.

3 Discussing leisure activities

3·1	1. F 2. F 3. T 4. T 5. F
3·2	1. Je suis désolée. Pourquoi (est-ce qu') elle ne te plaît pas? / Pourquoi ne te plaît-elle pas? 2. C'est la psychologie humaine. 3. Oui, je sais. C'est vieux! 4. Moi, elle me plaît, cette pièce! / Moi, cette pièce me plaît! 5. J'apprécie les bonnes pièces. 6. Tu ne penses pas que tu es un peu dur? 7. Qu'est-ce que tu penses des acteurs? 8. Tu vois! Tu apprécies quelque chose! 9. Je suis ravie. 10. J'espère que tu ne vas pas être déçu.
3·3	1. d 2. c 3. e 4. f 5. b 6. a
3·4	1. T 2. T 3. F 4. T 4. T
3·5	1. plaît 2. dégoûté, navet 3. as l'air 4. horreur 5. Quelle 6. On devrait 7. Il ne faut pas 8. On devrait
3·6	1. On devrait / nous devrions aller voir ce film. 2. D'accord. Il n'y a rien que des sports à la télévision / la télé aujourd'hui. 3. Nicole dit que c'est un navet / que c'est horrible, mais je ne la crois pas. 4. Quel genre de film est-ce / est-ce que c'est? 5. C'est la biographie du fondateur de Facebook. 6. Jean m'a dit que c'est un bon film. Allons-y!
3·7	1. T 2. T 3. F 4. F 5. T
3·8	1. emmènes 2. achètes 3. acheter 4. Pressons-nous / Dépêchons-nous 5. génial 6. Pressons-nous / Dépêchons-nous 7. Emmenons 8. emmène
3·9	1. Dépêche-toi, Karen. Nous sommes en retard. 2. Je suis essoufflée. Arrête de courir comme si on avait le feu aux trousses. 3. Je ne peux pas être en retard à ce concert. C'est mon groupe favori/préféré. Compris? 4. Je comprends mais je ne peux pas aller plus vite que ça. 5. Eh bien. Tu n'es pas en forme, ma petite. 6. Toi non plus / Toi, tu ne l'es pas non plus, Josette. 7. Bon/Bien. On y est! / Nous y voilà! 8. Je suis aux anges! 9. Voici Thomas avec les billets! 10. Que ça nous serve de leçon qu'il vaut mieux partir / s'en aller tôt / de bonne heure. 11. Oui, tu as raison. J'ai eu peur. 12. Remets-toi! Amusons-nous!
3·10	1. T 2. F 3. T 4. F 5. F
3·11	1. de la tarte flambée 2. mieux 3. Depuis 4. quand même 5. fait envie 6. en 7. meilleures 8. Tant mieux

3·12   1. a   2. e   3. f   4. c   5. b   6. d

3·13   1. La comédie que je veux voir depuis des semaines joue finalement dans le quartier. J'ai hâte de la voir.
2. Tu sais très bien qu'on va au ballet ce soir.   3. Tu as raison. Je suis quand même très déçu de ne pas
pouvoir voir mon film.   4. Je comprends, mais j'ai des billets chers pour le ballet ce soir.   5. Le ballet ne
m'intéresse vraiment pas. J'y vais seulement pour te faire plaisir, tu sais.   6. Et moi, je vais au cinéma et je
regarde les matches de rugby à la télévision pour te faire plaisir.   7. C'est vrai. Le ballet n'est pas si mal/
mauvais que ça et on peut aller au cinéma la semaine prochaine.

4   Discussing current events

4·1   1. F   2. T   3. T   4. T   5. F

4·2   1. Ici   2. Quoi de neuf   3. grève   4. poisse   5. Pas de   6. Zut   7. comme ça   8. On dirait
9. Ça arrive   10. en pleine saison   11. non   12. ce sera super

4·3   1. Zut! Quelle poisse!   2. Oui, j'en ai.   3. Tu plaisantes? / Sans blague?   4. Pas de nouvelles du tout!
5. Je vois. On dirait que tu as raison!   6. Ça dépend! Pas si bien quand tu aimes ton cours / quand ton
cours te plaît.   7. On verra.   8. Tu penses/trouves qu'elles sont super, ces grèves, n'est-ce pas? / non?

4·4   1. T   2. F   3. F   4. F   5. F

4·5   1. c   2. d   3. a   4. b   5. g   6. h   7. e   8. f

4·6   1. neige   2. Zut   3. On dirait que   4. être de retour   5. Veinard   6. plaisanter
7. Franchement   8. raison

4·7   1. F   2. T   3. T   4. T   5. T

4·8   1. c   2. f   3. a   4. b   5. d   6. e

4·9   1. où en est-on   2. Il paraît   3. Je me demande   4. qui circule   5. batteries   6. écologiques
7. Décidément   8. on parle   9. évident   10. tant que ça

4·10   1. Mariette, regarde la vidéo que je viens de trouver en ligne. Tu vas l'adorer!   2. Il s'agit de quoi?   3. Il
s'agit du mariage de...   4. La mariée est magnifique en blanc et le marié est beau comme un dieu.   5. Je
me demande combien coute un mariage pareil?   6. Ça coûte plus que tu ne peux imaginer ou t'offrir.

5   Watching sports events

5·1   1. F   2. T   3. T   4. T   5. F

5·2   1. e   2. f   3. d   4. c   5. a   6. b

5·3   1. Oui, bien sûr. Qui joue?   2. Tu penses que l'équipe française peut gagner?   3. Oui, mais la Croatie est
vraiment bonne.   4. D'accord. À quelle heure est le match?   5. Je veux bien. Tu peux faire le petit
déjeuner.   6. J'y serai.

5·4   1. T   2. F   3. T   4. F   5. F

5·5   1. d   2. c   3. b   4. f   5. a   6. e

5·6   1. toi   2. simplement   3. j'aimerais   4. tant que tu y es   5. Tu crois   6. heure   7. heures
8. chez   9. Il faudrait   10. à toi

5·7   1. T   2. F   3. F   4. T   5. F

5·8   1. regarder   2. un match amical   3. remarque   4. D'ailleurs   5. Il faudrait   6. Ne t'en fais pas
7. moi-même   8. si tu veux   9. C'est prévu   10. À demain

5·9   1. Qui joue?   2. Deux équipes excellentes. Génial!/Super!   3. D'accord. Je viens te chercher?   4. Ne
t'en fais pas. Je serai chez toi à l'heure.   5. Ah! C'est déjà prévu, je vois.   6. Merci, Martine. À demain.

5·10   1. Mon équipe favorite, Montréal, va gagner contre Toronto, c'est sûr et certain.   2. L'équipe de Toronto a
gagné ses trois derniers matchs. C'est une équipe super-bonne!   3. C'est facile de gagner un match amical.
4. Tu es gonflé! Même les matchs amicaux sont importants.   5. Ne t'en fais pas! Même si Toronto perd, ça
ne veut pas dire que c'est une mauvaise équipe.   6. Si Toronto perd aujourd'hui, il faudra que je t'offre un
verre mais ça m'étonnerait.   7. De toute façon, j'ai l'intention de faire un barbecue. Alors je t'invite à
célébrer la victoire de Toronto ou de Montréal.   8. J'y serai!

6 Celebrating and having fun

6·1   1. F   2. T   3. T   4. T   5. F

6·2   1. était   2. des fous   3. avait   4. vraiment   5. du succès   6. Et comment   7. rappelle   8. Ah bon   9. pense   10. une ambiance

6·3   1. C'était / Elle était super!   2. La bouffe était excellente.   3. Oui, ça/elle m'a plu. Et toi?   4. Et pourtant, ils ont eu du succès.   5. Il y avait de l'ambiance, n'est-ce pas?   6. Eh bien, mes amis et moi, on s'est amusés.

6·4   1. T   2. T   3. F   4. F   5. T

6·5   1. d   2. f   3. e   4. a   5. b   6. c

6·6   1. e   2. c   3. g   4. b   5. i   6. h   7. j   8. d   9. a   10. f

6·7   1. F   2. F   3. T   4. F   5. T

6·8   1. d   2. e   3. a   4. b   5. c

6·9   1. à la campagne   2. célèbre   3. pas encore   4. plutôt   5. fort   6. renseignements   7. des choses   8. Plus tard   9. demoiselles d'honneur   10. Ça tombe bien.

6·10   1. Je ne peux pas croire que notre copain Jordan a déjà trente ans.   2. Je suis d'accord. Il a maintenant le même âge que nous.   3. La cuisine mexicaine est super. Qu'est-ce que tu en penses?   4. J'adore tout ça. C'était mon idée à moi.   5. C'est la meilleure idée que tu aies jamais eue. C'est toi qui as fait tous les sombreros comme décorations?   6. J'ai simplement suggéré le thème mexicain pour la fête.   7. Quelle belle toilette tu portes aujourd'hui!   8. Pourquoi es-tu si impressionné? Tu m'as vue avant dans cette robe avec le chapeau assorti.

7 Accomplishments

7·1   1. T   2. T   3. F   4. F   5. T

7·2   1. Ça ne va pas   2. si   3. fallait   4. tout ce que   5. depuis une semaine   6. défendue   7. Ça s'est bien passé   8. valait   9. Félicitations   10. parles

7·3   1. e   2. d   3. f   4. b   5. a   6. c

7·4   1. F   2. T   3. T   4. T   5. F

7·5   1. Je me sens si heureuse/contente   2. J'ai été acceptée à l'université de Paris   3. C'était mon seul choix, mon chou / ma chère   4. Tout ce que j'ai fait, c'est de réussir à mon baccalauréat   5. Oui, ça valait la peine d'étudier dur

7·6   1. c   2. d   3. a   4. b   5. e

7·7   1. T   2. T   3. F   4. F   5. F

7·8   1. d   2. g   3. c   4. a   5. h   6. f   7. b   8. e

7·9   1. d   2. c   3. f   4. e   5. a   6. b

7·10   1. f   2. h   3. e   4. g   5. c   6. a   7. d   8. b

7·11   1. T   2. F   3. T   4. T   5. F

7·12   1. Chapeau! C'est / Elle est super   2. Non, elles sont bien   3. Quand il s'agit de l'environnement, je suis pessimiste   4. Je ne pense pas / Je pense que non   5. Ne t'en fais pas! C'est vraiment bien

7·13   1. h   2. a   3. f   4. e   5. g   6. c   7. d   8. b

7·14   1. T   2. F   3. T   4. F   5. F

7·15   1. b   2. e   3. a   4. c   5. f   6. d

7·16   1. bonne nouvelle   2. tu attends   3. J'ai été promue   4. Quel soulagement   5. J'ai le poste.   6. faire une commande chez le traiteur   7. chouette/super/cool   8. Je te félicite.   9. me vanter   10. nous réjouir

7·17   1. Pourquoi as-tu l'air si heureuse, Nathalie?   2. Quelles nouvelles est-ce que j'attends depuis un mois?   3. Que je suis bête (de te le demander)! Bien entendu, tu es heureuse parce que tu as réussi le baccalauréat!   4. Que je suis soulagée! J'ai réussi.   5. Je te félicite, Nathalie! Maintenant tu mérites de belles et longues vacances.   6. C'est exact. Tout ce que j'ai fait cette année c'est étudier.   7. Maintenant je peux vraiment me vanter d'avoir une fille très intelligente.   8. Quand il s'agit de l'école, je fais toujours de mon mieux.

8 Making comparisons

8·1   1. T   2. F   3. T   4. F   5. T

8·2   1. veux   2. réduit   3. modèle   4. marche   5. combien   6. un forfait   7. des promotions   8. profiter

8·3   1. e   2. a   3. d   4. c   5. b

8·4   1. F   2. T   3. T   4. T   5. T

8·5   1. Oh que oui, ma petite/chère Sophie.   2. Oui, mais ne te tracasse pas / ne t'inquiète pas. Tu peux acheter une nouvelle robe.   3. Tu es si/tellement originale avec tes vêtements/habits. Crée un nouveau style!   4. Il faut avoir les moyens de/pour suivre la mode de près.   5. C'est pareil pour nous, les hommes.   6. C'est gentil/sympa de dire ça.   7. C'est pareil pour moi.   8. Dans des boutiques/magasins haut de gamme?

8·6   1. d   2. e   3. f   4. a   5. b   6. c

8·7   1. T   2. F   3. T   4. F   5. F

8·8   1. Cette chambre est plus grande que l'autre.   2. Ces cuisines sont plus petites que les autres.   3. Regarde ces appartements! Celui-ci est beau. Celui-là est horrible.   4. Qu'est-ce que tu penses / vous pensez de ces maisons? Celle-ci est disponible immédiatement / tout de suite. Celle-là n'est pas disponible en ce moment.   5. Le prix de cette maison n'est pas aussi élevé que le prix de celle qu'on a vue / que nous avons vue ce matin.   6. J'aime ces deux studios. Celui-ci est aussi confortable que celui-là.   7. Et le loyer? Ce loyer-ci est plus élevé que celui-là.   8. Je veux ce studio(-ci). Il est plus mignon que celui d'avant.

8·9   1. b   2. e   3. g   4. c   5. f   6. d   7. a

8·10   1. F   2. T   3. F   4. T   5. T

8·11   1. i   2. e   3. h   4. j   5. b   6. a   7. d   8. c   9. f   10. g

8·12   *Answers will vary.*

8·13   1. épouser   2. ne charrie pas   3. le cœur   4. J'espère bien.   5. À croquer   6. Il ne manquait plus

8·14   1. Viens voir la nouvelle voiture de sport du voisin   2. J'arrive! Quelle merveille   3. Elle me plaît beaucoup, cette voiture. Je crois que c'est une voiture électrique   4. Il a toujours de belles voitures de sport, le voisin. Mais celle-ci est la plus impressionnante de toutes   5. Tu ne trouves pas que cette voiture ressemble beaucoup à ma Smartcar   6. Ta Smartcar est aussi petite que celle-ci, mais c'est tout ce qu'elles ont en commun   7. Bon. Je suis d'accord que ma Smartcar n'est pas aussi luxueuse que cette voiture, mais elle est tout aussi mignonne   8. Ne t'en fais pas! Tu n'as peut-être pas la plus belle voiture du monde, mais tu as la plus belle femme, n'est-ce pas?

9 Asking for help

9·1   1. F   2. F   3. T   4. T   5. F

9·2   1. Excusez-moi, madame, je cherche le rayon des vêtements de femme.   2. Ce rayon est en bas, mademoiselle.   3. Nous sommes au premier étage? / Est-ce que nous sommes au premier étage? / Sommes-nous au premier étage?   4. Oui, mademoiselle.   5. Je vous remercie, madame.   6. De rien. / Il n'y a pas de quoi. / Je vous en prie, mademoiselle.

9·3   1. T   2. F   3. F   4. T   5. F

9·4   1. reviens   2. le rayon   3. lasses   4. comme tout   5. faim   6. quelque chose   7. blagues   8. t'ai eue

9·5   1. c   2. f   3. d   4. e   5. a   6. b

9·6   1. F   2. T   3. T   4. F   5. F

9·7   1. Ce n'est pas très gentil   2. Mais je suis pressé   3. il te faut   4. J'ai besoin de / Il me faut de nouveaux pulls et de nouvelles chemises   5. il me faut   6. dès qu'on aura / aussitôt qu'on aura   7. c'est gentil/sympa de ta part   8. C'est où / Où est-ce / Où est-ce que c'est   9. c'est à cet étage / est-ce à cet étage / est-ce que c'est à cet étage?   10. suivez-moi

9·8   1. F   2. F   3. T   4. F   5. T

9·9   1. monsieur   2. plaisir   3. déranger   4. droite   5. mauvaise   6. mademoiselle

9·10 1. T   2. F   3. F   4. F   5. T

9·11 1. à vélo   2. balades   3. comprend   4. forfait   5. d'où que   6. ne trouves pas   7. guide-interprète   8. C'est bien

9·12 1. Je voudrais quelques/des renseignements concernant les tours de Paris, s'il vous plaît.   2. Je préférerais des tours à pied   3. Et les tours à vélo   4. D'où que nous partions, c'est le même prix   5. C'est bien ce qu'il me semblait / C'est ce que je pensais

9·13 1. Madame, s'il vous plaît, pouvez-vous m'aider à trouver un livre de cuisine?   2. Monsieur, le rayon des livres de cuisine est en haut au premier étage.   3. Monsieur, s'il vous plaît, où est le rayon des livres de cuisine?   4. Quelle sorte de livre de cuisine cherchez-vous, monsieur?   5. Je cherche des livres de Julia Child.   6. Il y a deux rayons de livres de cuisine dans la librairie; le rayon des livres de cuisine française à cet étage et un autre rayon de cuisine internationale au deuxième étage.   7. Je vous remercie, monsieur. Pouvez-vous me montrer où exactement?   8. Certainement. Je vous accompagne au rayon en question / au bon rayon.

10   Departures

10·1 1. F   2. F   3. T   4. F   5. T

10·2 1. dommage   2. accueillir   3. Bien entendu   4. miens   5. manquer   6. plus longtemps   7. pays   8. la tienne   9. hâte   10. retrouver

10·3 1. Ça y est. Noah est reparti/retourné aux USA.   2. Il était vraiment à l'aise avec nous. C'est vrai.   3. Bien sûr, mais il était / a été bien accueilli dans notre famille.   4. J'en suis sûre.   5. Et vivent les grandes vacances!

10·4 1. T   2. F   3. F   4. F   5. F

10·5 1. g   2. i   3. j   4. d   5. e   6. c   7. a   8. b   9. h   10. f

10·6 1. la rentrée des classes   2. Vivement   3. dans un endroit tropical   4. par hasard   5. faire une déprime   6. humeur   7. peu dire   8. En fin de compte

10·7 1. T   2. F   3. T   4. F   5. T

10·8 1. ton blog   2. un commentaire   3. commenter   4. mes adhérents   5. Qu'à cela ne tienne   6. Ça m'embête   7. Rassure-toi   8. lancer   9. les passionnés   10. D'accord

10·9 1. c   2. f   3. e   4. a   5. d   6. b

10·10 1. F   2. T   3. T   4. F   5. T

10·11 1. nouvelles   2. e-mails   3. D'accord   4. s'ouvrir l'esprit   5. carrément   6. un bon voyage   7. à ta santé   8. comme ça

10·12 1. Où (est-ce qu') il va, René? / Il va où, René?   2. Tu te sens triste? / Est-ce que tu te sens triste?   3. Tu ne pouvais pas y mettre ton grain de sel quand il a pris sa décision?   4. Alors c'est comme ça!   5. Tu es carrément/vraiment folle!

10·13 1. J'ai hâte de commencer mon année à l'étranger, mais en même temps je suis triste de te quitter.   2. Je comprends. Tu me manqueras beaucoup aussi.   3. En tout cas, on restera en contact par e-mail.   4. Je te conseille d'acheter une webcam pour ton ordinateur; comme ça nous pourrions communiquer par Skype et nous voir.   5. Ce n'est pas une mauvaise idée, ça. Mais je n'aurai peut-être pas bonne mine sur ton écran.   6. Ne t'en fais pas! Je n'inviterai que deux ou trois copains pour te voir.   7. Eh bien merci! Qu'est-ce que tu penserais si je mettais ta pire photo sur Facebook alors?